INFORMATION AND COMMUNICATION TECHNOLOGIES IN EDUCATION

AF734849

Dear MyCopy Customer,

This Springer book is a monochrome print version of the eBook to which your library gives you access via SpringerLink. It is available to you at a subsidized price since your library subscribes to at least one Springer eBook subject collection.

Please note that MyCopy books are only offered to library patrons with access to at least one Springer eBook subject collection. MyCopy books are strictly for individual use only.

You may cite this book by referencing the bibliographic data and/or the DOI (Digital Object Identifier) found in the front matter. This book is an exact but monochrome copy of the print version of the eBook on SpringerLink.

IFIP - The International Federation for Information Processing

IFIP was founded in 1960 under the auspices of UNESCO, following the First World Computer Congress held in Paris the previous year. An umbrella organization for societies working in information processing, IFIP's aim is two-fold: to support information processing within its member countries and to encourage technology transfer to developing nations. As its mission statement clearly states,

IFIP's mission is to be the leading, truly international, apolitical organization which encourages and assists in the development, exploitation and application of information technology for the benefit of all people.

IFIP is a non-profitmaking organization, run almost solely by 2500 volunteers. It operates through a number of technical committees, which organize events and publications. IFIP's events range from an international congress to local seminars, but the most important are:

- The IFIP World Computer Congress, held every second year;
- open conferences;
- working conferences.

The flagship event is the IFIP World Computer Congress, at which both invited and contributed papers are presented. Contributed papers are rigorously refereed and the rejection rate is high.

As with the Congress, participation in the open conferences is open to all and papers may be invited or submitted. Again, submitted papers are stringently refereed.

The working conferences are structured differently. They are usually run by a working group and attendance is small and by invitation only. Their purpose is to create an atmosphere conducive to innovation and development. Refereeing is less rigorous and papers are subjected to extensive group discussion.

Publications arising from IFIP events vary. The papers presented at the IFIP World Computer Congress and at open conferences are published as conference proceedings, while the results of the working conferences are often published as collections of selected and edited papers.

Any national society whose primary activity is in information may apply to become a full member of IFIP, although full membership is restricted to one society per country. Full members are entitled to vote at the annual General Assembly, National societies preferring a less committed involvement may apply for associate or corresponding membership. Associate members enjoy the same benefits as full members, but without voting rights. Corresponding members are not represented in IFIP bodies. Affiliated membership is open to non-national societies, and individual and honorary membership schemes are also offered.

INFORMATION AND COMMUNICATION TECHNOLOGIES IN EDUCATION

The School of the Future

IFIP TC3/WG3.1 International Conference on
The Bookmark of the School of the Future
April 9–14, 2000, Viña del Mar, Chile

Edited by

Harriet Taylor
Louisiana State University
USA

Pieter Hogenbirk
CPS
The Netherlands

SPRINGER-SCIENCE+BUSINESS MEDIA, B.V.

Library of Congress Cataloging-in-Publication Data

IFIP TC3 WG3.1 International Conference on the Bookmark of the School of the Future (2000 : Viña del Mar, Chile)

Information and communication technologies in education: the school of the future: IFIP TC3 WG3.1 International Conference on the Bookmark of the School of the Future, April 9-14, 2000, Viña del Mar, Chile / edited by Harriet Taylor, Pieter Hogenbirk.

Includes bibliographical references and index.

DOI 10.1007/978-0-387-35403-3

1. Educational technology—Congresses. 2. Information technology—Congresses. 3. Computer-assisted instruction—Congresses. I. Taylor, Harriet G. II. Hogenbirk, Pieter. III. Title.

58.

LB1028.3 .I33 2001

371.3'34—dc21 00-054597

Copyright © 2001 by Springer Science+Business Media Dordrecht

Originally published by Kluwer Academic Publishers in 2001

MyCopy version of the original edition 2001

All rights reserved. No part of this publication may be reproduced, stored in a retrieval system or transmitted in any form or by any means, mechanical, photo-copying, recording, or otherwise, without the prior written permission of the publisher, Springer-Science+Business Media, B.V.

Printed on acid-free paper.

www.springer.com/mycopy

Contents

Section 10: Focus Group Recommendations

Message from the Conference Chairmen

At the start of a new century, it was very appropriate to reflect on the progress in education and consider the potential for the future. Chile 2000 – The bookmark to the school of the future provided an excellent opportunity to do just this.

This international conference not only marked the turn of the century, but also itself made history. This was the first IFIP event ever to be held in Chile, and also the first TC3 event to be held anywhere in Latin America. Viña del Mar offered a beautiful and effective venue for this working conference and attracted experts in the field of Information and Communication Technology and secondary education from across the world. Forty-five delegates from nineteen different countries came together for the week to debate the issues which will affect us all over the next few years.

The papers presented there, and published in this book, were high quality and stimulated excellent debate. The focus groups enabled delegates to discuss the issues at great depth and their reports offer an insight into the concerns we must all address as we consider the schools of the future.

We have seen many changes in our lifetime and we know that the rate of change is accelerating. We can be assured therefore that the future for which we must educate our young people will be very different.

It is challenging to note that the teachers we are training today will be teaching the children who will lead us into the next century. We believe that you will find the papers and outcomes from our conference helpful and supportive in designing the education to support these children – our future.

Doug Brown
Chairman
Programme Committee

Sebastian Lagos
Chairman
Organising Committee

Chile 2000 Committees

Programme Committee

Chair: Doug Brown, UK

Members:

Herminia Azinian	Argentina
Pieter Hogenbirk	The Netherlands
Sebastian Lagos	Chile
Raymond Morel	Switzerland
Ferran Ruiz Tarrago	Spain
Harriet Taylor	USA
Deryn Watson	UK

Editors:

Harriet Taylor	USA
Pieter Hogenbirk	The Netherlands

Organising Committee

(from Universidad Metropolitana de Ciencias de la Educación)

Chair: Sebastian Lagos

Members:

Eduardo Cabezon
Daniel Frias
Jimena Sepulveda
Juan Vargas

Chile 2000 Sponsors

Chile 2000, the Bookmark to The School of the Future, could not have been a success without the help and support of many people.

The Organising and Programme Committees are particularly grateful to the following organisations without which the conference would not have been possible:

Universidad Metropolitana de Ciencias de la Educación

Arthur Andersen Business Consulting

Rowntree Trust (Through Head to Head Consulting)

Fundación Andes

Xerox Chile S.A.

Head to Head Consulting

Celestron

CPS, educational development and advice

Introduction

Pieter Hogenbirk and Harriet Taylor

Education is changing or will change. It is our intention to discuss the causes of that change extensively in this book. But in general we could state that the main factors that contribute to these changes all have to do with the transition from an industrial to an informational society. In that new society, the amount of knowledge is tremendously increasing and the skills to be productive are thoroughly changing. This gives a pressure on education to evolve from learning "facts and figures" into "learning to learn" and from learning as a personal achievement to learning as a result of a global social process.

Therefore IFIP Working Group 3.1 decided to elaborate on the possible changes and impact of those changes in secondary education through organising the Conference "Chile 2000, the Bookmark of the School of the Future." To discuss these future developments the programme committee invited approximately 20 experts from all over the world to contribute to the conference and to prepare a paper. Three keynote speakers were invited to give their general views. There were four discussion groups focussing on the different issues involved. All of these papers and contributions addressed one or more of the following conference themes:

1. the learning process and new learning environments
2. the role of the teacher in the school of the future
3. schooling, school culture, organisational aspects and the school in an information rich society
4. the role of connectivity and networking in the school of the future.

The quality of these papers was extremely high. The authors made a sincere attempt to look over the border of present education. They tried to give perspectives and views on the possibilities that Information and Communication Technologies (ICT) provide to improve the quality of our education, our schools and the way we learn and teach. In order to do justice to the variety of these contributions the editors decided to make a somewhat different classification in this book, which contains all of the invited papers. We think that this classification makes it easier for the reader to sharpen his or her view on future education. The following sections provide a brief description of the chapters of this book.

In section 1 Ana Luiza Machado describes in her keynote the present situation in Latin America's education. She also elaborates on the future perspectives and the needs of the countries involved to reach these potentials.

In section 2 Betty Collis analyses in her keynote the use of the Internet and of a school Intranet in an educational setting. She states that the use of an Intranet learning environment contributes much more to the development of future education than the use of Internet resources.

Section 3 is about *School culture*. Herminia Azinian describes two projects in schools where the introduction of ICT led to a change in the relationship between the pupils. Kwok Wing Lai examines the effect on teacher behaviour that the use of the Internet has in the classroom. Jaap Westbroek derives a new concept of school building from an analysis of the changes in society.

Section 4, *Teacher development*, looks in more detail to the way we could prepare teachers for their changing role. Bernard Cornu and Clara Danon describe the essence of the change role of teachers. Iliana Nikolova presents a model for building an informal professional society of researchers, trainers and teachers who communicate, collaborate and share. Vittorio Midoro describes a collaborative online learning environment for teacher training.

Section 5 handles the *Change and impact on learning* of ICT. David Passig expands Bloom's taxonomy for thinking skills with the new ability of "melioration." Toni Downes and Katina Zammit argue that learning processes in networked learning environments require substantially different literacies. James Issac converts an experience with a training course for ICT into a proposal for a "core-competency" course on information literacy and information skills.

Section 6 deals with *Distance and online learning*. Klaus-D Graf and Kiyoski Yokochi describe an environment for German-Japanese education projects using real time interactive distance learning between remote classrooms. Don Passey draws on the outcomes of a range of current evaluation and research studies focusing on home-school links. Antonio Saldano and Miguel Reyes introduce the concept of "edunetmatics" (education assisted by a telematic net), a new learning space constructed over an innovative educational paradigm. Jan Hylen uses the European

Schoolnet project to elaborate on two complementary concepts: the diminishing school, a reduction of schools and the role of the teacher, and the expanding school where the need for life-long learning puts the school in the centre of the development. Finally, Jef Moonen explores costs and financial benefit issues and gives some examples of the way one can use a costing model to measure the increase in learning productivity and the return on investment.

Section 7 presents views on *Cultural and historical perspectives.* Gail Marshall calls for a thorough investigation of the community's social, economic, political and cultural values before establishing a school of the future. Alnaaz Kassam reports on a research project and concludes that achieving a reflective approach to studying others is not merely a matter of making contact by the Internet but also includes changing attitudes and acquiring an ability to work in a more constructivist manner. Humberto Maturana and Eduardo Cabezon discuss the intriguing statement "Education is a process by means of which adequate relational behaviours are triggered through which another (or oneself) arises as a legitimate other in coexistence with oneself."

Section 8 gives some *National examples.* Sigrid Schubert examines the potential value of modelling in informatics education. Paul Jansen, Petra Fisser, and Cees Terlouw describe the elements of digital learning environments by the different interactions and communications between the student, teacher and materials. Lea da Cruz Fagundes presents a project which developed new models for educational virtual networks.

Section 9 concerns *Future perspectives.* In his closing keynote Jim Ridgway brings all the different contributions of the conference into one framework.

The final section contains the results of the four Focus Groups. These groups discussed the four conference themes that were mentioned above. Each group produced a position paper with a forward look on aspects of the conference themes. They also made concrete recommendations based on individual experiences.

We, as editors, enjoyed working on these outstanding papers on a subject that addresses one of the most important issues at this time, the future of our children. We sincerely appreciate the efforts of the authors and attendees at the conference in putting forward their thoughts and experiences. Furthermore we want to thank Deryn Watson for editing two of the papers. We hope that many readers in the educational community will benefit from these contributions as well.

Current status and perspectives for education in Latin America

Ana Luiza Machado
Director, UNESCO Regional Office – Santiago
Enrique Delpiano 29
Santiago, Chile Codigo Postal 6651692

Abstract: Education in Latin America is an important part of social policy. Although huge strides were made in the last decade, a region of disparity between the rich and poor needs to focus on the reduction of inequality of access and provision if it is to hope for qualitative change. Detailed achievements and challenges are presented, with an emphasis on improving school enrolment and a change to curriculum relevant for the future and local community and business involvement. Change will be achieved by a combination of new teachers, new management and leadership, and the involvement of all society.

Keywords: Latin America, change, literacies, inequities, society

1. INTRODUCTION

Education has become increasingly important within governmental policy, and particularly social policy, in Latin America. As a sector, it receives a large proportion of public resources. A review of declarations from meetings of the region's Presidents and Education Ministers during the last decade reveals the high expectations that policy makers and society have for education. The causal links between education and individual and social development, education and overcoming poverty, education and living together in peace, are recurrent themes in the political discourse.

In view of these high political and social expectations of education, it is important to start with the context of our region, and consider some factors regarding the status of education during the last decade. Then, we can look ahead to the future social and economic contexts and the challenges that the education sector faces.

In the last 10 years, the population of Latin America grew by 18%, from 430 to 508 million inhabitants. Of this increase of 78 million, almost all - 76 million - were born in urban areas. Less than 2% of the increase - 1.5 million – were born in rural areas. This increase was accompanied by moderate economic growth – averaging 3.6% annually. Latin America has the most unequal income distribution in the world. 40% of the poorest homes earn between 10 and 17% of national income, while the 10% of the wealthiest homes account for between 30 and 40% of total income. Poverty remains at high levels; by the end of the nineties, 36% of households were below the poverty line. Economic progress during the decade merely permitted the continent to return to 1980 levels.

Politically, the nineties were marked by the attainment of peace within the Central America subregion and by the recovery and consolidation of democracies throughout the continent. Nevertheless, the region continues to suffer from high rates of violence rooted in exclusion and poverty. From the cultural perspective, and seen from outside, our continent appears to be one of the most homogeneous groups of nations in the world. But viewed from inside, the region is a polychromatic mosaic of cultures with hundreds of dialects, dozens of languages, and countless ethnic groups, customs, and beliefs.

2. STATUS REPORT OF EDUCATION IN LATIN AMERICA

The following status report is largely the result of the Assessment of Commitments to Education For All in the Year 2000. The commitments of this programme were:

- Expansion of early childhood care and development activities;
- Universal access to basic education and the satisfaction of basic learning needs of the entire population;
- Reduction of the illiteracy rate by one-half by the year 2000, and increase of basic education and training services for young people and adults;
- Increasing availability of basic skills education and training for young people and adults;

Providing, through education, knowledge and skills to help people maximise their potential and improve the quality of their lives.

A general assessment of the development of education over the past decade reveals that although there has been real progress in the region, the goals proposed at Jomtien in 1990 have not all been achieved. There is much to be done in order to turn 'education for all, education from birth, education as a lifelong process, inclusive education' into a reality. But the decade witnessed the construction of the political and technical foundations necessary to make the achievement of these goals possible. So there is now an awareness, a national consensus, some clear diagnoses (including about what we do not know), and some examples of successful policies for further development. Some significant points of recent years for each level of education can be reported.

2.1 Early childhood care and education

Coverage of early childhood care and education programmes increased for the ages closest to primary school entry level, principally in urban areas, producing a substantial increase in the numbers of boys and girls who now enter primary school with some formal early education experience. But programmes for younger children - from birth to 3 years - are still limited.

This phase has benefited from a growing participation of parents and the community in these programmes, particularly for the age groups and social classes that receive less State attention. It should be noted that the countries that have the greatest coverage at this level are those in which the State participates widely in the provision of such services under various guises – both formal and non-formal, conventional and non-conventional.

2.2 Primary education and learning results

Formally organised primary education was the principal vehicle used by governments to deliver education services to the majority of the population. The last decade witnessed the achievement of universal access to primary education, except for some population groups in rural areas. Still, a serious and persistent problem is the high numbers (between 30 and 40%) of children who do not stay in school until the fifth grade (see Figure 1).

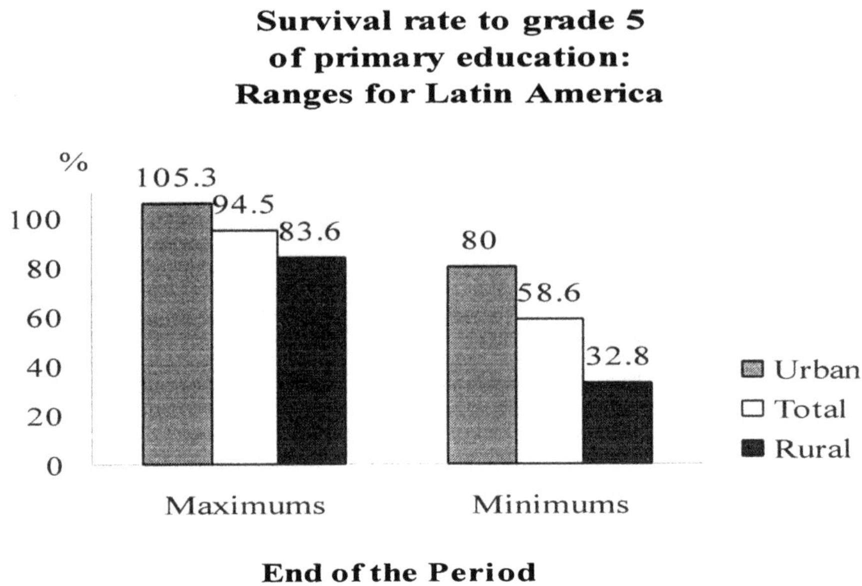

Figure 1. Attendance rate to grade 5 of primary education: Ranges in Latin America

Among major strategies used to improve quality and promote equality were:

- Strategies aimed at general improvement in:
    1. Curricular reform
    2. School autonomy
    3. Provision of teaching resources
    4. Initial and in service teacher training
    5. Increasing the time dedicated to learning;
- Focused strategies aimed at improving quality with equity by applying 'affirmative action' criteria;
- Programs for accessing and measuring the quality of education.

Although there is no consensus on the meaning of 'educational quality', there is agreement regarding the importance of measuring learning results, in order to estimate the levels of knowledge, skills, and abilities that students acquire. For an over-all view of learning results, we have used information from the Latin American Laboratory for the Assessment of Educational Quality, which published comparable data for 13 countries within the region. The principal findings of the study show the following.

1. A high percentage of student achievement scores are best explained by factors outside of the school itself. Among those that best correlate to student test scores are social and family context variables.
2. But an important percentage of the variance in student achievement is explained by factors linked to the school. This is encouraging because it means that significant opportunities exist to develop policies aimed at changing the current situation and at considerably improving student achievement.
3. Girls perform better than boys in language, while boys have better scores in mathematics.
4. With the exception of one country, urban schools showed better student results than rural schools.
5. The level of language achievement is low when pedagogical objectives are not met. Children are learning to read, but not to understand or to interpret what they read. They learn *how* to read but not how to *learn* while reading.
6. In mathematics, the results are, in general, poor and not uniform among countries. Students are not assimilating knowledge. Nor are they developing expected skills in mathematics. They do recognise symbols and structures on a basic level, but have difficulty solving both simple and complex math problems encountered in everyday life.
7. Achievement differences between schools are not explained by where a school is located or how it is funded; rather, differences between schools are related to teaching practices and to school management.
8. Most importantly, a favourable classroom learning environment, by itself, is more important for learning than the combined effect of all the other factors studied.

Although policies give high priority to equity, results are still modest. For example, although primary education increased in rural areas, only a smaller percentage of boys and girls reach the fifth grade. In general, girls do not suffer discrimination in terms of access to primary school. But such discrimination may exist in indigenous, rural, and marginal-urban contexts. Information about equity is scarce and not always reliable, so it is difficult to report confidently about education services for marginalised groups.

Financial investment in primary education has remained constant in most of Latin America, varying between one and four percent of gross domestic product. Although the decade saw a slight increase in public expenditure per student, this has not been significant. Lack of data on issues such as distribution of resources, relative weight of policy priorities, percentage of expenditures directed at marginalised groups, efficiency of spending, and private expenditure on education, inhibits strategic action.

Teachers are key actors in improving the quality of education. They are the major source of instruction in most societies. In Latin America, except in rural areas, the supply of teachers, in absolute numbers, has been sufficient to meet demand. But approximately 20% of teachers do not meet the minimum qualifications set by their governments. There are great disparities between countries in their requirements for teacher certification. And although there are measures to promote better initial and in-service training, these have not yet produced significant changes in classroom practice.

2.3 Literacy and education of young people and adults

Within the region during the nineties, literacy training and education for young people and adults were not among policy priorities. This, together with the inefficiency of school systems, which in Latin America discard between 6 and 42 percent of students before they reach the fifth grade, caused increases in the total numbers of illiterates in some countries.

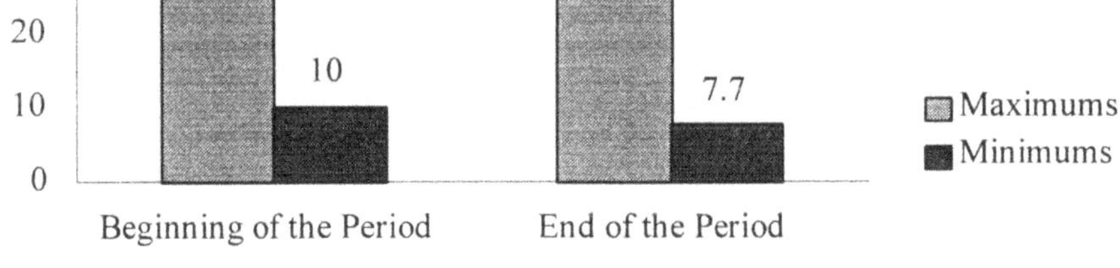

Figure 2. Adult literacy rate of the population aged 15 and older: Ranges in Latin America

Illiteracy rates however fell in all countries, but without reaching the Jomtiem goal of reducing rates to half of the 1990 levels. Illiteracy is concentrated in the 24 years plus age group, in rural areas, low income zones of large cities, and among indigenous groups. Higher illiteracy in rural areas is due to delay in primary coverage reaching these areas and their poor performance in terms of retaining students in school until the fifth grade. There have been important changes in literacy training models.

Literacy training is now often combined with other education activities for young people and adults, such as job training; training increasingly occurs outside of the formal education sector. Also work preparation components have grown, in order to increase worker flexibility and mobility in a rapidly changing labour market. Literacy training programs have embraced multiple actors, from within and outside government.

In our continent, the majority of those attending adult programs are young people. There is a consensus about the priority areas for young people: a) preferential attention to post-primary education for those who live in poverty and have dropped out of primary programmes; b) the creation of programmes that stimulate active participation by young people and the full recognition of their responsibilities and rights; c) programmes that support and stimulate job training for young people living in poverty.

2.4 Training in basic skills and education for a better life

Schools in most countries now include learning components in human rights, values, ethics, concern for the environment, sexuality, and health. 'Education for life' themes occur across disciplines and as separate subjects. But with no assessment tools or systematic data, we do not know to what extent these subjects are addressed in schools; nor the impact that exposure to 'education for life' themes have on the daily life of students. Some countries make intense use of the media such as radio in the education of children and adults, particularly in rural and indigenous areas. The media is used for education in almost all the countries. The region does not have industries to develop and produce educational programmes for students, teachers, and the general public.

The use of computers and the Internet as teaching aids is only beginning in the region. Almost all countries have carried out projects to adopt these technologies in schools; some have set up national networks linking schools. A key question is how to utilise these new learning tools to encourage inclusion in education, and how to avoid hardware and software becoming factors resulting in greater inequality.

2.5 Achievements, pending themes, and challenges

Thus, among the major achievements in education during the nineties were:

- Universalisation of coverage of primary education
- Significant increases in coverage of early childhood education

- A relative decrease in illiteracy
- A concern for quality
- A concern for equity
- The inclusion of education for life themes in both formal and non-formal, or alternative education programs
- Participation of multiple actors: NGO's, parents, social groups
- Education became a national priority.

The decade also left a number of themes pending:

- High rates of repetition and drop-out in primary school
- Scattered coverage for early childhood education, particularly for the 0 to 3 year age group
- Low priorities were placed on literacy training and the education of young people and adults
- Low student learning levels
- The persistence of social inequalities in the distribution, efficiency, and quality of education services
- Lack of communication and co-operation between different actors involved in the tasks of Education For All
- The need to strengthen governmental policy-making
- Small increases in investments in education.

So the major challenges faced by education in the future are:

- To transform education into a task for all through consensus- building, participation and co-ordination among actors
- To achieve greater participation from parents and communities
- To respond effectively to the multiple dimensions of education problems through policies that cut across all sectors of society
- To increase coverage of early education by promoting quality alternative programs
- To substantially improve primary school quality and to achieve effective learning of reading, writing, and math
- To substantially reduce rates of grade repetition and school drop-out
- To give greater priority to literacy training and to the education of young people and adults
- To improve opportunities for girls to learn math and science in the classroom
- To promote greater gender equity in rural areas and in indigenous communities
- To assess the impact of the teaching of education for life themes in both formal and non-formal programs

- To encourage the use of the media and information technologies in order to promote equity
- To substantially increase public spending on early childhood education, primary education, literacy training, the education of young people and adults, education for life, and the use of the media and information technologies
- To increase the production, quality, and utilisation of data on education in order to improve decision-making at all levels of the system
- To increase education system efficiency and achieve greater transparency in the use of resources
- To substantially improve the initial training, work conditions, and social status of teachers.

3. SECONDARY EDUCATION

Secondary education was not included in the Education For All assessment. Nevertheless, the progress achieved in primary education during the nineties increased the demand for secondary education. The gross enrolment trends in secondary show a 10 percent growth between 1990 and 1997, from 50.9 to 62.2%. This increase represents both a quantitative advance, and also suggests access to secondary education by sectors that have hitherto been excluded through geographic, social, economic, and cultural factors.

Countries are implementing policies aimed at improving this secondary level. But it is the weakest link in the learning chain, with few clear definitions of its purposes, its structure, and functions, causing ambiguity and disfunctionality in approaches to secondary curricula. Traditionally, the secondary phase has been seen from two perspectives: either a scientific and humanistic bridge to higher education, or a specialised technical and vocational training leading to the labour market. This traditional view is lamentably out of date, exhibiting an unrealistic social perspective, disconnected from the concerns and needs of the population, society, and culture in which it is immersed. Traditional education based upon a juxtaposition of academic subjects, each one of them usually with a separate teacher, does not lend itself to a necessary unity and cohesion of approach. One damning criticism of secondary education is that it is divorced from the realities of everyday life, and that school knowledge is not transferable to day to day living.

4. THE FUTURE CONTEXT

So what of the future, the context in which education will develop, the demands it will face, and the services needed to satisfy these demands and aid in constructing a more just society. This requires thought on future economic and social contexts for education.

4.1 Sustainable development and the environment

There is a consensus that projected world economic growth cannot be sustained unless we change current life-styles. What are the cultural obstacles to such a change - a change demanding new life styles, new beliefs, and new social relations. The idea of predictable market liberalisation ignores the fact that poorer nations need, besides a basic infrastructure, social investments in areas such as family planning, environmental protection, health care, and education - major public investments in social programmes.

During the last fifty years, the world's production of wealth has increased six-fold, never previously experienced. One cost has been pollution and environmental deterioration. The hope is that future, new, 'clean' technologies will aid heavy industries to develop non-polluting, earth-friendly processes; this requires educated and qualified people. Clearly, future generations must be able to live in a cleaner, healthier world, and the best way to protect the environment is through the development of technology and of education.

The last few decades have seen an ominous widening of the income gap in Latin America. A high proportion of children and young people remain outside of the school system through economic necessity. Malnourished millions live on the streets. Women, particularly rural women, have been doubly hit by the increase in poverty. Often it is difficult for women to attend class because either as children as adults, they are heads of households. Currently, women head 20% of households of Latin American families. So, one challenge for the future is to reverse this trend toward ever-greater poverty and assure that the education systems themselves do not reproduce social inequalities.

4.2 Knowledge and information

The production and accumulation of knowledge are the driving force for development. Currently, the production of scientific and technological knowledge in the region is precarious. It is necessary to come up to speed internationally to be part of the technological revolution and to survive in an increasingly competitive world. Training must be intensified in scientific and technological research, so people can face the new challenges of the global economy.

Information technology will profoundly transform the way that people organise their lives, interact with others, and participate in all areas of social life. We should be aware, however, of the social impact of these new information technologies – the effect they will have on work, education, culture, health, business, and public services.

4.3 Demographic aspects

The population growth rate has decreased in wealthy countries, and has remained high in poor countries. The fertility rate is inversely related to the literacy rate of adult women; consequently, the population of developed countries is ageing, while the demographic structure in developing countries is younger.

Nevertheless, in Latin America, population growth projection curves show an important downward trend. From the 16% growth figure for the years 1995 to 2000, they should drop to 10.6% between 2015 and 2020. The proportion of the population below 16 years is estimated to fall from 31.6% in the year 2000 to 24.9% in the year 2020.[1] So the increase in demand for education will grow for young adults, and relatively diminish for the 5 to 14 year group. For OECD countries (*Education at a Glance*. OECD Indicators, 1998), in 1996 the percentage of the population between 35 and 44 years with studies after secondary school was 65% for men and 60% for women. In Latin America and the Caribbean, these percentages are 26% and 33%. Enormous efforts will be required, for our region to at least equal the situation of the developed countries in 1996.

Education impacts on population growth rates. For each additional year of education that a girl receives, the infant mortality rate drops and the birth rate falls. Access to more and better education also raises education levels of parents leading to decreasing dropout rates and raising achievement levels of their children.

5. EDUCATION SERVICES: DEMAND AND SUPPLY

What about the future demand for education and the response from education systems?

[1] Boletin Demográfico Nro. 64, CELADE - CEPAL, julio 1999.

5.1 Future demand for education

Among the demands placed upon education, we should note those directed at: a) assuring human development and improving the quality of life, preservation of the environment, overcoming poverty, and achieving education that excludes no one; b) contributing to regional integration and to strengthening citizenship skills; c) strengthening the development of science and technology; and d) improving working conditions.

a. Human Development and the Quality of Life

Education is the key for the development of individuals as well as the development of society. At the World Education Conference in Jomtien in 1990 it was declared:

> Each person, children, young people, and adults, should be able to have access to education options in order to satisfy his or her basic learning needs. These needs include essential learning tools (such as reading, writing, oral expression, arithmetic, and problem-solving), as well as basic learning content itself (theoretical and practical knowledge, values, and attitudes) necessary to permit human beings to survive, to fully develop their abilities, to live and work with dignity, to fully participate in development, to improve the quality of their lives, to make basic decisions, and to continue learning.

This recognises that:

> The satisfaction of these needs confers on people the possibility and, at the same time, the responsibility, of respecting and enriching their cultural, linguistic, and common spiritual heritage, of promoting the education of all, of defending the cause of social justice, of protecting the environment, and of being tolerant of social, political, and religions systems that are different from their own, respecting humanistic values and commonly accepted human rights, as well as working for international peace and solidarity in an increasingly interdependent world.

The Delors Report (UNESCO 1996) established four pillars as the foundation for tomorrow's learner - learn to know, to do, to live together, and to be.

In *learning to know*, people require:

1. The ability to concentrate, to use memory and thought as the basis for learning;
2. The ability to seek out and analyse available information;

3. The ability to take active control of their own education, to adapt to the environment and to existing possibilities;
4. The understanding that learning is not a linear process nor a single event, but rather a wide process that moves forward by means of a great variety of experiences outside of the classroom.

In *learning to do*, people require:

1. To recognise that learning is a practical process which is not solely based on abstraction and theoretical discussion;
2. To go back and forth between school-based learning and every-day experience in order to integrate knowledge an action;
3. Aptitudes and abilities to act based more on general competence than on specific task-related skills;
4. Scientific and technical reasoning skills due to the importance that this kind of knowledge has for human development.

In *learning to live together*, people require:

1. The ability to participate in democratic processes within a spirit of building peace;
2. An open and accepting attitude toward peoples and cultures;
3. The ability to learn anywhere and to recognise that the community is responsible for the education of its members;

In *learning to be*, people require:

1. Self-responsibility and participation in the common goals of the community;
2. Integrated knowledge of the potentialities of human beings, including an aesthetic sense, an appreciation for sport and for culture;
3. An understanding that having is not the same as being;
4. Education that contributes to their full spiritual, physical, and ethical, development.

An important trait for young people is the ability to adopt a pro-active, autonomous and self-confident attitude toward life. Quality life-long education for all should encourage creativity, flexibility to adapt to change, the development of intelligence, the ability of self-initiative, sociability, solidarity, self-esteem, self-confidence, and ethical integrity.

The greatest challenge faced by education in Latin America is to effectively contribute to overcoming poverty and social inequalities. Most poor children still receive poor quality education that does not enable them to break out of the vicious circle of poverty. An accepted meaning of equality of educational opportunities is for all to be able to enrol in an education system. But who enters, into what kinds of establishments, and with what kind of 'cultural capital'? For education to become an effective tool in the struggle against poverty and inequality, we must differentiate the financing so the State can provide compensatory resources for those children entering with less 'cultural capital'.

b. Regional Integration and Globalisation

Globalisation has made us aware of the need for Latin American integration as a means to strengthen cultural identity. Cultural trends in the past were distinguished by lack of recognition, or even disdain between neighbours; as if one built cultural identity by affirming one's own traditions and rejecting those of others. This kind of thinking must change. People must learn to recognise and value differences as positive factors in the construction of a durable regional cultural identity.

This has direct implications for the school curriculum, such as the obligation to teach foreign languages, a history that emphasises common projects and achievements more than wars and divisions, a history that takes a positive, rather than a negative view of neighbouring countries. More effort is needed to certify study, from primary to university, taken in other countries to facilitate our social, economic, and cultural integration.

Education is being called upon to play a key role because it is uniquely able to encourage the positive aspects of globalisation and reduce possible negative ones.

c. Generation and Incorporation of Knowledge and Technologies

The production and utilisation of knowledge are increasingly important so that countries may achieve long-range, sustainable economic growth. Education must be both efficient and responsible in training citizens able to produce new knowledge and use it creatively. In the future, such a focus has the advantage of remaining up to date as it constantly seeks to narrow the gap between education systems and the future requirements of societies.

Everyone should have access to and use technology. Without this, we will increase the distance between more and less developed countries. Train for its use and development, incorporating it into daily life is a task for education. Developing countries have invested little in preparing scientists. This should create a concern to extend science education to all, to increase the training of scientists, and to demystify the daily use of technology.

The link between scientific and technological development and education has been absent, in most cases, in the definition of education policies. Improving training in science, particularly on the secondary school level, requires more and better-trained teachers. Countries that do not develop integrated policies of scientific and technological development with education components are taking a short-range view. But in an integrated policy, a high priority should be given to those aimed at financing national investment in science and technology. To do so we must be highly creative and original, as well as being aware of financing models successfully used by developed countries.

The relationship between competition and education has never been closer. We must make great efforts to diminish the gap between developed countries and us. It is not only the case of the need to produce and make use of knowledge. We must ensure that knowledge and technologies are widely disseminated and used by all of the population.

d. The World of Work

It is predicted that in the coming years the labour conditions of the population will change. People who remain in the same job will change the way they work. The informal sector of the economy will continue to grow, and with it the vicious cycle of unstable occupations, low productivity, low incomes, and the impossibility of absorbing advanced technology.

Education, therefore, must look into the future and visualise a labour situation both different and more vulnerable that the present one. The ability to work in small groups; to use of communication technologies; to be a 'self-starter' and to develop and adapt to the informal market; to make more and better use of free time (shorter working days), should all be the objectives of training in both the formal and non-formal education sectors.

Most of these changes will have profound impacts on education. Among areas that require attention is higher education, which is not yet fully sensitive to the demands of the market. Adult education and informal, leisure learning will be affected as well. We do not need to know precisely for which kind of occupation we should educate our young people, or re-train adults. Education must be more open in order to train individuals who are creative, able to solve problems, and who can accept change. Since technological innovations create new occupations or eliminate others, countries that are not prepared to train or re-train their labour force will be at a serious disadvantage.

5.2 The supply of education services

Education systems must respond to demands for the need for a new kind of school, a new kind of curriculum, a new kind of teacher, and new actors.

a. New Schools that are Open and Autonomous

If we want education to change, we have to change school. Schools are among the institutions most alienated from our societies. Generally, most of the important decisions are taken outside of the school itself. Decisions such as the nomination of its teachers and directors; regarding curriculum, tests, and assessment; about the training of its teachers, have been based more on central plans than of considerations of teachers' real needs. Decisions on resources and how they are used come from a central administration.

The new school must be based on administrative, financial, and pedagogical autonomy. Each school should manage its own personnel, make decisions regarding the school calendar and strategies to track and assess learning achievement. It should be able to include in the curriculum subjects that are of interest to the community of which it is a part. School management should be a joint responsibility between teachers, parents, and local authorities. In order for this autonomy to function well, all actors should be prepared and trained to work together. Inputs and processes should be subordinated to student learning. An efficient school should establish a longer, more assiduous, more intense school day. Current education reforms have witnessed some interesting experiences aimed at providing incentives for autonomy and creativity in schools. These positive trends should be strengthened until schools are transformed so that, besides carrying out their fundamental missions, they become true socialising agents and community centres.

b. A New Curriculum and Education Resources

School curricula should be profoundly transformed in order to change the current compartmentalised, subject design. Crosscutting themes should be incorporated which contribute to the integral training of students, and which respect multiple intelligences. It could be a curriculum more centred on facilitating learning to know, to do, to live together, and, especially, to be. This kind of knowledge would thus help to counter one of the most worrisome fears of our times: the fear of not finding a meaning to life.

Education systems should consider new styles of learning marked by greater autonomy of the learner and the utilisation of new technologies. The communication media and information technologies within the school system can make education available to more people – even the most distant. A more flexible system is needed that makes learning opportunities available to people throughout their lives. The new curriculum must take into account the multiple possibilities of learning that occur outside of the classroom. By doing so, the school can both develop and strengthen in people critical thinking in regard to the media. Course content in the curriculum cannot be an end in itself. It make no sense to study language if the purpose is not to communicate more effectively orally and in writing. Nor does it make sense to study history if this does not serve to develop a critical and constructive attitude vis-à-vis society. Memorising is not learning; learning must be used to progress in the world, more autonomously and more creatively.

c. The New Teacher

A pending task is the training of a group of professionals able to introduce and carry out these profound changes that the education system needs. To educate in new skills for a more developed society demands teachers with different characteristics, teachers who are innovative and have self-initiative. To prepare such teachers, we must support initial and in-service training. This requires: a) the creation of in-school meeting places where teachers can reflect, exchange experiences, provide mutual support, and create teaching materials; b) national and international policies for exchange of teachers and innovative experiences; c) resources for research and creative thinking; d) reform of teacher training courses. Special attention should be given to experiments with teaching programmes based on the use of new information and communication technologies.

Schools will not change without first changing the teachers. We need less bureaucratic teachers, teachers willing and able to take the initiative and who can use their professional knowledge to help solve the learning challenges of their students. A teacher with initiative does not need to directed from someone outside the classroom. Assessments of the learning achievements of the students of such a teacher do not have to come from outside. He or she does not have to be told that such and such a content must be given in such and such a time. So the education system must remove bureaucratic barriers, and create necessary conditions for freeing the self-initiative and creativity of teachers. A teacher with self-initiative knows how to diagnose the learning problems of each student, propose adequate measures, and track the situation until the problem is solved. This is to say that, as a professional, the teacher should assume responsibility for student learning. But such a teacher deserves and requires a better salary and better working conditions than are the norms in our region. We should think about systems with flexible, competitive salaries which reward good teachers, salaries with fixed and variable components, with criteria that reward merit, with control systems that are close to the municipality and to the school. All of this means that much effort must be given to the selection and training of teachers who have a new mentality. We must create new stimuli such as premiums, scholarships, training courses, and salary incentives for those who work under difficult conditions in rural or distant areas. A teacher with self-initiative is the single most effective tool in the school, such a teacher both teaches and learns at the same time.

Education systems should concern themselves with themes of university-based initial and in-service training of science teachers, particularly for the secondary level. Reinforcing national capacity for the development of education material in science is fundamental if we wish knowledge of science and technology to be presented appropriately to students.

A new school requires a new school director. Besides the technical competence required for the position, besides pedagogical and administrative skills, the school director must have leadership skills as well. This is important not only in order to create a team spirit in the school among teachers and students. It is vital in order to involve the community in the life of the school and the school in the life of the community. The success of a school is in large measure dependent upon the dynamism and competence of its director.

d. New Actors

If we wish the whole society to be educated, we need new actors who participate in the tasks of education. A policy of inclusion requires a change of responsibility in school management. This raises a number of questions about the roles of the State, the private sector, and society in educational change. Besides a more marked and more dynamic participation of teachers and of parents in the process, education should be a responsibility shared by all: journalists, business people, churches, legislators, and other governmental authorities not connected to education. Quality education for all, throughout life, demands from everyone a new viewpoint. Each sector of society should reflect on its role and do all it can in the creation of a more human and more just society, with citizens who are better educated and more able to live in an ever more complex world.

6. CONCLUSIONS

These reflections allow us to identify a set of requirements for consideration when thinking about education systems in the future. All of them apply to the world as a whole, but they have special relevance in Latin America.

- Because of the complex demands placed upon them in terms of human development, quality of life, integration, globalisation, the challenges of the knowledge and use of technology and it effects on work, the education system is of the utmost importance.

- We need to imagine the building of an education system that is flexible, open to all, independent of age or life conditions; a system that guarantees that education as a right throughout life. We need to imagine a system that is open to those who have already been to school, allowing them to return. We need to think of an open system that incorporates all educational resources in the society, including the media and new communication technologies.
- We need to achieve an educating society, involved and aware that responsibility is shared, and that education is everyone's task, not only that of those traditionally involved in the sector.
- The development of science and technology must be undertaken with responsibility not increase the gap between rich and poor countries. We need more scientists; we need to increase the use of technology, particularly for the improvement of learning.
- We should move towards education that considers both the transmission of knowledge and the development of all of person's potential. The strengthening of democracy, the maintenance of peace, the fostering of development all demand education with a profound ethical meaning; an ethics of solidarity which is manifested in daily life, in politics, in business, and in interpersonal relations.
- It is evident that people must be trained to adapt themselves to changing situations, to possess cultural fluency with respect for other cultures, to be able to prevent and to solve problems, and to be self-motivating, able to become permanent learners.
- Regional integration, globalisation, and respect for one's identity demand an education that respects diversity, that allow us to successfully face the tensions between the world and the community, between tradition and modernity, between what is global and what is personal.
- Improving the professional and social status of teachers is crucial for a new kind of education appropriate for the new millennium. Initial and in-service teacher training must convince teachers that they are not only teachers, but learners as well.
- As in any other system, the education system needs to be managed with competence and accountability. Until recently, the use of management tools in education was unheard of; today it is clear without such techniques, it will be more difficult to obtain the financial, material, and human resources required for transformation.

What happens in the coming years will have a decisive impact on the future well being of our planet and all of us who inhabit it. Much will depend on the kind of education that we offer our citizens. Schools, as they have always been, are our last and best hope.

BIOGRAPHY

Ana Luiza Machado has been Director of UNESCO's Regional Office for Education in Latin America and the Caribbean since 1997. She holds a degree in Social Sciences from the Federal University of Minas Gerais (Brazil) and completed post-graduate courses in Business Administration offered by Columbia University (NY) in collaboration with the João Pinheiro Foundation and FUMEC (Brazil). In addition, she is certified in Organizational Consulting by the Business Administration Council of the National Business Studies Service (SENAC, Brazil). She worked as a planning and research specialist at the João Pinheiro Foundation (Brazil) from 1971-1988, and as a consultant in business organization for the private and public sectors, principally in the area of education. She was Deputy Secretary of Education of the State of Minas Gerais from 1991-93. From 1993-1996 she was that State's Secretary of Education. Under her leadership, the state successfully carried out major reforms in education. In January, 1995 she was elected President of the National Council of State Secretaries of Education (CONSED), serving in that post until December, 1996. She was a member of Brazil's National Education Council from 1996-97.

The school of the future: The WWW and learning processes in new learning environments

Betty Collis
Faculty of Educational Science and Technology, University of Twente, P.O.Box 217, 7500 AE Enschede, The Netherlands.
Collis@edte.utwente.nl

Abstract: The IFIP WG 3.1 Chile 2000 Invitational Conference addresses the topic of the school of the future via four overlapping themes. The WWW and Web-technologies can have a key role in one of these themes: learning processes and new learning environments. This key role will be explored by using a reference matrix that involves two main dimensions: a dimension relating to the location and ownership of learning resources, and a dimension relating to the difference between the WWW as library or marketplace and the WWW as workspace for learners to create and share resources. The impact of the WWW in the school of the future in relation to learning processes will be predicted and examples given of how this impact is already occurring will be described.

Keywords: Web-based systems, Web-resources, pedagogy, learner-centered learning

1. INTRODUCTION

The WWW, or the World Wide Web, the Web, websites, have become commonplace terms in society, so certainly they will be familiar terms in the school of the future. But familiarity does not necessarily mean centrality; the examples of the telephone and television attest to the fact that some technologies that are central to everyday life rarely become central to the core functioning of the school, in the classroom and in the direct teaching and learning process. Will this also be the case with the WWW?

2. THE USE OF THE WWW IN THE SCHOOL

Before addressing this question, it is useful to make some clarifications about technology. There are many distinctions about Web-technology that are important to the school of the future. The most important may be:

- the distinctions among external websites, an internal intranet system, and a personal website;
- the distinction between using the WWW to find and interact with information or resources put there by others and using Web-technology to publish one's own information and artifacts or as a workspace;
- the distinctions among the different types of communication that can be supported by the WWW.

The first point is important to mention because sometimes it is assumed that the WWW has little application for schools because of the technical problems and high costs associated with accessing the WWW via the Internet as well as the social issues resulting from allowing children to be exposed to inappropriate external sites. An intranet system offers full Web-functionality but does not have to involve making use of the Internet, or can control this access. All that is needed for a Web-based system running as an intranet is a local-area network in the school and one computer designated as a server. In addition, individual webpages can be made and used as standalone files without needing any network connection at all. Such files that can be copied via floppy disks and thus shared with others in a local environment, again without needing a network connection. In the discussion that follows about the potential role of the WWW and Web-technologies in the school of the future, there will be made a regular distinction between externally available WWW sites and resources, intranet systems, and individual websites and pages. Each has its potential contribution to the school of the future.

The second point, if one thinks of the WWW as an external repository which can be browsed and from which items can be selected, or if one sees the Web as a working environment via which new materials are developed and made available, has critical implications for the role of the WWW in the school of the future. The WWW as a library, or increasingly, as a marketplace, brings up different issues than those that pertain if the Web is primarily used as a working space. As a metaphor, it is the difference between giving a learner access to a library with a skilled librarian to steer him to find things efficiently, or giving the learner his own word processor and printer along with tools that facilitate his working together with others on the production of some sort of document. The different issues involved with the WWW as marketplace and the Web as working space are important for the school of the future.

The third point relates to the number of persons receiving a communication (none, one, designated group, anyone), the degree to which the communicator knows those who will receive her messages and those who respond to her messages, the reusability of the messages, the structure of the messages (formal, structured, informal, non-structured), procedures relating to initiating a message, the use of text, audio, video, images, or some combination of each of these for communication and the intention of the messages (initiating a question, giving feedback, stating an opinion, giving an instruction). The degree and manner in which Web-functionality's are used to support different aspects of communication will affect the nature of the impact of the WWW in the school of the future.

3. A GRID FOR WEB USE IN THE SCHOOL

The first two of these points can be used to form a form a reference grid for Web-use in the school of the future, as shown in Table 1 where the columns relate to location and ownership and the rows relate to the marketplace/working space distinction. Numbers are given to the cells for convenient referencing in the subsequent discussion. Within each of the cells of the grid, different forms of communication can occur.

Table 1. Reference grid for WWW use in the school

	External websites	Intranet system	Individual sites
USE RESOURCES OF OTHERS	1.	2.	3.
CREATE RESOURCES	4.	5.	6.

This grid can help us in the analysis of the role of the WWW in the school of the future in relation to the learning process and new learning environments. If we look from a learner's perspective Table 1 can be filled in as shown in Table 2.

Table 2. Characteristic activities relating to learning processes

	External Websites	Intranet system	Individual pages or sites
USE RESOURCES OF OTHERS	1. Can range from library-type reference use to provision of traditional computer-based instruction.	2. Generally the same as Cell 1, except that the source of what is in the system is local.	3. Limited access and distribution, as has been the case with traditional computer-based resources.
CREATE RESOURCES	4. Can be used as a reference source for what is being created, also as a publication medium.	5. Same as Cell 4, but what is created can be labeled and integrated with other resources; access can be controlled.	6. Learner uses the WWW pages as a medium for personal expression; later they can be shared.

3.1 Using resources of others

The strength of using external websites as sources of information is the fact of the vast quantities of information available, sometimes information that is not only timely but beyond what could be possible to obtain from a school library or textbooks. In addition, the use of external websites as sources of information sometimes allows direct communication with the person supplying the information, or with others interested in the information, highly unlikely to occur with non-WWW-resources originating outside of the local context of the learner. Counteracting these benefits is the difficulty of finding appropriate information. Copyright and cost issues, inefficient information-handling skills (inefficient skills in finding, evaluating the appropriateness of, and making use of information in terms of copyright and citations), and also the lack of quality control and cultural and language control of information in externally available websites will increasingly limit the amount of appropriate resources that learners are able to obtain from such sites. However, the use of the WWW for information will be a common, recurring activity in society as a whole; learners must develop these skills, not be sheltered from them. Intranet systems increase the chance that information will be appropriate, but at the cost of only offering a limited amount of information. Also, the information must be created or placed into the intranet (see Cell 5), a task that will require substantial time and effort at the local level.

In terms of hoping to find appropriate structured learning materials (in the sense of tutorials or other forms of teacher-independent materials), external websites are less likely to be of value, at least at the school level. The many variables that need to be aligned to the local situation of a learner before learning materials are appropriate for a learner are rarely going to be found in materials located on the Internet; tailoring of those materials by the teacher will need to occur (which then moves the activity into the second row of cells in the matrix in Table 2). As was the case with informational resources, structured learning materials available via a local Intranet will be much more likely to fit local conditions. But the time, skills and effort to create such materials will limit their realisation, just as it has limited the creation of computer-based learning materials by teachers for several decades. This is even more the case with standalone webpages, where access to a database of materials such as can occur with an intranet Web-system, cannot occur.

3.2 Creating resources

There is much more potential for new forms of learning activities when the focus is on using Web-functionality's to support the process of creating one's own resources. The emphasis shifts from (a) trying to find and supply just the right resource to (b) strengthening the learner's own communication and organisational skills. Resources as hyperlinks or externally obtained information can be incorporated into the materials being created, but are not the major focus of the learning experience; the process of creating one's own webpage or site as an exercise in reporting and communication is what is primary. If such a page or site is published on the Internet, if it is only available through an intranet, or even if it is only available as a local file, may not be important; this will depend on the learning context of what has been created. If children are creating reports to be shared with learners outside of those served by their Intranet, then publishing on the external WWW is a valuable motivation activity. But the majority of learner-produced materials do not have meaning for the external world; their meaning is in the doing, and thus can be limited to Intranet or local-file sharing with others.

Web-based course-management systems are offering new ways for instructors and students to add learning resources that they create or tailor themselves to an Intranet system (Landon, 1998; Robson, 1999). These materials can be integrated with other resources and information relevant to a given course, class, or project; and can be used by other learners. New pedagogies are developing whereby learners are co-creators of learning materials for their peers or for other (Collis, Winnips and Moonen, 2000). Web-based course-management systems make it easy for learners to input such self-created learning materials into a website accessible to all their classmates, and to share and even add to such resources. Web-based tools can support learners working collaboratively on the creation of such resources; such tools are helpful even for learners who are working together in a face-to-face manner. Shifting learners into the role of co-producers of learning resources also is a response to the problem of locating materials for use in an Intranet system: let some of these be from the learners themselves.

4. PREDICTIONS ABOUT LEARNING PROCESSES AND LEARNING ENVIRONMENTS

Given the above, my predictions for the major impact of the WWW in the school of the future with respect to learning processes and learning environments are shown in Table 3.

Table 3. Predictions (given in italics within parentheses) about the impact of the WWW on learning processes and new learning environments

	External websites	Intranet system	Individual pages or sites
USE RESOURCES OF OTHERS	1. Can range from library-type reference use (Common but limited) to provision of traditional computer-based instruction. (*No*)	2. Generally the same as Cell 1, except that the source of what is in the system is local. (*Impact highest when learners share in the creation of the resources to be used by others, see Cell 4.*)	3. Limited distribution, as with traditional computer-based resources (*No*)
CREATE RESOURCES	4. Can be used as a reference source for what is being created, also as a publication medium to make learners' work available to the external world. (*Common but limited.*)	5. Same as Cell 4, but what is created can be labeled and integrated with other resources; access can be controlled to those within the school or class. (*Impact can be high.*)	6. Learner uses the WWW pages as a medium for personal expression; later they can be shared. (*As HTML editors are more common, this becomes relatively easy to do, but publishing requires WWW server access or intranet system.*)

In terms of impact on the school of the future, this suggests a scenario where learners, of all ages, systematically learn search skills, skills in identifying appropriate information, and skills in how to properly make use of information produced by others. Learners and teachers will routinely look up information and resources via external websites, and if the information is about local situations, via an Intranet. How this information is used will depend on the teacher; it is not likely to be self-contained learning modules which replace the teacher even in an intranet system. Information-handling (finding, evaluating, selecting, using properly) literacy will be a major learning skill, relevant in different degrees in all subjects and at all grade levels. It must be learned in an incremental way, just as learners learn how to communicate. It will be part of the curriculum in the school of the future.

In terms of new learning processes, the use of a Web-based system with easy ways to upload learner-created resources offers the strongest potential, especially if learners can create such resources without having to learn a type of programming code, such as HTML, but only need to use editors (text, image, video, audio, HTML). At the least, learners have the experience of self-expression, but the potential is much stronger. Learners have new ways to work collaboratively on a complex document or multimedia product. Learners have new ways to share their work with others and to have their work become part of the study resources of the class. The process of communication is the focus, but it serves a double purpose, because what is produced as the result of this process can be a resource that can be studied by others. The problem of how to get adequate resources into an Intranet is addressed by using students as a source of some of these resources. The role of the teacher takes on a new dimension: that of guide and quality controller of learner production.

5. EXAMPLES FROM PRACTICE

At the University of Twente in The Netherlands, students in the Faculty of Educational Science and Technology are engaged in new learning processes using new learning environments in ways that illustrate the above predictions. Although these are university students, the pedagogical ideas involved can be scaled down for use with school-age students. Between 1994 and 1998, there was extensive use of the WWW in terms of Cell 6 in Table 2; via standalone sites created by pioneer instructors and used as environments to guide and support student activities. Most of these activities involved the students, working in groups, creating resources that were then evaluated by other students, all as part of the assessed learning processes in the courses (Collis, 1997; 1998). External websites were used for ideas and as links within the pages and sites made by the students (Cell 4 in Table 2). Because the faculty did not have a Web-based system available, all work was isolated and dependent on the technical skills of the instructor. Student-produced work had to go on the WWW in order for students to share each others' work, a situation that led to problems when external visitors to the course sites misinterpreted the work-in-progress aspects of the students' pages. The whole process was not likely to scale up to other instructors beyond the pioneers, as it was too labor-intensive for the instructor and required too much technical skill.

In 1998 the faculty moved from a pioneer-only approach in the use of the WWW to the use of a Web-based course-management system, called *TeLeTOP* (http://teletop.edte.utwente.nl). This Intranet is based on a set of design principles emphasising the need to make it easy for both instructors and students to create and input their own resources into a course website and the underlying database, and to share and reuse these materials (Tielemans and Collis, 1999). TeLeTOP is now being used by all instructors in the faculty, as well as in several other faculties. Underlying TeLeTOP there is an educational philosophy called C@mpus+ which has as major aspects the idea of students becoming more active and of gradually becoming professional in their behaviours. Thus new pedagogical ideas, supported by the new form of learning environment, the TeLeTOP system, are evolving at the faculty. Some examples of these are listed below.

5.1 Students search external websites to select example and study materials for the course

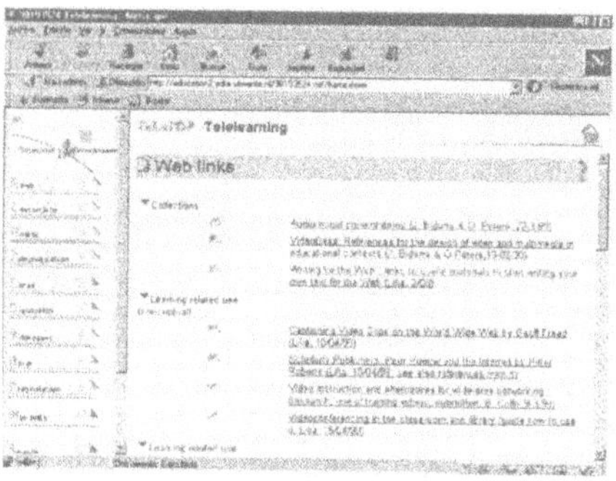

Figure 1. Weblinks

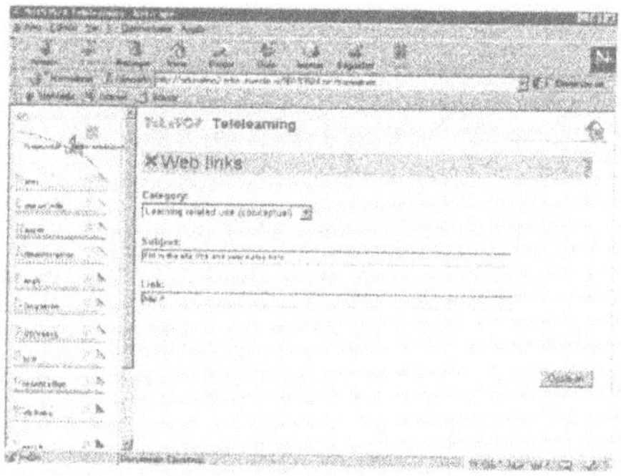

Figure 2. Fill-in form

In the course Tele-Learning the first assignment for the students is to locate examples of websites that are being used for certain types of educational purposes, and to enter these into a portion of the course website. These links are then used repeatedly throughout the course as a basis experiences and for students to compare and contrast in a number of subsequent assignments. The instructor reviews the choices made by the students and if not appropriate sends the student an e-mail explaining why and asking the student to delete the entry and upload a new one.

Figure 1 shows example materials added to a course environment, used subsequently by all students as examples and resources for the course.

Figure 2 shows the submission of such example materials to the course Web-environment simple via the use of a fill-in form which when submitted adds a copy of what was submitted to the course data base.

5.2 Students create multiple-choice questions which are part of the resources for the course

In the course General Psychology each student created two multiple-choice questions for each topic in the course and submitted these, along with comments relating to each of the four options offered for each question, into the course website. Students used a Web-based tool that was available via the Web-system for creating multiple-choice questions. The instructor checked the questions and only gave feedback when a question was weak in some respect. Students studied for the final examination of the course using the submitted questions as a resource. By the end of the course, over 600 questions for self-study were submitted into the database, and could be reused in subsequent years.

5.3 Students create an instructional manual for subsequent classes

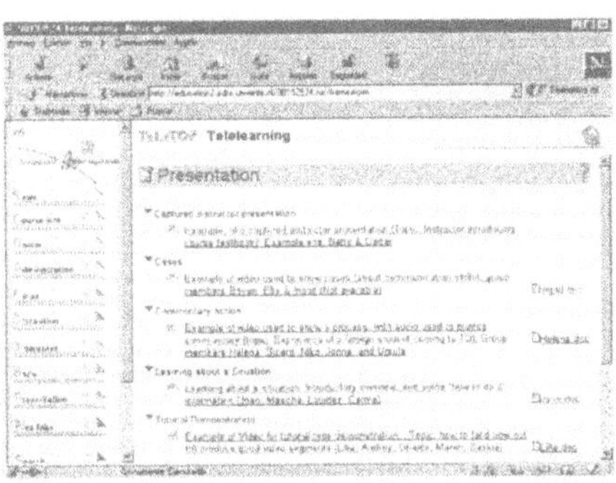

Figure 3. Presentation area

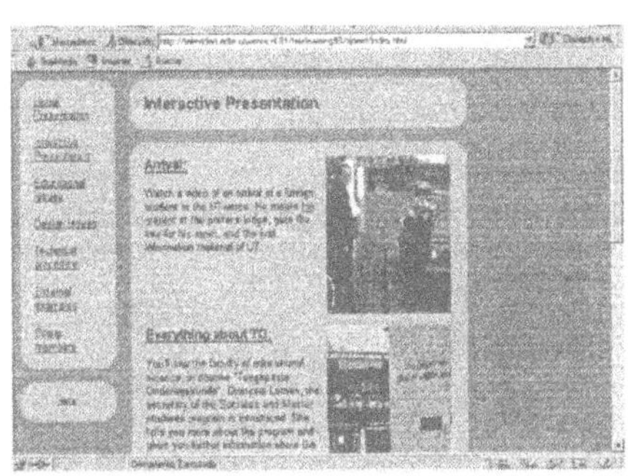

Figure 4. Menu of a manual

In the course Tele-Learning students work in groups to create a multimedia product, and then created an instructional manual based on what they had learned through their own experiences, to be used by subsequent groups of students doing the same assignment. The manual is available via the database system, and is linked to the final projects of the students.

Figure 3 shows the links to four of such instructional manuals added to the Presentation Area of a course website in the TeleTOP system. Figure 4 shows the menu page of one of these manuals, created as a Web-based resource making use of text, visuals, audio and video segments.

5.4 Students create additional study resources

In the course Instrumentation Theory 2 students work in groups of three, where each group focuses on one of the topics of the course, selects an article or articles to complement those already in the reader for the course on the chosen topic, and then prepares a document or website to summarise the new materials. When approved by the instructor, the new document or website is added to the course website, and becomes part of the study material for the course. The students also prepare a short video segment, explaining the main points in their new materials. These video segments are also uploaded into the course website and are meant to be used as additional support materials for the other students in the course. Figure 5 shows one of the Web-based reports integrated into the TeleTOP course website.

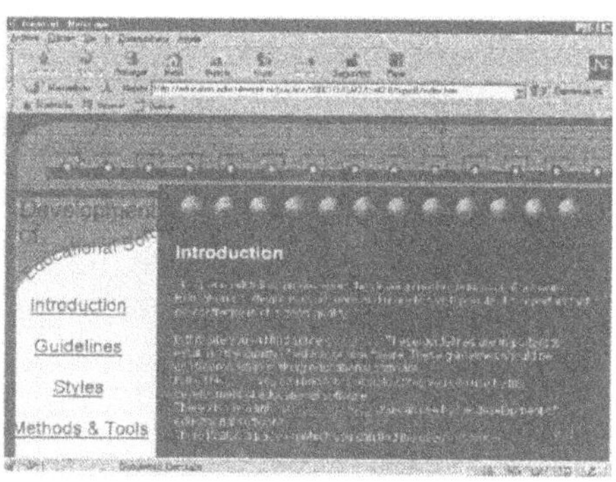

Figure 5. A Web-based report

5.5 Students perform peer evaluations

In a number of courses students use structured forms in the course website to provide formative evaluation of the work of other students, as well as for self-evaluation of their own work. There can be posed the questions to guide peer comments after a class presentation. Also the comments can be submitted via the course website by the end of the class period by students who were present at the presentations, and later, by students who were not present but could look at the class presentation materials via the website and add their comments later.

5.6 Students take the responsibility for some of the lectures and associated study materials

In the course Network Systems students work in groups. Each pair of groups is assigned to one of the lecture periods of the course. One group must prepare and deliver the lecture, making all support materials available via the course website. The other group must prepare a set of study questions based on the lecture, make these available via the website, and provide feedback as far as possible to the questions of students about these study questions. The instructor works closely with each group, to make sure the material presented is accurate and adequate.

In all the of above examples, the students are evaluated and graded on these activities. In this way, thousands of items with potential re-usability value as learning resources have been entered into the TeLeTOP database during its use to support the teaching and learning process. All of these items have been created by the instructors and students themselves. No special time, funding or training was required to produce the resources; in general, instructors only use a word processor or PowerPoint to create materials, while students also use HTML, image and video editors as well as word processors and PowerPoint. Entries can also be typed directly into the TeLeTOP system or copied and pasted in from a word processed document or a webpage. While the resources may vary in quality, based on external criteria, their primary value was in the process by which they were created, and as examples of student work and as extensions and supplements of the course study materials. It is not the case that these locally created items replace the textbook, but rather make the textbook dynamic. They share the benefit of fitting well with the local culture and context, as they were created within those. The TeLeTOP WWW-based course-management system supports Cells 2 and 5 of Table 2 and also allows access of external websites for ideas and links (for Cell 1 and Cell 4).

6. CONCLUSIONS

While the pedagogical strategy of learners being active and creating resources and sharing those with their classmates as part of the learning experience is not a new idea, the WWW and in particular a Web-based course-management Intranet allows possibilities that were not feasible before. The Intranet allows easy uploading, easy access by all classmates, easy reuse of learner-created resources, and can support group production of resources. Learners do not have to be at the same place at the same time to work together or to make use of each others' resources; all that learners (and teachers) need is a web browser and Intranet or Internet-access. Such ideas are relatively easy to realise technically, with access to a well-designed Web-based course-management system. The bottleneck will be not at the technical level, but at the human level. A number of barriers will confront a more regular use of learner-created resources.

Norms

Learners, parents, administrators, teachers all have deeply established views about learning resources; almost all of their experience has been to use materials made by "experts" and learn what is in them. The movement toward learning from each other raises the immediate fear that quality will be lost. Students themselves feel more comfortable mastering what is in a book than being told they have to extend what is in the book; students, parents, and administrators alike may argue that this uncertainly is not appropriate. Setting standards in advance for performance in a course becomes more difficult as students' work is taken seriously as study materials. Administrative procedures that require detailed specification of course content and evaluation criteria will not be compatible with an approach emphasising learner creation. The evaluation of the learning that occurs during the process of creating learning resources will be difficult to measure and grade.

Time and effort

It will take more time and work for both instructors and students alike as soon as learners move away from following a single prescribed textbook and doing assignments where all come up with the same, known-in-advance answers. As learners begin to locate their own supplemental study materials via external websites, the instructor must familiar him or herself with these materials, in order to guide the student as to the appropriateness of the choice. This can take much time, and require much time on-line, which may be very difficult for all involved. Students may complain that it takes too much time for them to find appropriate materials. More care must be taken with communication that is going to be used by others, not just submitted to the teacher. Communication skills for both learners and the teacher will be taxed in new and sometimes demanding ways.

Pedagogical creativity

Reorienting one's instructional approach to an active-student perspective will not be easy for many teachers, partly because some will not find it easy to think of manageable activities that can fit the new approach. Because the tools are new, and the type of activities that make use of those tools are also new to them, many instructors will fail to think of educationally useful ways to engage students in new forms of process-oriented learning. Many examples are needed, and these need to evolve over a period of time.

In the TeleTOP system, instructors can easily visit each other's course environments to get ideas from each other. The matrix-like *Roster* is used in different ways by each instructor but makes it easy to see at a glance the instructional activities chosen for a particular class. Figure 6 shows part of a roster in one of the TeleTOP courses.

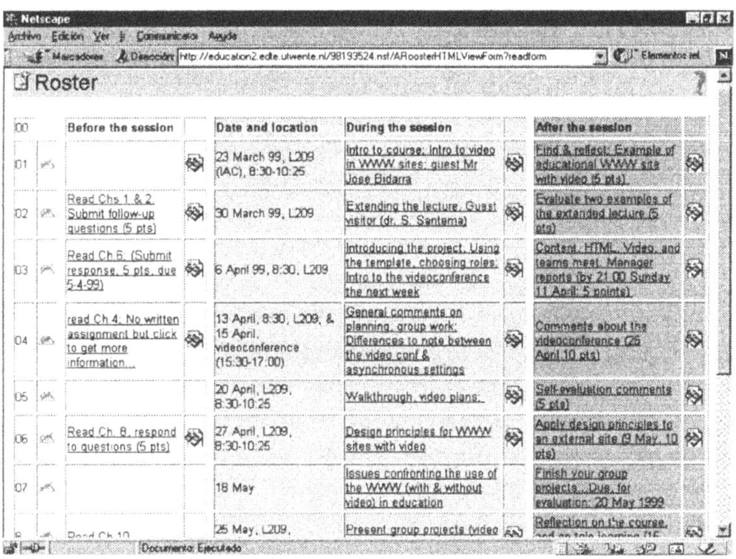

Figure 6. Part of the roster in one of the TeleTOP courses

Nonetheless, despite these possible constraints of local norms, time and effort, and the need for creativity, the use of Web-based tools and intranet systems offers so many possibilities for the school of the future that such tools and systems are likely to be part of the school even if not used to their full potential. These new learning environments will at the very least streamline various forms of communication and information handling. But because learners have the tools to communicate in many ways and to find and select resources from both external websites and an Intranet does not mean that they will do these things well. Doing them well requires good teaching and hard work on the part of the learners. In this respect, the school of the future with its use of the WWW will still resemble the school of the past and present.

REFERENCES

Collis, B. (1997) *Pedagogical re-engineering: A new approach to course enrichment and re-design with the WWW*, Educational Technology Review, 8, 11-15.

Collis, B. (1998) *Building evaluation of collaborative learning into a WWW-based course: Pedagogical and technical experiences,* Indian Journal of Open Learning, 7(1), 69-80.

Collis, B., Winnips, K., and Moonen, J. (2000) *Scaffolding and the use of the WWW: Does it pay off?,* Journal of Interactive Learning Research (in press).

Landon, B. (1998) *Online educational delivery applications: A Web tool for comparative analysis.* [http://www.ctt.bc.ca/landonline]

Robson, R. (1999) *WWW-based course-support systems: The first generation,* International Journal of Educational Telecommunications, (in press).

Tielemans, G., and Collis, B. (1999, 24 June) *Strategic requirements for a system to generate and support WWW-based environments for a faculty*, Paper presented at ED-MEDIA '99, Seattle.

BIOGRAPHY

Betty Collis is professor of Tele-Learning at the University of Twente in The Netherlands and also Chair of the TeleTOP Project. She has been working with WWW-based course-support sites since March 1994 and is thus a pioneer in this area. Prior to the WWW she has been involved in the use of computer-related technology for nearly two decades and has published an extensive amount in the area (see her home-site: http://users.edte.utwente.nl/collis/). Of particular current interest is the topic of instructors' reactions to possible uses of streaming video in WWW-based course support environments.

Dissemination of information and communications technology and change in school culture

Herminia Azinian
University of Buenos Aires, Miller 2377 - 8 C, Buenos Aires -1431 Argentina
azinian@dc.uba.ar

Abstract: School culture can be analysed through the relationships between people (students, teachers, and parents) and through the management of resources. This includes physical ones (like space), non-physical ones (like time), and people. In fact, each of the elements of the analysis affects the other, forming a cycle. Two schools where the principals had a strong belief in computers improving learning are analysed. The administrators and parents of these schools also felt that ICT was the core of education of future citizens. The kind of changes designed in each school, how these changes modified the school culture, and the changes that happened in the way teachers actually used ICT are compared. The main factors that seem to be responsible for the successful continuing use of ICT in one of the schools are presented.

Keywords: School culture, classroom changes, resource co-ordinator, ICT facilitator

1. INTRODUCTION

This paper describes a case study comparing two secondary schools in Argentina. The techniques used were interviews, observation of various aspects of support for ICT, taking notes about the observations and expanding notes through reflection and reading of the literature. When possible, descriptive data collected during the interviews were checked against data collected from direct observation.

The schools were chosen from approximately twenty public and private urban schools that the author, as a teacher educator, had visited. They were selected because the principals had a strong commitment to disseminate ICT in their schools. They believed that this technology should form the core of the education of future citizens. Both schools are private schools owned by parents in communities of high income families and each school has an enrollment of about 300 students.

Dissemination of ICT in Argentine schools is high as there was and still is a push to incorporate hardware. However, there is very little support for educational technology in a broad sense. Computers are placed in computer laboratories with a timetabled use for formal computing classes. Computing teachers are responsible for them because this is the easiest way to deal with the problems of managing the resources for learning and ensuring equitable access to ICT for all the students. Thus, ICT resources are more manageable, but they are isolated from the classrooms. Many teachers are unaware of what their students do while in the computer laboratories. Only a few schools are now in the process of integrating ICT resources physically into classrooms and other places.

The amount of ICT resources in schools has increased significantly during the last years. There is an important gap between the amount and the availability of ICT for educational applications. In schools with a non-supportive environment and with the obligation to use ICT, teachers typically send students to the computer laboratory to use a word processor or to look for some information on the Web. Thus, they show a "modern" face but they only reinforce strategies that don't meet the needs of students.The school of the future is the school that prepares future "worldzens" (better than citizens) who have developed critical thinking skills with a systemic view in a context of problem solving.

2. SCHOOL CULTURE

When discussing the future of ICT in schools we must begin with considerations about the school itself rather than with ICT because education is the main factor of the equation. Schools have always shaped instructional uses of emerging technologies to fit with existing practices (Cuban, 1986). Those planning for an innovative school making effective use of ICT must consider the school culture. Each school is unique not only because of its own educational philosophy, expectations of the community, moral culture, political skills of its leadership, and curriculum but also because each one has its own patterns of relationships and of management of resources that determine how innovations evolve. These patterns are dynamic, depending on other conditions that will not be discussed in this paper.

The school of the future is linked to a constructivist vision of education, with students constructing their knowledge by asking questions, solving meaningful problems, and interacting with others in their environment. It is important to articulate this vision of the potential of ICT, although it is also possible that teachers will come to a constructivist view through using ICT in the classroom (Sandholtz, Ringstaff, & Dwyer, 1997). Both aspects are considered when teachers deal with the power of ICT applications and also link these applications to clear curricular goals.

3. THE CASE STUDY

About three years ago, the schools of the case study, school 1 and school 2, appointed new principals. Both of them faced a new ICT general plan, intending that all students and teachers:

1. share a general knowledge and usage of tools so that they can take full advantage of ICT and
2. use ICT in the learning and teaching processes.

Before this time, both schools were working in the traditional way, but school 1 had been supporting teachers for curricular integration, though with scarce resources. The decision stage of the new plan in both schools included buying hardware and software and training of personnel. Compulsory courses were offered to teachers about the tools.

The set of tools selected for the first goal was similar for students of both schools (word processing, Internet, spreadsheets, graphics, presentations). It was different for teachers at school 2 (word processing, Internet, and curricular specific software) and teachers in school 1 (same tools for teachers at school 2 plus spreadsheets and presentation package).

School 1 provided courses and training in the use of the software and learning activities which demonstrated how ICT applications could be used in teaching. The teachers then had to draw upon effective models of computer integration, as recommended in Ehley (1992). Teachers were encouraged and coerced to use ICT for curricular purposes and coerced to use a computing system for grading students. After attending courses, nearly all of the teachers frequently used the Internet to find information for teaching purposes and made or let their students use the Internet.

Discussion about critical uses of Internet resources was promoted by the computer resources coordinator. Many of the teachers used content-specific applications with students (dynamic geometry, biology simulation, etc.), improving each time they used the software. A few of them haven't yet found software or an application package that adequately met their needs or their school had not yet acquired the software due to financial constraints.

Teachers in school 2 were encouraged but not coerced to use ICT for curricular purposes. They were coerced to use an internal communications system as all communications became paperless. Some of them used the

Internet to find information for teaching purposes and made or let their students use it. Nobody used subject-specific applications.

However, teachers in both schools viewed the computer about equally as useful for instruction. The researcher felt that this statement was made to avoid conflicts in the working place, as some of the teachers showed anxiety because of school demands. As to the availability of hardware, teachers reported to have ready access to computers for themselves in both schools, but the difference was in the support they had at school 1.

Teachers in school 1 had individual students working alone at computers, had them working in groups of two or three, took the whole class to a laboratory, or had the class working with a computer on a large screen. These options were possible because some computers were placed in the hallways and could be used there or moved to other places. There was also a computer at the sciences laboratory for specific purposes.

In school 2, computers were taken out from the laboratory and located in the hallways and in the library. It was decided not to have computing classes since "there is no need to learn, you can just use it" as the external advisor stated in his first presentation to teachers. After two years, students had timetabled computing classes again, as both the students and their parents pushed for this. Each class was distributed in three hallways, so the teacher had to go from one place to another during her lessons. This was a clear example of failure to consider school culture and community needs.

4. TEACHERS' EXPERIENCES

In both cases, institutional willingness to change classroom practices had been approached through inservice (but not during working hours) courses and/or workshops. Many teachers felt excited after the initial training and willing to use the new technologies. They wanted to adopt innovations but in some cases enthusiasm didn't last. This happened with the courses and workshops that lacked focus on solving educational problems, and the teachers could not transfer the skills to actual classroom implementation. Teachers with previous knowledge and experience using ICT adopted and implementated innovative practices quicker.

Teachers in both school systems have similar perceptions of what it takes to become effective users of computers for teaching and learning. They all rated courses and workshops in the school, self-training and experimentation with the computer, and encouragement and support from a facilitator as being the most important factors.

Since school 1 had a ICT resources facilitor in the staff and school 2 just an external facilitator, it is not strange that only teachers in school 1 developed implementation plans. They planned teaching materials, strategies, and management of change while using ICT, during in-service hours, supported by the computer coordinator and a pedagogical advisor. As experiences were successful, the use of ICT spread to other teachers.

Some innovators not only used ICT in their own classes and continued their own self-training, but also helped later adopters by becoming mentors (with no extrinsic compensation). As opportunities to come together in groups of related disciplines to share ideas and experiences were provided in the context of general changes in Argentine schools, ICT-based innovations were discussed. These meetings promoted reflection and encouraged others to attempt new projects. Teachers noted a shift from teaching to learning and a strong appreciation of their efforts by the students. As the three phases of change (adoption, implementation, and continuation) co-existed and demand of support increased, a computing assistant was also employed at school 1.

5. THE ROLE OF THE FACILITATOR

Each school had a designated ICT facilitator. In school 1 the facilitator (resource co-ordinator) was a person internal in the school while in the other school the facilitator was an external person who made regular visits to the school. The facilitators main tasks about ICT in education were:

1. helping teachers plan for the use of ICT, for the elaboration of educational goals, and for the development of projects to reach those goals;
2. assisting teachers in the classroom implementation of projects;
3. assessing the effects of ICT in the school, based on the quality of the integration of ICT resources in terms of students learning and the process of applying it.

In school 1 the facilitator's plan for integrating ICT considered the school's interpersonal culture, the history of successes and problems with ICT, and the configurations that offered promise of desired change. It provided a process for educating teachers and students in the use of a common set of tools, thus considering ICT education as well. The teachers had personal contact with the facilitator/coordinator and got individualized support. The facilitator spent plenty of time walking around, being where she was needed or where she could gather and give information about technical and policy issues.

Thus, in school 1, each teacher's level of knowledge about ICT, attitude toward ICT, and pedagogical practices were highly respected. Besides, the coordinator was a liaison between teachers, and facilitated teacher interchange. This was not the case in school 2. There external facilitation failed because the outside facilitator ignored the issues mentioned before. The needs of the school and of the teachers were not met.

6. MAJOR SUCCESS FACTORS

The researcher found that the principal's attitude towards ICT was the main factor that started the process in each school, endorsed by the community vision. The planning and the support of a facilitator was seen as indispensable by teachers. Last, but not least, some organisational factors were seen as obstacles to cope with. These included timetabling arrangements, the disposition of the school building, and the physical distribution of resources.

7. CONCLUSIONS

Both schools have allocated a great amount of internal funds to their plans to become "schools of the future." Real success with ICT ultimately comes at the level of proper individual planning and use.

The components that seemed to be responsible for the successful ICT-based change in school 1 were:

1. The development of a common technological culture;
2. A supportive computer resources coordinator guiding and developing the general plan, and at the same time involved in the curriculum of the classroom;
3. Courses and workshops given in a stimulating atmosphere which supported learning to use tools, reviewing programs, and making connections with appropriate curriculum goals;
4. Content modules on specific topics given to enable teachers to develop greater expertise in areas in which they wished to specialize;
5. Post-training meetings to help the participants make plans to generalize and integrate what they had learned;
6. Individual curricular support; and
7. Organisational support.

As an educator and a policy-maker, the computer resources co-ordinator's role made a significant difference in the school change with her technical expertise and her understanding of the classroom into the context of the school curriculum. The experience in these schools is published in order to promote factors of change. Since teachers in the schools of the future must be knowledgeable, there is a need to promote professional groups with teachers from different schools to determine not only how ICT can be integrated in the existing curriculum, but also how it can help shape specific curricula and help teachers support each other in implementing the curricula using ICT.

REFERENCES

Cuban, L. (1986) *Teachers and Machines: The Classroom Use of Technology Since 1920.* Teachers College Press, New York.

Ehley, L. (1992) Building a vision for teacher technology in education. ERIC Document Reproduction Service, No. ED 350 278.

Sandholtz, J., Ringstaff, C. and Dwyer, D. (1997) *Teaching with Technology: Creating Student-Centered Classrooms.* Teachers College Press, New York.

BIOGRAPHY

Herminia Azinian is a professor of ICT in Education at the Sciences Teachers College of the University of Buenos Aires. She has taught at all levels, from primary and secondary schools to university and in-service teacher training. She is an advisor to schools and the author of three books and many articles. She has worked internationally for the American States Organisation and is a member of IFIP Working Group 3.1.

Internet in the classroom: Teachers as custodians?

Kwok-Wing Lai
School of Education , University of Otago, PO Box 56,
Dunedin, New Zealand.
wing.lai@stonebow.otago.ac.nz

Abstract: This paper investigates the changing role of the teacher in the digital age. The recent increase of Internet connectivity in the classroom means that students will spend more time using the Internet to access information and inevitably they will access materials considered to be objectionable. Based on a recent study conducted in New Zealand, this paper examines the custodial role teachers have to play in using the Internet with their students. As well, this paper also discusses the legal and ethical issues involved and the strategies teachers used to deal with these issues.

Keywords: Internet censorship, role of the teacher, professional development

1. INTRODUCTION

According to a recent survey, Internet connectivity in public schools in the United States has skyrocketed from 64% in 1997, to 85% 1998, an increase of 21% over just one year (Market Data Retrieval, 1998). In New Zealand, there has also been a similar growth of Internet connectivity in recent years. For example, it is reported that in 1998, 83% of the 2,300 primary schools and 94% of the 340 secondary schools had access from at least one computer to the Internet (Ministry of Education, 1999). No doubt the growth of Internet connectivity would have an impact on learning and teaching strategies, classroom organisations, collegial interaction, as well as professional development of teachers.

As increasingly more students are using the Internet as a tool of learning, skills of information gathering and evaluation have now been considered as essential skills in schools. To successfully use the Internet as a teaching and learning resource, teachers thus need to become conversant with information and communication technology (ICT) as well. Frameworks or standards of ICT competencies for teachers have begun to emerge in recent years. For example, in the US, the International Society of Technology of Education (ISTE) has developed a set of foundation standards adopted by the National Council on Accreditation of Teacher Education (the full document is available at http://www.iste.org). In New Zealand, the recent Review of Education Green Paper (Ministry of Education, 1997) has recommended that information skills be included as a key element in the professional standards required for beginning teachers. It is also documented in an Education Review Office publication (1998) that a capable teacher should demonstrate informed professional knowledge of appropriate technology and resources.

Professional development has been clearly established in the literature as a key success factor if an innovation such as ICT is to be integrated into the learning process (Fullan, 1990). Developing "Internet literacy" for teachers thus has become a prominent focus of many professional development programmes. For example, the New Zealand Ministry of Education has recently launched a programme called *Interactive Education Strategies for Schools*, with one of its key components being the construction of an online learning centre to provide teachers with Internet-based resources. It is encouraging to see that policy makers have begun to recognise the importance of developing teachers' skills of integrating ICT into the school curriculum, as well as emphasising the role of the teacher as a facilitator in a computer-supported learning environment. However, the focus of the majority of these programmes is still very much on the cognitive aspects of ICT use, paying little attention to cultural and ethical issues, and the custodial role of the teacher has seldom been considered.

It has been demonstrated that the Internet could be used as a tool to support a constructivist and a student-centred approach to learning (Lai, 1999). However, if students are asked to take charge of their own learning and given the opportunity to retrieve information from the Internet, they not only will access unscrutinized and irrelevant materials, but will access objectionable material as well. This should be a major concern for Internet using teachers as students may be accessing materials which are not only unlawful to have in one's possession but may also be harmful to them. For example, under present New Zealand legislation (The Films, Videos, and Publications Classification Act 1993), it is unlawful to possess "objectionable" materials (information, pictures, moving images and sound). While the Ministry of Internal Affairs (through its Censorship Compliance Unit) attempts to ensure the unavailability of objectionable material in New Zealand, intercepting and controlling the availability of such materials through the Internet is difficult. In providing students with access to the Internet, school administrators and teachers therefore have to address some major custodial and educational issues associated with online access.

Increasingly teachers have to interpret what constitutes "objectionable material" both from a legal as well as a custodial point of view while being mindful of the importance of freedom of speech and information gathering. Schools are faced with the problem of imposing some form of censorship on Internet use in their classrooms to keep students safe and often make ad hoc decisions on practices and strategies to deal with these issues. Most teachers are unprepared to deal with these legal and custodial responsibilities in an Internet-rich learning environment.

Supported by data collected from a recent New Zealand study on Internet censorship in schools, this paper examines the extent to which New Zealand secondary teachers are aware of their legal and custodial role when using the Internet with their students. Strategies for controlling access will be discussed and recommendations proposed as to how teachers may deal with these issues in the future schools.

2. THE NEW ZEALAND EXPERIENCE

A study was conducted in 1999 to investigate the awareness of New Zealand teachers of ethical issues involved in accessing Internet resources and the strategies they used to deal with these issues. This research was divided into three stages. In the first stage an online questionnaire was sent to 983 primary and secondary schools (out of a total of about 2,640 schools). 280 schools (28.5%) returned their questionnaires. In the second stage, a follow-up hard copy questionnaire was sent to each of these 280 schools. 196 (70%) schools returned the questionnaires. 74 were secondary schools (out of a total of about 340 secondary schools). In the final stage of the research, ICT co-ordinators/managers of 16 secondary schools were interviewed during site visits. In addition, 65 students from these schools were also interviewed. This paper uses some of the findings gathered from the second and third stages of the study to illustrate the changing role of the teachers and the need for professional development in this area. These 74 secondary school respondents were mostly heads of ICT departments or ICT co-ordinators (62%), teacher-librarians (22%), and principals (9%). More details about the study can be found in Lai, Elliot, & Trewern (1999).

3. LEGAL AND ETHICAL RESPONSIBILITIES

3.1 Lack of awareness

To examine teachers' understanding of their legal responsibilities in accessing materials from the Internet, participants of this study were asked how much they knew about the Films, Video and Publications Act 1993, which defines whether a publication (including Internet resources) is objectionable or not. On average, the awareness of the respondents was low. Of the 74 secondary school respondents, only 16 (22%) knew about the Act. When asked to describe what they knew about the Act and its implications on Internet use, their responses showed that they had very limited understandings of its implications. The following comment, from a technology-rich school, which had a large proportion of teachers using the Internet at the time of the interview, was a typical response:

> "a lot of them had an idea that there was something they didn't know much about it. They had a feeling that there were some issues there, but they didn't know what they were…"

Secondary teachers seldom talked about ethical issues related to Internet use. For example, while over half (57%) of the respondents (mostly ICT co-ordinators) considered Internet censorship a moderately or extremely important issue in their schools, their colleagues only occasionally talked about it in the staff rooms ("No. It hasn't been raised…as a topical issue at all"). One teacher reported that the last time they talked about these issues was "probably last year… at the beginning of last year [20 months ago] when we organized the policy".

3.2 Lack of ownership of school Internet policy

Most of the schools had developed a policy on Web use for their students (82%) and nearly two-thirds of the schools (63%) had a policy on students' e-mail use, although fewer than one-third of the schools (30%) had a policy on staff use of the Internet. Although a high proportion of schools in this study have developed some kind of Internet policies for their students (e.g. an Acceptable Use Policy (AUP)), it seems that teachers had little ownership of these policies. Very often, it was the ICT co-ordinator who was responsible for the development of the policy, which was subsequently approved by the principal and/or the board of trustees, with little staff input. Parent and community support was also limited in developing these policies, with only 12% of the schools having some form of community involvement. Parent's involvement was not high either (31%).

3.3 Lack of professional development

The lack of awareness of the ethical issues had a lot to do with the lack of professional development in this area. Typically, schools spent very little time on professional development. According to one school:

"We had it as a staff briefing at the beginning of the year… we ran a workshop at the beginning of the year for all new staff, and all staff, and that was one of the issues that was raised, as to what are our legal and moral and ethical responsibilities…we spent probably 20 minutes to half an hour on that."

For those schools that had professional development on Internet censorship, not every teacher had the opportunity to participate. One respondent gave the following answer when asked whether he had participated in any professional development in this area:

> Teacher: "we had an advisor in"
> Researcher: "…and most people had an opportunity of participating?'
> Teacher: "Umm, not all of them. Only those ones who felt they had the need to at that stage were in line"

It is sometimes difficult for teachers to "feel the need" if they have not been informed about the issues. The lack of full participation may result in some kind of tension in some schools because of the lack of understanding and consensus of the school's policies. For example, the following incident was reported in one school:

"…We did have big trouble, at the beginning of this year where we got [a] new computer teacher, and he is in the computer room and the kids have got easy access to the Internet. And when they weren't doing things, they'd flip into the Internet and they'd be in all sorts of places…Of course, he was a new teacher…I even had to ban somebody from using the Internet for the way they were carrying on in that class."

A similar incident was reported in another school:

"...the child will not have the permission slip therefore they can't access the Internet but they [the staff] don't feel it's wrong to sit that person next to someone [who is] using the Internet. And that is a worry to me because to me it's wrong, the parents have not given us permission for their child to look at the Internet."

4. CONTROL, CONTROL AND CONTROL

While teachers in general have limited awareness of the importance of the ethical issues involved in Internet use, at the management level, principals and ICT co-ordinators were keen to have tight control so that students would be protected from accessing objectionable material from the Net. For example, close to three-quarters (74%) of the secondary schools in the study had developed a policy of tracking students' WWW use and about half (44%) of the schools tracked their students' e-mail use. From the study it is clearly noted that respondents were very concerned that their students might access materials they should not be accessing. For example, some schools did not allow students to use Web-based e-mail because of the lack of control over what they would send out. Teachers saw that it was their responsibility to supervise and monitor their students' Internet activities. They felt the need to provide students with a safe environment without exposing them to objectionable material. A number of the respondents suggested that they adopted a similar role to a parent when they used the Internet with their students.

Various strategies were used to control access to objectionable materials. These included: supervision (92%); signing an AUP (70%); using a filtering software (38%); educating students (39%); and setting up an Intranet (30%). Most schools used multiple strategies, although fourteen schools (19%) relied solely on physical supervision, two schools used an AUP alone, and one school used educational strategies to inform students about objectionable materials without employing any restrictive measures to block out access. For example, the following school used a combination of strategies to achieve tight control over access:

> "...We have a programme which checks for keywords in any e-mails sent and we have some programmes which check for particular stuff that's downloaded, and because the Intranet is set up [in] a particular way, we can identify every site, that every student has been to...most of the computers are visible by a teacher. And during lunchtime, they're still visible by a supervisor..."

4.1 Supervision

The main objective of physical supervision was to make sure that students had no opportunity to access inappropriate materials. The supervision process normally began by requesting students to get parental permission to use the Net for school work-related purposes. For example, "Students are asked to show their permission note which must be signed if they are on the Internet".

Sometimes tighter supervision might include:

"Teachers set tasks, nominate URLs to be used and keep a watch as it is done in the PC lab"

"use of bookmarked sites only...Actual searching under close supervision with discussion as to efficient key word searching first and supervision as to which sites to look at..."

Supervision almost always meant the physical presence of the teacher:

> "A staff member is expected to monitor the sessions by checking the screens every few minutes and advising as necessary"
>
> "Computer is in "visible" part of the room. Students can only access when staff is present"

Physical supervision has its limitations. For example:

"Experienced users know how to access a site in the background, fooling an inexperienced teacher that they are on task"

> "Teachers have 30 or so pupils to cater for. Supervision cannot be fully relied upon as a safeguard."

Also, time was a major factor, as "close supervision means loss of time to do other work" and "not many staff [are] willing to supervise due to lack of time".

4.2 Filtering software and Intranet

Some schools were quite happy with using filtering software to screen out inappropriate materials. For example, one respondent being interviewed was very proud of using *Cyber Patrol* for filtering out unwanted sites, although problems were encountered in the process.

> "... if we didn't have...a censorship programme with the *Cyber Patrol* software, that would be a big concern... [students] do a lot of things like downloading song lyrics, downloading games, downloading zip files that they never use and its just an overhead on the system...Alright, we paid $2000 to purchase *Cyber Patrol*...Everyday it downloads from the United States a new set of updated rules...identifies all the nasty stuff, and it goes from pornography to um, nudism in art to racism in art to racism, hatred, violence, sex, drugs, alcohol, general substance abuse, and anything unpleasant, and they create what they call these "Not rules"...we can look at the list of Not rules and we can tick whether we want to have...basically we tick the whole lot ..."

When asked whether this program has excluded students from going to sites that actually would have been acceptable, the teacher replied:

"Yes. A teacher came the other day, in social science, I think it was a history class, they were doing research on the KKK (Klu Klux Klan) in the United States and they couldn't get to the site that they wanted to get because it was blocked."

Although a high percentage of teachers using filtering software agreed that it was an efficient way of limiting access to the Internet, some teachers doubted its effectiveness. One respondent commented that it was "far too much effort for dubious results," as many appropriate sites were blocked and also because "it is like a challenge to some students to see if they can get around the system. It also limits and cuts out some useful sites."

Setting up an Intranet had similar problems. The following are some of the negative comments given by the respondents:

> "Information can be limited/dated"
> "No online access but it is impractical in terms of time taken to pre-cache. In that respect it is not effective".

"Very time consuming – removes many of the features of the Web – i. e., free thinking/surfing"

4.3 Educating students

It is surprising to note that just one school used only educational strategies to deal with problems of accessing objectionable materials. Views such as the following were rare:

"[educating students involves helping] them develop skills in finding out, [exploring] with assistance the range of information in specific areas they are studying and be discriminating in selecting info to answer their questions. Developing personal integrity in what they choose to view and access, understanding that the validity and content of many sites is very suspect – yet not denying the vital tool it is becoming to find out fast..."

In secondary schools, there was a view that at the end of the day teachers could not really do a lot about Internet censorship:

"Secondary students are old enough to know what they should and should not be accessing...ultimately we can no more stop them accessing some sites if they are really determined than we can prevent them from bringing a porn mag [pornographic magazine] in from home..."

While primary teachers placed greater emphasis on supervision, their counterparts in secondary schools put more emphasis on the responsibilities of the students.

"...Students are ultimately responsible for their choices and it is helpful for them to sign usage contracts upon entry to the school. These contracts can state clear consequences for abuse of Internet usage."

5. THE CUSTODIAL ROLE OF TEACHERS

While secondary schools in New Zealand are using a variety of strategies to limit access to objectionable materials on the Internet, teachers are not clear how to define objectionable materials, nor have they reflected on the implications of adopting restrictive measures on using Internet resources. One comment from a teacher summarises this feeling succinctly, "reasonably...who decides what is appropriate? Too many value judgement involved in the absence of a policy..."

Limiting access to Internet resources may not be compatible with a constructivist approach to learning where students are asked to actively explore, gather, and evaluate information. Decision making is an important component in the research process, particularly for senior secondary students, and limiting access may undermine independent research. According to one teacher,

"...so much stuff out there that would be stopped by using a filter. And I don't think it teaches the children how to evaluate what they're reading...we want them to decide whether its authentic or not...If we had filters on and stopped them having to make decisions, I think that's wrong..."

However, students have already faced the problem of information overload. There is simply too much irrelevant information available on the Internet. If teachers do not take up the gate-keeping or custodial role it may mean a waste a lot of students' time and resources. However, how much protection students should have from accessing inappropriate materials is a difficult question to answer. One teacher from the study illustrated the need for protection with the following example:

"Downloading Web pages about the Columbine High School massacre resulted in our students having access to document containing hateful and violent racism in the form of vocal statements recorded from court records."

How far should teachers' custodial role go? Should teachers keep track of students' e-mail and their Web browsing activities? Many schools contended that as long as they had included it in the policies it would be legal. If teachers go as far as the following comment by one of the respondents suggests, would it eventually come into conflict with teacher's role as facilitators?

"...we track where they have been...I go and check their mail...it is in the policy, they know its not private...I always go through and see where people have visited..."

6. CONCLUSION

From the questionnaire survey and interviews it is clear that teachers do have to take up a custodial role when using the Internet with their students. However, many teachers are unprepared to take up such a role. The tendency to impose control and limit access will clearly pose problems for those teachers who are willing to allow students to freely explore the Internet and make their own evaluative decisions. The lack of emphasis on educating students about their ethical responsibilities in these schools is a big concern. If there are no clear guidelines for teachers to follow, tension among colleagues on Internet use may result. The lack of professional support in this area may also mean that teachers may be discouraged from using the Internet in their teaching simply because it is too hard and time consuming to make ad hoc decisions.

Teachers cannot deal with these ethical issues alone. As one respondent commented, "you cannot stop inappropriate use if it is supported at home," teachers have to work closely with parents and the community to deal with these issues. Their involvement should begin at the stage when schools begin to formulate their policies. Perhaps the following procedure, reported by one of the respondents, could increase the involvement of both teachers and parents:

> "The technology committee introduced [the policy] at a staff meeting and then we went, split up into what we have as forums, which is 6 groups of teachers, and we debated the issues that were in here and came up with this as the consensus and said, yes, we'll live with that...last year, when were formulating the policy, I went to the PTA [parent-teacher association] meeting, we had a special parent teacher meeting on technology where we explained what we were doing and the implications and the contracts and other things, and they had a bit of input as to what they would like and what they wouldn't (like) for their kids"

Teachers of the future need to reflect on the kind of ethical issues involved in using the Internet with their students as well as the desirable strategies needed to deal with these issues. They need to decide whether student access should be limited and whether student e-mail and Web browsing should be tracked and recorded. In addition, teachers have to decide the optimal level of involvement of parents and the community. Equity issues involved in Internet access also need to be considered. The issue of accessing objectionable material from the Internet is used in this paper as an example to illustrate the new custodial role teachers have to take up in a Internet-rich learning environment.

Deciding what Internet resources should or shouldn't be accessed is a moral as well as a legal issue. Teachers clearly have a custodial role to play when they allow their students to access the Internet for their work. Professional development is needed to prepare teachers to take up this role in the new millennium. The question of whether, as well as how to, control or educate students so that they are aware of their legal rights and ethical responsibilities is a big issue for teachers to resolve in future schools.

7. ACKNOWLEDGEMENTS

This research was supported by the Otago Research Grant (LAMB03). The author wishes to thank Anne Elliot, Fieke Roozon, Nicola Elliot, Philip Munro, and Haidee Brash for their support in the data collection process.

REFERENCES

Education Review Office (1998) *The Capable Teacher*, Education Evaluation Reports, Wellington.

Fullan, M. (1990) Staff development, innovation, and institutional development. In *Changing School Culture through Staff Development* (ed. B. Joyce), ASCD, Alexandria, VA, 3-40.

Lai, K. (1999) Teaching, learning, and professional development: The teacher matters most. In *Net-Working: Teaching, Learning, and Professional Development with the Internet* (ed. K. Lai), The University of Otago Press, Dunedin, 7-23.

Lai, K., Elliot, A. and Trewern, A. (1999) Ethical use of the Internet in New Zealand schools: A preliminary study. *Proceedings of the ICCE*, Chiba, Japan, November 4-7, 1999, 451-468.

Market Data Retrieval (1998) Technology in Education, 1998. [WWW document]. URL *http://www.schooldata.com/publications3.html*

Ministry of Education. (1999) *Request for Proposal for The Learning Centre*. Ministry of Education, Wellington.

Ministry of Education. (1997) Review of Teacher Education Green Paper. [WWW document]. URL *http://www.minedu.govt.nz/ Teacher/Review97/*

BIOGRAPHY

Kwok-Wing Lai is a Senior Lecturer in the School of Education, University of Otago. He has been teaching and researching in the field of ICT since 1986. His research focuses on the use of computer-mediated communication in the school curriculum, as well as on teacher development.

The Esloo design for the digital elementary and secondary education

Jaap Westbroek
School Group Esloo, Rijnlandlaan 1,2273 CT Voorburg.
Esloo@svm.nl

Abstract: In the Netherlands near The Hague Schoolgroup Esloo will build a future school for prevocational education, with a focus on the technical vocations. It will be made with the people of the old school that is part of the Schoolgroup. The school will be named Corbulo College. Corbulo was a Roman soldier who built a village in the 1e century. The school will be opened in august 2001. In this article we will introduce the way this design was developed for a future school and the way we the design is implemented. We will accentuate the role of architecture and the role of ICT. Over the next few years, there will be substantial investment in the use of ICT and in the connection to internet in Dutch schools within the major programmes of the Dutch government. They are called "Investing in Progress" and "Education online" and Schoolgroup Esloo is one of the front schools for implementation.

Keywords: Ethics, building design, creativity, curriculum development, pedagogy

1. INTRODUCTION

To think about the future is only possible when it will take place on different levels. This means two things: we have to put the school in a sociological and historical context and we have to make philosophy part of the thinking process. Especially in times of great change we have to analyse the base of the change and when you want to do that in a profound way you get to philosophy.

Not only for analysing we used philosophy. When we want to make a demo of the future, it is not enough to describe the concrete situation we want to create. The starting school is part of a dynamic process so we have to consider the concrete situation in its historical perspective. Describing it on a philosophical level will make clear in which direction the process will continue.

This paper will elaborate on the way we think about education. Education has an ethical and a social aspect. It has to give our youth the possibilities to become citizens who are able to do their work in society. But they also have to be good citizens who are constantly asking questions to society about the developments going on. So education has to give the tool to the youth to ask the good questions as well. That is the ethical task of education. In the whole of history you can see that there is a contrast between the education to be a normal citizen and the education to be a good citizen. Being good means being abnormal as well. So education has to give way to both. The starting-point of this paper is that the paradigms of future society based on a richness never achieved before will give citizens more possibilities to be abnormal, creative, etc. So that the contrast between the normal and the good will diminish in the future.

In "The disciplined mind" (1999) Howard Gardner says: "I believe that three very important concerns should animate education; these concerns have names and histories that extend far back into the past. There is a realm of *truth* – and its underside, what is false or indeterminable. There is the realm of *beauty* – and its absence in experiences or objects that are ugly or kitschy. And there is the realm of *morality* – what we consider to be good, and what we consider to be evil." To realise this, education has to change a lot. This paper wants to give an impression how it may be possible. Our school wants to become an example of that.

2. MISSION

Esloo operates on the following educational principles:

- education must be made-to-measure;
- education is demand-driven;
- education must take place in a small-scale environment;
- education provides the culture exchange that students need to shape their future;
- education advances self-reliance;
- education links up with the social environment.

3. TRANSITION TO AN INFORMATION SOCIETY

"If knowledge is the centre of new society... It means that education is the leading branch of economy. How can we rethink that?

George Copa

These words say in a nutshell what Schoolgroup Esloo eventually wants to achieve through education. George Copa is a professor of Teaching and Learning of the University of Minnesota and one of the partners in thinking about both the shape and contents of the new school.

3.1 Transitional period

Maybe it has everything to do with the fin-de-siècle sentiment, but it is a fact that a lot of attention was given in the past to the mapping of the social changes brought to us by the 21st century. To be able to build a school for the 21st century, we first must have a clear picture of the changes society has been going through lately. These changes are described in many ways. They are sometimes referred to as the 3rd Wave Society (Toffler, 1980), the information society or the demand-driven society.

Fast economic growth in East Asia, globalisation of the economy, the world becoming smaller because of the Internet, the shift from an industrial economy to an information society with a "new economy" seems to be decisive. The share of the service enterprises in the western economy has been growing increasingly for the past few years.

Creativity, intelligent products, integration of production and service have become the new fashion. In trade and industry people refer to learning organisations, intelligent enterprises and paradigm shifts as mental model for the future.

Generally speaking we live in a transitional period: the industrial society is nearing its end and the information society has already begun. Knowledge is the core of the information society. New concepts are promoted and life long learning is one of them. Trade unions and employers reach agreements on employability and flexibility. ICT becomes more and more basic to our society. We live in a dynamic society in which not only the changes develop more rapidly, but also the concepts that are fundamental to these changes. To Esloo it meant that building a new school could no longer be undertaken starting from concepts from the past.

Developing a concept for a new school then became a quest. Wherever it was possible we included outsiders in the project and we consulted the available literature. We noticed that especially in the management literature many interesting points were to be found. For example the metaphors that map the social changes have been developed there. Applying these metaphors to education bring along the changes of perceiving knowledge as economic capital only. Describing the school as an enterprise could imply that the relation between education and fundamental questions is abandoned. On our quest we encountered the contrary. The metaphors of the management literature that describe enterprises on their way to the information society refer to a society and to organisations which have been able to realise the targets and propositions we formulated for our school too. In the future information society knowledge will not only be referred to as economic capital but also as social and cultural capital. It means that truth, beauty and morality will be part of this conception of knowledge. Enterprises are willing to play a different role in information society.

3.2 Life long learning

All this rotates around knowledge, around the part of the creative human being in the production process, around the service and the entrepreneurial capacities expected from everyone, around flexibility and employability. The early industrial society made a clear distinction between education and labour. Education was reserved to young people who were shaped into cultural and social beings with the aid of education. The labour period followed the learning one. The earlier someone switched to the labour process, the lower his position on the social ladder would be. Since the quality of labour wasn't exactly high, it was better for children to stay away from it as long as possible. Hence we may declare the fights against child labour in favour of obligatory education with the logical consequence that neither working nor learning was fun.

The organisation of society based on this paradigm has been broken open in two ways since the fifties. First of all the dynamics of society led to the development of a totally different perception of the relation between labour and learning in adult life. This caused education to spread over the entire life span (life long learning). Secondly young people became more important economically; first as consumers, but later also as producers. Both developments made the principles of elementary and secondary education more and more contradictory to social reality. Students with lower levels of education, to whom education has less to offer, experience this even more strongly. So instead of referring to the division of life in consecutive learning, working and resting periods we refer to life long learning, working and, as a third item, personal development can be added.

3.3 Learning in the information society

Until now in general secondary education there is not really a relation between learning and working. This means that elementary and secondary education lacks the potency of life long learning by which it is excluded of contributing substantially to shaping the 21st century in which society will function on a much higher level. The principles of the information society oblige education to connect more to real life in stimulating young people more in their economic roles. Life long learning and life long working must be linked. Life long learning teaches people to get grip on their personal development through strategic knowledge and skills. This applies to both their producer and consumer role.

In the process of life long learning, learning can be reduced to only three strongly related learning areas: the own mind, the own body and the own environment. One spends a lifetime getting to terms with these three areas. This has to do with the three realms pointed by Howard Garner: the realm of truth, beauty and good. The acquired knowledge is put to use (= working) in the social and thus cultural context within which one operates. Meanwhile every culture of all times has always been permeated by this, it won't be until the information society, that the use of this knowledge will be given a full social implementation.

So we can see learning as a divergent and a convergent process. When a child is born it is seeking its way through the surrounding world and it is learning all the time and the surrounding world is growing during his whole life. This is the divergent process. But in puberty the identity of the adolescent makes his learning position convergent. He wants to know his own position in the environment. What will he do, who will he be, etc. The link between learning and working is a good metaphor for describing this converging process. It means that prevocational education can be the bridge and must be introduced in all forms of secondary education. As result education can address fundamental questions in an entirely new way. Not surprisingly this has strong effects on the learning contents, learning processes and learning environment. It gives content to the constructivist paradigm.

By all this education will be brought into the centre of society. It will develop new models for learning of which eventually enterprises and other social organisations will benefit. Herewith education plays the crucial part, which it is expected to play in a knowledge society.

Enterprises and schools will support the importance of the concepts of learning organisations and they will describe which qualities are needed. Hereby the role of general and purely factual knowledge strongly decreases, while the importance of metacognitive abilities, of development of other forms of intelligence, and of the management of abilities that belong to a learning organisation strongly increase.

It is necessary from both a social and economic point of view that these transformation processes do not intensify social splitting but strengthen unity. The creative capacity of the entire world population should contribute to the shaping of the 21st century society. A real transformation of society can only take place if the changes in education regard all students.

4. INNOVATION IN EDUCATIONAL PERSPECTIVE

The innovations of education that are in accordance with the changes in society can be classed as follows:

1. the change of the curriculum;
2. the change of the role of both the teacher and student;
3. the change of the organisation;
4. the change of the physical learning environment.

These four classes are closely related: one change can't take place without the other. Our school is active in all classes. This is an important point because most of the rethinking of education until now is about the creation of a new didactical situation. In our vision this concerns only the second subject. Real change can not occur without redefining the other subjects as well.

4.1 Curriculum

We call the core of this transformation "context-oriented education". A "learning route" shapes life long learning educationally. Through such a route a student is prepared for his future. It describes a process from today to the future. For every student the learning route is divided in learning paths and the learning route co-ordinates the learning paths of students with the same future. For secondary education students, this future can either be the labour market or prolonged education. The learning route is a description that makes the consecutive situation the starting point of education. The notion "learning route" assumes a dynamic and future oriented culture exchange. The student always is the starting point of education. The cultural context of a student is dominant in composing the learning contents. Life long working is an integrated part of this culture. The educational learning situation is not anymore an isolated environment with no relation to real life, but exactly a situation that forms part of real life.

The curriculum is based on contexts of which the origin lies in real life. Within these contexts a broad range of skills is necessary to get to grips with the future. Not only cognitive skills are the issue here, but certainly also the development of reflective and emotional intelligence. With that education gains a much more strategic value by which it functions as a crowbar to make way to the future. Especially fundamental questions like the ones described by Howard Gardner as mentioned before can be brought under discussion in these contexts, and so context-oriented education does not only teach "how to learn" and "how to do" but also "how to live together" and "how to be" (Delors, 1996).

The thought structures of the general subjects are the basis of the contents. In the current educational organisation and examination programme these general subjects do not build a strong learning environment, because the contents do not relate to the demands of education, but mainly to reproduction. Therefore these general subjects do not really contribute to the raise of the educational level. The emphasis is put on the acquisition of declarative knowledge (facts) in the majority of the cases in stead of on the acquisition of the thought structures and of the interpretation framework with which the facts can be analysed. But the thought structures of the different subjects are the most important to learn. They form the cultural and historical basis of society. They give us the different ways in which we are able to look at and act in the world.

So in this new education we will finish with the dividing learning in the different subjects, a way of thinking that started after Renaissance. We integrate them in the contexts we mentioned. During the first two to three years of secondary education we use at school the program "City Works", from Boston. "City works" supplies the contexts within which the core targets of the fifteen obligatory subjects in secondary school can be combined. The three learning areas for context-oriented education are the mind, the body, and the environment, and they are given their completion in "City Works". Contacts with art and sport institutes etc. supply the contexts. It is the metaphor for the surrounding world.

The vocationally oriented subjects[2] form the logic sequels for the contexts of the higher levels of secondary education. They build a strong learning environment by connecting life long working to life long learning.

[2] Traditionally a lot of attention is given to the vocationally oriented subjects in the Dutch lower training levels of secondary school. In the transition from 'City Works' to the real vocational education after secondary school, these subjects build an excellent basis for students to support their choice for a vocational training. The four professional categories for which the students can opt are technology, service, economy, and agriculture. Each context teaches the student to discover and develop his own qualities and wishes. Agriculture is seen as an environmental education; economy as the education how to be; service is the education how to live together, while technology shows the material standard of society.

They will be able to teach productive knowledge that can be used in real life. Within the context of the vocationally oriented subjects, with their strong learning environment, and their orientation on teaching productive knowledge, the thought structures of the general education subjects are thought to raise the general level of education. The demands of the general subjects should therefore be limited to learning the thought structures relevant tot the subject. They give the real tools to handle real life problems. The factual knowledge does not belong in the examination program and will be liable to change in the curriculum depending on the contexts being offered.

4.2 The role of teachers and students

To the teacher this change means a change of role. He won't be a "know-it-all" any longer. To the contrary even: very often the students know more about dynamic developments than the teachers will do. Many students for instance have skills the teacher does not have. The most important role of the teacher is the role of coach in the learning process. Thus his pedagogic role is given a new content. The learning organisation will change as well. The class will be broken up into teams of for example seven students, and one teacher supervises seven of these teams. The breaking up of the class unit means that the discipline paradigm will be transformed. Consider that the teacher is playing his pedagogic part in the much more small-scale environment of seven students, either of one team or of the seven representatives of each team, while the other students work on their own. This brings forward the possibility to reinstall the master-apprentice relation, which is impossible in a class of thirty students.

This means a change in the role of the students as well. The students have to loose their reproductive role and will have a productive role mastering in a team their own learning process. Consider also the possibility that it is very easy to have tutors, composed of senior students, joining the small-scale unit. These senior students learn to make, as they tutor, their knowledge productive. Besides, the younger students are given positive role models that are more close to their own cultural environment. This means that working and learning go together here as well and that learning to communicate knowledge, essential to everyone in a knowledge society, is acquired during the tutoring. Besides, students learn to co-operate as a team, just as in real life. This new form of learning relations gives a view to many other changes. The tutorial situation doesn't stop at the frontiers of the school. On the contrary, it links the different parts of the learning community together. And it even links learning and working. Next to that it gives another change necessary in knowledge society. Kuhn (1996) described the present situation of schooling. He says that teachers are always teaching the paradigms that they studied themselves at the university. It means that our youth at school is structurally confronted with the knowledge of the past in stead of the present. In knowledge society it has to change. The structural integration of tutor systems in the learning environment can be an important step to leave the dilemma.

4.3 The organisation

The change in the role of teachers and students is described as a change in the organisation as well. We want to transform into a network organisation and we think about it as a fractal or Matrushka organisation, as we call it. But you can also define it in a more detailed way in biological terms describing the relation between different organisational levels. The work of Maturana and Varela (1980) about autopoiesis can be used in this way. It means that the change of class organisation proliferates through the entire school organisation in which for instance teams of seven teachers are made responsible for the education of about 200 students. And this will go on until the management of the school. The entire school organisation becomes an example of a network organisation and we can even introduce it in the way we work together with exterior organisations. It may be evident that this effects the occupational profile of the teacher and the manager. Their roles will not differ from each other so much. They have all a primary responsibility, a co-responsibility in the team in which they are a member and an end responsibility for the team they have to lead. The difference is set in the subject of responsibility. In the training plan of Esloo is established that in the development of the pedagogic qualities of the teacher and the manager attention should be paid to the teacher in his role of curious creator, inspirator, team player, coach, learner, planner, designer, entrepreneur, innovator, and ICT technologist.

4.4 The architecture of the building

All these changes can be expressed only if the physical learning environment, the school building, fits the task. The design of a new building will have to process all these new concepts. New construction on the basis of pedagogic and educational concepts is an enormous challenge. By preparing for the actual educational insights and anticipating the social developments, the new school will be an example in the almost unexplored field of educational innovation.

A school is built to be used last at least for 30 years. Thus, the new Esloo building will still have to meet the requirements of the year 2030. In translating the sketched developments into clear targets for the new school, we deal with a momentary impression. Therefore flexibility is essential to the plan. Insights of today can be old-fashioned tomorrow and it is by all means important to keep that in mind. Will the school in 2030 resemble the current school? Will there still be a bell ringing to announce the next hour? Will there be any breaks? Maybe not, since the students determine their own study program and their own breaks. Anyway, the school will become a place where there is room for the unexpected, for the unpredictable. This will finish the school built on the Napoleonic army barracks design with classrooms for 30 students next to each other. The concept of the classroom as an instruction locality with the teacher as the commanding officer and the schoolbook as the handbook for soldiers has finished. The school can't be built anymore on this concept in which external discipline equals learning, where there is no room for curiosity and where the unexpected and the unpredictable are not allowed.

When working and learning will be bridged the relation with the environment also must be redefined. Often secondary schools were built with a big gate all around the building like a prison and put in the middle of nowhere, so that the direct environment has no nuisance of the huge amount of adolescents. This has to change in the future as well. Older people have to come in the school for their life long learning process while our adolescents have to leave the school to work partially and learn in real life. So the gates must disappear and the school must become a learning centre in the middle of the community for example as part of a shopping centre, virtually linked to each other as virtual communities.

So the new building of our school is constructed as follows. At first it will be built on the place of the former school, that is happily for us next to a shopping centre, a two-floor building. It has a basic plan in the form of a U on the ground floor and on the first floor but the first floor has the U-form upside down. The front of the ground floor is twice as high and marks the place for festivities, the forum. At the back of the building there is an opening in the ground floor because of the U form while the opening in the U form of the first floor is filled by the height of the forum. The problem of security, important for the employees of the school, is solved: though there is no gate around the school, it will be possible to close the U at the back.

As said, the place of the school makes it possible to be part of a shopping centre, in order to connect the school with a real life situation of working. We organised it on the ground floor. The glass front of the school with the room for festivities can be opened so that this room can be used as a grand café. Students can train the skills to run such a business. The working places of the mostly technically oriented prevocational contexts are positioned at the two sides of the U of the ground floor. They can be opened to the outside as well so that they can be used as shops and be part of the shopping centre. So the ground floor is very flexible like a shopping centre. When the curriculum changes, the shops will change.

The first floor is positioned as an office. It is an open room with about one meter fifty high walls to get room for teams to work. Some parts have at the moment flexible walls to the ceiling so that working in a classroom situation will be possible. With ease these walls can disappear when the learning environment doesn't need them any more.

The building is an example of the bridging between learning, searching and working in the surroundings. Real life and all forms of activity take place on the ground floor. Reflection and study can take place on the first floor. Next to that not only adolescents will be in the building but also the whole community will get access.

5. THE ROLE OF ICT

ICT will lead to a different social and economic structure of society. As described above, the industrial society will have to be transformed into the information society. ICT is the tool for that like the steam engine has been it for the industrial society. That is in short the importance of ICT. So ICT is a facilitator. We think that in future society ICT will have the strongest impact on education.

To know about the role of a facilitator you have to know at first about the situation it will facilitate. That is one of the reasons why we described the changes in society in such an extensive way. We needed it to know more about the role of ICT in education. Let us recall what Copa said: *"If knowledge is the centre of new society... It means that education is the leading branch of economy. How can we rethink that?"*

When we apply this thesis on the role of ICT in education we have a good point saying that ICT will have the most impact on education. It makes also clear why the introduction of ICT in education has just started while it has already a role in other parts of society. Its role in education will be the most complex one and that means that the ICT apparatus must be developed enough. It will take a huge lot of bits to play a role in education. Just Internet gives us that huge lot of bits. It is obvious why it will take so many bits. The automation of processes of education has much to do with taking over actions of the brain by a machine. In industrial society these actions play a central role in organising society and they are much related to the way intelligence is defined. It has much to do with the education possibilities to become a citizen who is able to do his work in society as we described before. We think therefor that we are just at the start of the revolution generated by the introduction of ICT in education.

5.1 ICT in society

While we can only fantasise about the changes that will come, we are able to give some examples of the function of ICT in companies. The first automation wave strengthened the island structure of a company. It was organised from the inside to the outside. For every question the client had to go from one counter to another. This organisation structure was reinforced by the first automation wave. Every counter was automated separately. The cohesion within the company was reduced. So at first the organisation has to redefine itself so that ICT could support the integration. ICT can support companies for real only, if the organisation turns itself inside out. So by the redesigning organisations are not anymore reconstructed from the inside out (bureaucratically), but from outside in (as a network). The whole of the organisation becomes subservient to the existing and future client through any counter anywhere in the world. ICT makes it possible that the communication in the enterprise will speed up and get another interactive non-hierarchical approach. The organisation becomes demand-driven in stead of supply oriented. A good example is the way you get your money from a bank in the past and nowadays. ICT facilitates and accelerates this paradigm shift by its integrating possibilities.

Also skills needed by staff workers are changing. For example, in supermarkets adding is not a necessary skill anymore but has been automated. So whole production processes with all the skills needed by employees are now automated. When we speak about the new curriculum that enterprises need for their staff in information society and about the change from cognition abilities towards skills, it is just because of that. Many of the procedures that are organising society now will be taken over by ICT. And the brain damage people got by learning themselves all these procedures will probably for a big deal belong to the past.

5.2 ICT in education

The description is supporting the changes we foresee in education. At first the integration. We described the integration of the traditionally subjects in contexts. It may be clear that this complex process can be fixed by ICT. No more fifteen subjects (fifteen counters) with each its own (partly) automated educational materials, but integrated educational materials designed around the demand-driven contexts. ICT facilitates the production of these made-to-measure products. It makes education indeed demand-driven. "City Works" will become "Working with the Global Village" by the possibilities of Internet.

Next to that it gives a total new way of communication. We see that in the new sort of contact between teachers and students, between schools, etc. by e-mail, tele-learning and videoconferencing. These communication possibilities can be mixed with others. In education the process side (the learning process) is at least as important as the product side (achieving the curriculum). This certainly applies to these days as more and more attention is paid to the coaching of students, for which a good student monitoring system is a prerequisite. The tool used for this, what we call the SDRE-circle (See, Diagnose, Remediate, Evaluate, and da capo) is a wonderful aid. Similar ways of assessment are automated well with ICT. A sufficient database can monitor the student's entire learning process and interfere continually if the learned items do not stick. It gives the student its own Learners Information System (LIS). And we can use this tool also to get a Management Information System (MIS). Both can help to accelerate the learning process significantly. It is necessary, however, that students log in on the computer for all their central activities. So the new learning won't start anymore from books supported by computers, but it will start from the computer supported by books. Every student will have his "personal assistant", which will support his learning. This makes very clear the changing in the learning organisation. With the MIS it can support also the organisational changes of the schools, that mean the coaching and team role situation described before.

We think that the most important influence of ICT in education has to do with the curriculum. Many things we are learning at school nowadays are not necessary to learn any more. We are just at the start of thinking about these things but we think the upgrading of the intelligence level of society has to do with this. The spelling control of my computer program is an example of it. But the role of all procedures that we have in education will be questioned. They are until now necessary to become this citizen that can play its working role. When ICT will take it over it gives us time and opportunity to get to the real goal of education described by Howard Gardner. So ICT possibilities will question what we have to learn.

You can combine this all with other new possibilities of ICT. Ever since printing was invented an enormous acceleration of knowledge has taken place because the image language made by artists (in the churches) was replaced by textual language. The latter made knowledge accessible to large groups. Multimedia again allows an acceleration of knowledge. It is achieved by partly replacing text by image. With the aid of images it will be possible not only to learn faster, but also more thoroughly, because the very, not or only hard to express, unknown can be known through images.

5.3 The implementation

We have already done quite a lot to implement the changes we want to introduce. The architecture of the building is the most important part of it. We introduced back-casting as management tool for changes. Back-casting is used in environmental policy. One has to describe at first the future situation. After that one uses the nearby future as a transition situation from today to the future. It means that the nearby future will not be a blow-up of today but really another situation that refers to the future.

As said before, we started to transform real life. From there we can use the possibilities of ICT. So next to the change in learning environment we are busy with the three other mentioned changes: the organization of the school, the role of the teacher and the student, and the curriculum. Next to that we are trying to use ICT to support the different changes.

5.4 The internal process

At first we will give you a description of the internal process in the school on the three subjects. The most important and the most difficult is the change in the curriculum. As we have seen there are two basics for context-orientation: "City Works"/ "Working with The Global Village" for pupils from 12–14 years, and prevocational subjects for pupils from 14–16 years. We have many choices of ourselves in the curriculum for the years 12–14. But the curriculum for 14–16 years has to lead to a national examination. There is a huge national discussion about the curriculum at the moment. We try to play a role on this subject but the outcome is still not clear. Because of that we have chosen in the school to start our transformation and to learn how to manage it by working on "City Works". The program is functioning in more schools in The Netherlands and it has governmental support. We started in one group in the first class (12–13 years) with two teachers. They made their own program for 4 hours a week. So in stead of fifteen subjects these pupils had sixteen subjects because parts of the other subjects were put in "City Works". We had good results with it, so we started last year with a new group in the second class; and more teachers are involved in it. In the meantime we started in the first class to digitise parts of the program as the first school in The Netherlands. At the moment we are busy to plan the transformation from "City Works" as extra subject into "City Works" as the only subject of the first class. In this new environment we are experimenting with the new role for teacher and student as well. All teachers of the school are participating in introducing ICT and Internet skills. As an ICT front school we have relatively much ICT-equipment. Searching and introducing good software is nowadays becoming more urgent.

Next to and in co-ordination with it we are changing the learning organisation. We are diminishing the amount of teachers in a class. So they have to teach in different subjects. Duo-teaching has started. Two teachers are responsible for a double group while they help each other in their own learning process. We are busy to build a network organisation in the whole group of schools as well. So the directory of the whole group participates in all the changes we are managing. Like all other schools in The Netherlands we are busy to automate our management organisation so that we can communicate in a stronger way. We are also experimenting with these assessment programs leading to the so-called "personal assistant". So we are really doing a lot of work in the internal implementation of the design.

5.5 The external process

Maybe the external implementation is giving the most problems. In The Netherlands education is in permanent discussion these days. The design of the school plays a role in the discussion. And we are constantly busy to scale things up by starting new initiatives and taking part in others. The problem is that real changes are only possible when generally introduced and old thinking still has many roots in society. So the changing process has to get its time. It means that the coupling of the internal and external process is very complex. The ambition of the school is to be an example of new education. But the general organisation of the curriculum diminishes the possibility to be it. Co-operation is a central issue. Here we will mention only two forms of co-operation that we think are essential for us.

At first we are strongly related to the influential non-governmental organisation of principals in The Netherlands. As said before the management of the school plays an important role in school organisation. A national board of principals can give strong support. This board in The Netherlands is the organisation VVO. It is part of a European counterpart called ESHA and an international one called ICP. All these non-governmental organisations will play a crucial role in the transitions made all over the world. Our school is closely related to the national board and has its relations with the international ones. It gives our school a more structural position in the country.

The second co-operation is a starting public private partnership in The Hague between the educational field, the local government and the international Telecom Company KPN. The partnership is meant to organise the participation of 13000 students in The Hague mobile linked to a virtual educational community. We think that this project will be the real start of the transformation. In our view a change between the public and private domain is essential for the forming of a knowledge society.

6. CONCLUSIONS

As described in this paper we did a lot of thinking but we acted a lot as well. One will understand that other schools of Schoolgroup Esloo are changing as well. This performs a climate of changing all around our group of schools. We taste this climate nation-wide and the possibilities to work on our design wouldn't have been so big without this atmosphere. We have been in a lot of countries now and we have read a lot of relevant literature.. So we know that this atmosphere is world-wide. School managers are in a crucial position. The changes can't be introduced anymore in a hierarchical way far away from our schools. So school managers have to take their responsibility. National boards of principals like the VVO in the Netherlands will play a crucial role as initiators of the transformation process.

ICT has a lot to do with these transformations. But is no more than a tool. We have to rethink the learning process and the position of the learning process in the knowledge society at first. During and after the transformation process ICT will play its facilitating role. By acting this way we are able to give education its important position where it can give room at the realm of the truth, the beautiful and the good.

REFERENCES

Delors, J. (1996) *Learning, the treasure within,* Unesco, Paris.
Gardner, H. (1999) *The disciplined mind,* New York.
Kuhn, T. (1996) *The structure of scientific revolutions*
Maturana, H. and Varela, F. (1980) *Biology of Cognition, in Autopoiesis and Cognition,* edited by D. Reidel.
Toffler, A. (1980) *The third wave,* London.

BIOGRAPHY

Jaap Westbroek is chairman of the board of Schoolgroup Esloo and member of the VVO, the Dutch national board of principals in secondary education. He has studied biochemistry and was a teacher in biology, physics and chemistry. He wrote many articles about education in The Netherlands and is co-author of the Esloo-design.

Teacher development in ICT: Vision and implementation

Iliana Nikolova
Department of Information Technologies, Faculty of Mathematics and Informatics, University of Sofia, FMI – KIT, P.B. 48 , 5, James Bouchier, Sofia 1164, Bulgaria.
iliana@fmi.uni-sofia.bg

Abstract: The paper presents the philosophy and practices of the Department of Information Technologies and the Teacher Training Center at the Faculty of Mathematics and Informatics, University of Sofia, related to teacher development in Information and Communication Technologies. The conceptual framework for teacher development calls for an integrated approach to the problem: the various forms for teacher training and continuing support are combined with activities, aiming at influencing the system in which the teachers work. The approach embeds "teachers as change agents" paradigm and aims at creating sustainable links, both vertical (between the research and training units and teachers) and horizontal (among teachers themselves), finally building an informal professional society of researchers, trainers and teachers who communicate, collaborate and share. The teacher development processes are initiated in a university environment in which research, development and teaching are closely interrelated. This creates added-value opportunities and experiences for the participating teachers. The scope of activities includes workshops and seminars for teachers; strategy and curriculum development in ICT; educational software and learning materials development; carrying out educational and researches projects; building WWW support environment for teachers.

Keywords: Flexible learning, Internet, Logo, multimedia

The Information and Communications Technologies will have a substantial effect on what we do in schools just as the advent of the pen and paper did in the past. *Seymour Papert*

1. INTRODUCTION

One of the greatest achievements of this century is the remarkable development in the area of ICT. The rapid technological changes affect many aspects of our lives, including the way we learn. The school of tomorrow will embed learning in technology rich educational environments. This will be natural for the new generation of children for whom the technology is already part of their everyday life. How will teacher's role evolve? How will schools cope with the change? What can be done today to prepare for tomorrow? Such questions seek their answers at the threshold of the new millenium.

This paper presents the philosophy and practices of the Department of Information Technologies (DIT) and the Teacher Training Center (TTC) at the Faculty of Mathematics and Informatics, University of Sofia, related to teacher development in Information and Communication Technologies (ICT). First the profiles of DIT and TTC are briefly outlined. Then a vision for the role of the teacher in the future is presented. Next the milestones of the conceptual framework for teacher development are discussed and current problems are identified. The ideas are illustrated by a number of examples, some including WWW solutions for teacher support. Finally, implications for future teacher education in Bulgaria and other countries are drawn.

2. THE DEPARTMENT OF IT AND THE TEACHER TRAINING CENTRE (TTC)

The Department of Information Technologies (DIT, http://www-it.fmi.uni-sofia.bg) was established in 1993 as an ancestor of the Educational Computing Systems Laboratory founded in 1984. The Department's activities involve teaching, research and development in the field of ICT and their applications in education. DIT is responsible for teaching informatics and computer education topics in a B.Sc. program, where teachers in mathematics and informatics are prepared. It offers also two M.Sc. programs: "Information and Communication Technologies" and "Artificial Intelligence". In 1994 a functional unit - Teacher Training Center - was established to deal with in-service teacher training for the integration of ICT in schools. The Center is not a separate administrative unit with own staff and budget – its activities are carried out by the staff of the Department and by external collaborators, including teachers.

3. A VISION FOR TEACHER DEVELOPMENT

3.1 The role of the teacher in the future

The teacher will be teaching in an Information Society, i.e. in an information and technology rich environment. The way people learn will change and this change will be accelerated by the "kidpower" (Papert, 1999): the computer oriented generation of children now entering the educational system. ICT will play a substantial role in this change by offering new educational media and provoking new educational paradigms. Teachers have to adapt to this change, even more – to act as "change agents" and help shaping new school cultures. They should be fluent users of ICT themselves and capable to employ ICT to empower students' learning, but also recognise uses of ICT, which can disempower learning.

The variety in the forms of learning will increase. It is very likely that the school of the future will be differently organised and the traditional classroom-based learning with fixed timetables will decline. The curriculum will be restructured to support more resource-based and project-oriented learning. The role of the teacher will evolve into navigating learning in technology rich educational environments and into designing learning environments that allow more flexible learning, mediated by technology.

3.2 Conceptual framework for teacher development

At Tele-Teaching'98 Niki Davis said: "Preparing teachers is perceived as the main critical success factor in deploying ICT in education. Teacher trainers and teachers have key roles to play. They can spread the benefits of the Information Society through their enthusiasm and by the innovative new work techniques, which many are adopting. Often these changes to working practice are occurring by teacher trainers altering the processes and organization within their institutions."

3.2.1 Goals, methods, tools and roles

Goals. Teacher development should contribute to building a coherent and consistent professional culture for using ICT in teachers' practices. ICT should become a natural component of school everyday life. Teachers need to be able to recognise powerful ICT uses for learning purposes and to design appropriate ICT solutions for practical cases. To keep up-to-date they have to learn to learn continuously (considering also tele-learning options).

They need to develop a positive attitude and culture for professional collaboration.

Methods. To be effective and to build transferable skills, teacher education and training has to be based on constructionist learning principles (Paper, 1999) and to embed active, experiential learning. The teacher development processes have to be supported by rich environments (Nikolova, 1999), in terms of educational, technological and human resources. These environments should offer powerful ideas, methods, tools, technologies and examples of good practices. Teachers' have to be involved in multifaceted activities, which give them different kinds of experiences, and create opportunities to develop various competencies. In this way valuable experience is gained which allows such teachers to serve as change agents in their school environment. Further (on-the-job) support to teachers is important for the success of the school innovation processes. Internet and Intranets can play an important role in designing such support solutions.

Tools. Traditionally, DIT values interactive software environments for learning which support exploration and creative expression (i.e., embed some sort of language) and allow teachers to develop their own applications. Such environments are a powerful context for constructionist learning. Examples of such environments are Comenius Logo, Geomland and MATCH, mentioned further in this paper.

Roles. This conceptual framework is based on the active learner assumption. The learner (in this case, the teacher) is a citizen of the cyberspace with access to on-line information, learning resources and communication facilities. The teacher trainer is a facilitator, a navigator of the learning process, consultant in the selection and utilisation of the learning resources. The teacher development processes vary from formal, fixed in time and space instructional sessions to informal, self-initiated, flexible in time and place learning, supported by off and on-line resources and by collaboration with peers and communication with experts.

3.2.2 Key ideas (from an implementation perspective)

There are three main target groups to whom DIT's and TTC's deliver training in ICT: pre-service teachers, master students in ICT and AI, and in-service teachers. *Establishing links among these three groups* in order to facilitate mutual enrichment and create synergy effects is one of the key ideas in our approach to teacher development. It is realized by forming small teams, involving people from the three groups and consultants from the

Department. These teams work on different tasks, e.g. curriculum development, project work, development of software applications and teaching and learning materials, building WWW support environments, testing research outcomes in school settings. Examples of such cooperative work are VALUE, MATCH, development of ICT curriculum, NETLogo Teachers' Course (see the paragraph Examples from practice).

Another key idea is to make the teacher training *more flexible and multifaceted* in terms of methods and forms. The traditional classroom based teaching is minimized in favor to more hands-on experience, seminars, discussions, individual and small group project work, individual consultations with teachers and schools, and, where possible, involvement of teachers in real research and development projects carried out at DIT.

The third key idea is to build *rich environments for learning and continuous support to teachers.* After the formal period of training is over, i.e. when the teachers return to their school environment, they often need advice and further support. We try to help in different ways: (a) by building full range of support materials around the educational software environments, which we consider appropriate for school use (examples are Comenius Logo, Geomland, MATCh); (b) by building WWW support environments for teachers (examples are VALUE, GEOMLAND and School Resource Bank - see "Examples from practice"); (c) by being available for e-mail support, telephone and face-to-face consultations.

The fourth key idea is to facilitate the change – the integration of ICT and accommodation of teachers and schools to it – by *influencing the system itself.* At EUROLOGO'99 Seymour Papert said: "Educational change is possible, but the educational system has to be allowed to evolve itself, rather than attempting to impose changes on it." To achieve this, we act both "top-down" and "bottom-up":

(a) Collaboration is established with educational institutions: the Ministry of education, educational institutes, regional ICT –co-ordinators, school masters. Examples are: participation of leading researchers, teacher trainers and teachers in the development of the National Strategy for integration of ICT in schools (Eskenazi et al, 1998) and in curriculum development at national level (see "Curriculum development" in the "Examples from Practice"); formal and informal discussions with local educational authorities and school administration.

(b) The "teachers as change agents"-paradigm is employed: Opportunities are provided for motivated teachers to get deeper involved in various kinds of activities at the Department. Thus they can feel the spirit, to benefit from the collaboration with staff, affiliated members, and other teachers, to discuss extensively "the message" of our concept for integration of ICT in schools and to practice it in different ways. When "well armed" with vision and experience, these teachers are "implemented" in schools, keeping close contact with us, bringing innovative practices to the school and influencing colleagues and school administration.

The fifth key idea is to *build an informal professional society* of researchers, trainers and teachers who communicate, collaborate and share. The aim is to establish sustainable links, both vertical (between the research and training units and teachers) and horizontal (among teachers themselves). Throughout the teacher development process we are building a "human network" (supported by an electronic database) and encourage peer support and collaboration among its members. Web support tools are also employed for this purpose (examples are VALUE, GEOMLAND, NETLogo Educational Site).

The sixth key idea is to *facilitate international co-operation* at teacher and school level and help establish direct channels for communication via Internet. This is done by organising international events and enabling teachers participate in them (one recent example is EUROLOGO99 hosted by the Department), by helping teachers establish partnerships and start projects, by involving teachers in development, evaluation and validation activities within DIT's projects (examples are MATCH, NETLogo Educational Site).

3.2.3 Current problems

Currently, DIT and TTC do not have the capacity (technical, human, organisational and financial) to offer this kind of development to a vast majority of teachers. To go to a large-scale implementation, the above principles need to be made operational, a relevant methodology has to be developed to support the adopters of the framework. We work mostly with informatics and ICT teachers (this is a speciality of our educational system). Recently primary teachers were also addressed. All subject teachers at secondary school level should be involved in teacher development as well.

Another serious obstacle to building ICT school cultures is the low level of technological infrastructure in most schools. Also the low social and financial esteem of teachers is inadequate to the effort expected from the teachers.

4. EXAMPLES FROM PRACTICE

One specific feature of our approach is that the teacher development processes are initiated in a university environment in which research, development and teaching activities are closely interrelated. This creates added-value opportunities and experiences for the participating teachers.

4.1 General examples

Curriculum development

Teams of researchers and teachers were involved in the development of curricula for "Integration of ICT in primary school", "Informatics in Logo style", "Internet for beginners", "Internet for advanced". A set of accompanying materials and services is under development around each curriculum: workshops, teacher manuals, software, online resources.

The Project "Learning by Developing"

This project was initiated in the frames of the program "School initiative of IBM for Bulgaria". The "learning by developing" paradigm (Blaho & Kalas, 1998) and Comenius Logo, an attractive and sophisticated environment with much conceptual and operational power, were employed to involve teachers and students in attractive and meaningful activities using ICT. The goal is to teach and learn better and to strengthen the creative spirit in using technology in our schools. We use LOGO because it enables children to deal with real ideas. It is a tool for carrying out engaging projects. Comenius Logo gives the possibility to create interactive applications (microworlds) in different subject areas. Teachers can tune existing microworlds to their classroom needs and/or build microworlds on their own.

The target group involved initially 16 schools. Gradually more schools and individuals joined. An integrated approach was used to spread Logo ideas and tools across the educational community and helping teachers integrate them in schools: the software was adapted to the Bulgarian language, Bulgarian online help was developed, and a whole range of reference, teaching and learning materials (lessons, problems, projects, and microworlds) was produced. In all these teachers were involved. In this sense the project is a good example for initiating and supporting educational innovations (Fullan, 1994). A "web" of Logo professionals who support each other and collaborate effectively was built.

WWW support for teachers

Maintaining educational websites does not only save time and help reach more users. Feedback from users is facilitated, two-way communication channel and mutual collaboration can be established. A positive effect is, that offering meaningful material and helpful interactions to teachers in such a way, they get used to using Internet for educational resources and motivated to make their own Web developments. One inconvenience is that educational Web sites need frequent updates and constant maintenance. Another aspect of websupport to teachers is the opportunity for tele-learning. A majority of online courses is already available. Teachers need guidance and some kind of brokerage service to be able to orient in it.

VALUE: A Virtual Almanac for Logo Users and Educators.
VALUE (the Virtual Almanac for Logo Users and Educators (Nikolova, 1997) was created to support the implementation of the project "Learning by Developing". The Web was used as a supplementary channel for reaching teachers, delivering materials to them, getting feedback and establishing collaboration. A rich collection of developed materials is uploaded to the site, communication and discussion are embedded (Conference Room), announcement (Current Events), building virtual Logo community (Guest Book). For easier orientation a site map is developed (see figure 1). Teachers contribute to the further development of VALUE (many of the resources there have been developed by our "change agents"). Many teachers benefit from VALUE, but the vast majority of teachers still do not have the habit and/or technological infrastructure to use virtual support like this. New culture has to be developed in this respect.

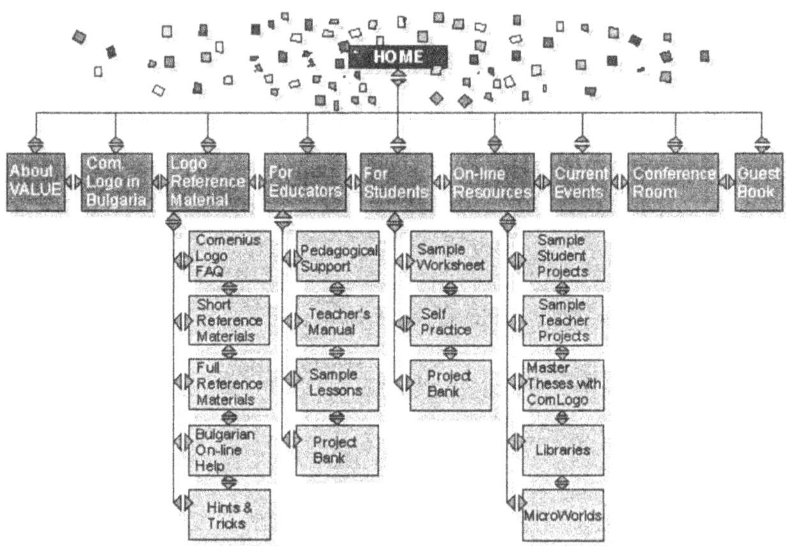

Figure 1. Sitemap of VALUE

NETLogo Web course for Teachers
Within the NETLogo project (Sampson et al, 1998) an online course for teachers (figure 2) is being developed collaboratively by a Hungarian and a Bulgarian team. Teachers are involved at different levels in this initiative.

GEOMLAND: Laboratory for Mathematics Explorations in Logo Style
GEOMLAND (Sendov & Sendova, 1997) is a powerful Logo style learning environment for mathematics explorations, developed at ECSL, the Department's predecessor. The system is used in teacher training and in secondary schools. A recently developed Web site (Figure 3) provides teachers with the software, research and methodology papers, demonstrations and examples for school use, contact with the authors.

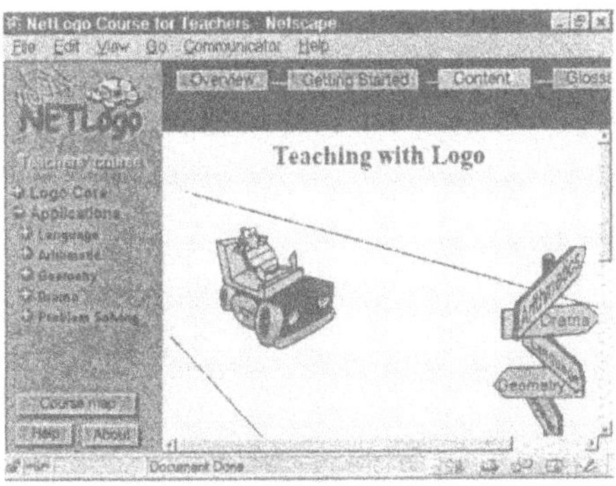

Figure 2: NetLogo Web Course for Teachers

Figure 3: A Geomland Web page

School Resource Bank: A Subject-Oriented Web Catalog
This is a useful collection of annotated online educational resources to ease teachers in finding online subject-oriented materials. It was developed by a master student in cooperation with teachers. The site was offered to the Bulgarian I*EARN section for use by schools with Internet access.

MATCH: A Multimedia Authoring Tool for Children
In this recent European project (Triantafillou et al, 1997), where DIT collaborated with partners form Slovakia, Hungary, Holland, UK and Greece, an environment for multimedia authoring for children, MATCH, was developed. The system employs the constructionist learning philosophy and supports creative thinking and expression by means of multimedia technologies. We use multimedia authoring for children, to provoke children's thinking, imagination, expression and active learning; to enable them to taste the process of creating multimedia and to personalise the basic concepts of the multimedia world surrounding them; to create a context, in which each child can participate in an enjoyable collaborative activity with what she or he is talented for.

4.2 APPLICATIONS DEVELOPED IN BULGARIA

Several applications were developed with MATCH which demonstrate the power of the environment and served as system testbeds.

Multimedia Screen Cards

The application (figure 4) faces children with most popular European traditions and festivals related to children. A multimedia screen card is a moving, speaking, singing card, the child can play with, print, modify, export into a Web page. Sample cards for different occasions were developed and built into a consistent Screen Card World.

Figure 4: Entry to the Screen Card World

Figure 5: "Save the Animals" game

Save the Animals

This application (figure 5) illustrates the possibility to design multimedia games with MATCH. It is a story where the child plays the role of a Zoo Detective, trying to help an animal in danger. The application has a modular structure and allows modification and extension by teachers and students.

Children's Projects

While testing the system and applications in school, children made their own production with MATCH – individual screen cards and class projects "Meet our class" and "Class album". This work kept both children and teachers very much involved and provoked learning about multimedia technologies and numerous ideas for multimedia projects.

5. TEACHER INVOLVEMENT

Teachers (our "change agents") were involved in the development of MATCH applications and in testing the system and the applications in schools. MATCH was used in teacher training to illustrate "learning by developing" paradigm and ideas for using multimedia for creative expression. In the near future it will be made available to more teachers for use in their classrooms. These teachers will contribute to the production of the Bulgarian version of the system and the applications.

5.1 Implications for future teacher education

It is inevitable that in the near future all teachers will have to cope with UCT in one way or another (Collis, Nikolova & Martcheva, 1995). It is important that they have a deeper insight in the ways ICT could help learning. When featuring the direction, in which he would like to see the educational system going (in his academic speech, "The Future of Learning", at the Ceremony for awarding him with Dr. Honoris Causa of Sofia University, in August, 1999), Seymour Papert talked about Constructionism as a theoretical foundation for education using a more project-based approach. He pointed out, that currently many teachers have difficulties embedding powerful ideas in projects and/or recognising powerful ideas embedded in existing projects. He felt the need for developing epistemologies of powerful ideas to be explored in computationally rich environments. To cope with the tendency for globalisation of education, future teacher education has to take into account the explosion of tele-learning. A global electronic brokerage system would ease the orientation of teachers in the global learning space. The time has come for teachers using technology to become an actively learning and collaborating professional society. Internet provides good opportunities to build virtual professional communities.

6. CONCLUSIONS

The educational research is a longitudinal process. It is too early to say if the approach presented in this paper is a good solution to the problem of teacher development or not. The university setting addressed in the paper is one of the main places in Bulgaria where secondary school teachers in informatics and IT are prepared. Nevertheless, there is still a way to go before the approach presented in the paper can be considered a large-scale example. In this respect DIT and TTC act as "change agent" themselves.

Every opportunity is used to bring our vision and experiences to the professional community. The teachers, "change agents" are our advocates.

REFERENCES

Blaho, A. and Kalas, I. (1998) *Learning by Developing with Comenius Logo*, Longman Logotron, London.

Collis B., Nikolova I., and Marcheva, K. (Eds.) (1995) *Information Technologies in Teacher Education: Issues and Experiences for countries in transition*, UNESCO, Paris.

Eshkenazi, Assenova, Michnev, Nikolova, and Lakyurski (1998) *National Strategy for integration of ICT in the Bulgarian Secondary Schools*, Ministry of Education, Sofia

Fullan, M. (1994) *The New Meaning of Educational Change*, Cassel.

Nikolova, I. (1999) *Teacher Training in Informatics and ICT*, In Peicheva, R, (Ed.) New Approaches of ICT in Teacher Training, Phare -TEMPUS (in Bulgarian)

Nikolova, I. (1997) *Towards VALUE - A Virtual Almanac for Logo Users and Educators*, Proceedings, Eurologo'97: Learning and exploring with Logo, Budapest, p. 240-248. http://iea.fmi.uni-sofia.bg/value/

Papert, S. (1999) *Constructionism: Putting Logo into Pratice*, in Nikolov, Sendova, Nikolova, Derzhanski (Eds.) Proceedings of the Seventh European Logo Conference EUROLOGO'99, Sofia.

Sampson et al (1999) *NETLogo: The European Educational Interactive Site*, in Nikolov, Sendova, Nikolova, Derzhanski (Eds.), Proceedings of the Seventh European Logo Conference EUROLOGO'99, Sofia, Bulgaria.

Sendov, B. and Sendova, E. (1997) *Tuning a Logo-like learning environment to a knowledge domain,* in Proceedings, Eurologo'97: Learning and exploring with Logo, Budapest

Triantafilou, S., Pixton, J., Kallenbach, K., Kalas, I., Turcsányi-Szabó, M., Pintelas, P., and Nikolova, I. (1997) *MATCh: a Multimedia Authoring environment for Children*, Eurologo'97: Learning and exploring with Logo p. 80-84

BIOGRAPHY

Iliana Nikolova is a chief assistant professor at the Department of Information Technologies, Faculty of Mathematics and Informatics, University of Sofia, Bulgaria. She has been working for more than 12 years in the following areas: applications of ICT in teaching and learning, teacher development in ICT, educational multimedia, and tele-learning. Her recent research, development and teaching activities involve methodology and tools for Web-based course design, multimedia authoring and applications for children, integration of Logo-style computer environments in schools. She has a M.Sc. in Computer Science (University of Sofia, Bulgaria) and a M.Sc. in Educational and Training Systems Design (University of Twente, The Netherlands). She is a member of IFIP Working Group 3.6.

How teachers and teacher training are changing

Vittorio Midoro
Istituto Tecnologie Didattiche, CNR, via De Marini, 6 , 16129 Genova, Italy.
midoro@itd.ge.cnr.it

Abstract: While the 20th century school focused on teaching, the 21st century school may well focus on learning. The role of teachers is changing to reflect this trend, and consequently teacher training processes are also changing. Teachers are becoming managers and facilitators of learning. To enhance children's learning, they design, adapt, manage and evaluate learning environments. These functions require competencies pertaining to three domains and their interrelationships: pedagogy, subject area and ICT. As far as the relationships among these domains are concerned, teachers should be aware of the changes brought about in the their subject area by the introduction of ICT. They should know how the didactics of their specific subject area are evolving and what new ways of learning are being opened up by ICT. To construct these new competencies, new teacher training processes, environments and policies are required. This paper describes a collaborative online learning environment for teacher training. It is shown how online education can be used to train teachers to create a learning community of European teachers. Researchers have developed "Medea", an online teacher training course in environmental education developed and run in the context of both a national programme and the European project "T3: Telematics for Teacher Training".

Keywords: Teacher training, online education, educational policies

1. HOW TEACHERS' WORK IS CHANGING

Information and Communication Technologies (ICT) are modifying our ways of communicating, sharing information, co-operating and learning. In the near future, teachers' competencies need to be enriched to embrace these changes.

1.1 The traditional pillars of teachers' competencies

Knowledge of subject matter and basic pedagogy are the traditional pillars of teachers' competencies in modern day schooling. The importance of these two elements changes according to the school level. While pedagogic issues are crucial in primary school, those related to the subject matter assume greater importance for secondary school as the students' age increases. It is said that primary school teachers love their children, secondary school teachers love their curriculum area and university professors love themselves. Although the situation is changing, in some European countries aspiring primary teachers still commence studying a student teacher curriculum for secondary education (focusing mainly on pedagogical issues), while no specific pre-service training is provided for secondary school teachers, who merely require a degree in a given subject matter in order to teach it.

As to the subject matter, the problem is how to cope with the rapid growth of knowledge in specific curriculum areas and consequently deciding what teachers need to learn.

Regarding pedagogical issues, present-day schooling focuses more on teaching than learning. The transmissive paradigm not only affects approaches and methods, but also determines the layout of premises and classrooms. The higher the school level, the more the transmissive paradigm determines school structures. In this context, teachers should be capable of communicating, able to evaluate the impact of this communication on their students, and, more generally, have all those skills needed for effective transmission of their knowledge.

Within each subject area, a pedagogy has developed that relates specifically to that area, be it mathematics, foreign languages, history, etc. This fact can be thought of as the relationship between the subject matter and pedagogical knowledge applied to it.

Besides the subject and pedagogical knowledge, teachers' competencies involves skills that are hard to classify, such as the capacity to deal with conflict, to empathise with students and to operate in the school context (knowledge and practice of school laws and rules, active participation in school life, etc.).

1.2 How children's learning is changing with ICT

Computers and the Internet are changing the ways of learning adopted by children who use these tools. Working with the computer generally requires autonomy and independence. Novices continuously face problems when seeking to use the computer. Depending on their individual learning style, children either ask for help or try to solve problems by themselves. However, in the long run, frequent users acquire considerable autonomy, allowing them to solve most of their problems without any help. It is reasonable to assume that this independence applies not only to difficulties posed by computer use, but to cognitive problems in general. Moreover, the use of a computer application affects the ways in which related cognitive activities are performed. For example, a word processor changes writing styles. A browser or search engine affects the ways of searching for information. A graphic editor affects the ways of drawing. A database or spreadsheet influences the ways of organising data, a music editor those of composing music. Electronic mail and computer conferencing systems change ways of communicating using written language and so on. It is reasonable to assume that children, who use computers and the Internet, acquire new powerful learning skills through frequent interaction with virtual environments (computer games, editors, courseware, e-mailers etc). In this way, learning by doing and reflecting about one's own ways of operating become the main learning mode, in contrast with conventional schooling, where the main learning activities often consist of listening in classroom and performing pencil and paper tasks at home. Thus, the gap between school and children's lives widens, as does that between children who use computers and the Internet and those who do not have access to these resources.

1.3 ICT: A new pillar in teachers' competencies

As teachers cannot be excluded from the new ways of learning and new tools for improving individual productivity, communication and co-operation that have been brought about by computers and the Internet, their competencies should be improved to comprise a new fundamental pillar: skills pertaining to ICT. This competency will involve the ability to use the computer and web not only as individual productivity tools for writing, storing data, communicating, and sharing information, but also as tools for improving and facilitating their students' learning.

Computers and the Web are becoming ordinary tools for people who deal with information and knowledge. Thus they should also become thinking and working tools for teachers, to use both in class and in course management activities like writing reports, compiling statistics, communicating, collaborating with colleagues and parents, and so on. The systematic use of computers and the Internet will enrich teachers' competencies in directions not yet completely explored. Computer skills will soon become a prerequisite in any intellectual profession, and in particular for teachers, whose role it is to facilitate children's learning processes.

Teachers' ICT competencies should involve aspects strictly connected with their role, covering both the curriculum area and the ways of learning. As far as the subject area is concerned, teachers should be aware of the changes being brought about by ICT. For example, using a word processor has changed the writing style of many professional writers. Computer simulation models have heavily affected "hard" sciences. Even in fields that are traditionally distant from hard sciences, such as music, painting etc, computers are used as a powerful tool for enquiry and expression.

But the aspect specifically related to teachers' work is the capacity to use computers to improve and facilitate children's learning within subject areas. This use entails changes in both content and methods. As to the former, numeric calculus in physics allows with the study of topics that were not previously dealt with since they required analytical calculus. In mathematics, evaluating the correctness of the results will acquire greater importance compared to calculus ability. In science, the ability to build computational models will become more important than recalling specific facts and figures. Historical databases will allow students to answer open questions and make hypotheses about connections between events.

The other aspect of the ICT-pedagogy coupling regards the ability to use applications for individual productivity and specific courseware in order to improve and facilitate personal reconstruction of knowledge. Teachers should know how to use the most effective courseware related to their subject, but should also know how to exploit fully the personal productivity tools suitable for their curriculum area.

1.4 The teacher's new role

Teachers' competencies will also involve the capacity to reflect on their own role and how it changes when the boundary conditions are modified. ICT develops children's autonomy and creates conditions for an independent reconstruction of knowledge by means of interaction with a social and bio-physical environment. The teacher's task will increasing become one of adapting and developing learning environments to accommodate different learning styles. This task will be accomplished by reusing learning material available in different forms (print, off line and online, local or remote etc.) or producing new material, which can be shared with colleagues. Teachers' explanations will be replaced by rich audio-visual presentations available on CD-ROM or the Internet. Unsolved problems may be discussed with peers or eminent scientists. Students who are not able to perform an assigned task might ask peers for help or access a database of solutions. Formative tests could be automated to diagnose students' strengthens and weaknesses, along with possible reasons for failures and hints about what remedial material to use, and so on.

2. ORIGINAL SOLUTIONS FOR IN-SERVICE TEACHER TRAINING

Teachers' competencies will change to embrace knowledge and mastery of ICT, in such a way that they will become able to use and/or develop learning environments which both reflect how children learn outside school and facilitate the understanding of curriculum areas. This change is required now; we cannot stand by and wait for new generations of teachers to bring it about. But how can the retraining of several hundreds of thousand of teachers be achieved? Decision-makers have to tackle a crucial issue: how to promote quality learning processes in such a way that ICT skills become a basic pillar of the competencies possessed by all those in-service teachers. Solutions to this problem require a range of different strategies, the most promising of which seem to be those based on ICT and especially on online education (OLE) (Davis, 1998). The features of OLE allow the development of high quality learning processes for in-service teachers on a mass scale.

2.1 Quality

Like other forms of distance education, online education removes space and time constrains, but it also features a new characteristic which makes it more powerful than the others. In OLE, the availability of tools for rapid, reliable and cheap communication allows the implementation of forms of social and co-operative learning based on asynchronous written messages. As a result, not only are the time and space constrains typical of a classroom situation removed, but also the learning paradigm is changed. While the transmissive paradigm predominates in the classroom, in OLE the learning paradigm is social construction of knowledge, an approach far better suited to the needs of expert teachers. Here a community of experienced professionals uses the technology to share information, communicate, and co-operate, and learning takes place as a result of co-operative activity. In this process, new knowledge and material are created which become available for other teachers involved in future teacher-training processes. Three features characterise OLE:

1. a learning community, involving participants, tutors, experts, observers, etc;
2. a pool of resources;

3. a telecommunications infrastructure with related services.

The community uses the telecommunications infrastructure and related services to communicate, access and share information, and co-operate. The material is available online on the Web or off-line. It may also be developed and sent out by tutors or other community members. A more detailed model of OLE is described by Midoro (1998). The strong points of this type of learning are its co-operative features and interaction among the participants. Moreover, written communication allows the storage and reconstruction of the co-operative process, providing the basis for evaluation and tuning of the whole learning process.

2.2 Scale

The ideal participant/tutor ratio is about thirty to one. A single course cannot be expected to meet the needs of a large number of trainees. However, the reusability of materials, methods and technology means that any online course can be repeated many times over, in series or parallel, provided that enough tutors are available. Moreover, courses are progressively enriched with each edition run, since they acquire new materials and management expertise. The apparent drawback of the OLE approach is the large number of tutors required to run courses in parallel sessions. But this problem can be overcome, considering that any run of the course "produces" people who are potentially capable of tutoring in an online course. Little effort is required to transform this potentiality into an effective availability of tutors, a point that will be discussed later in the paper.

Let us now see how these general statements have found practical application in a case of in-service teacher training.

3. MEDEA: AN ONLINE TEACHER TRAINING PROGRAM

At the outset in 1994, MEDEA was an online teacher training course regarding environmental education (EE). The idea behind MEDEA was to respond to the needs, constraints and structures of EE by adopting online education approaches (Briano, Midoro and Trentin, 1997). The course originated within the framework of LABNET, an R&D project carried out by the Italian Research Council's Institute for Educational Technology (ITD) under the INFEA Programme, funded by the Italian Ministry for the Environment.

In MEDEA, a computer mediated communication system, First Class, was used to support learning activities that involved groups of teachers living in various Italian cities.

The course was based on a methodological approach proposed by ITD for the development and management of EE projects using educational technology. The chief objective was to give teachers the skills for designing and carrying out EE projects using this methodology. The approach comprises a number of phases (Midoro and Briano, 1996) and involves the planning and management of EE projects by groups of teachers from various disciplines. Rather than dealing with individual teachers, MEDEA addressed groups of teachers, the aim being to encourage local face-to-face interaction as much as possible. These groups met up at local EE centres or in their schools in order to use the necessary network links.

Ten groups of teachers located in various Italian cities were enrolled in MEDEA, and the course was led by three tutors, who were also experts in the specific subject matter. Five observers with an interest in the project also followed the course, without taking an active part in group work.

The course was organised into three main phases, each composed of a series of modules that ranged in length from 2 to 4 weeks (Table 1).

Table 1. MEDEA's schedule

	Introduction	
Module 0	Course presentation and ice-breaking	2 weeks
	Educational Project	
Module 1	Choice of environmental issue	2 weeks
Module 2	Definition of objectives	2 weeks
Module 3	Choice of specific environment	2 weeks
Module 4	Definition of a model for the specific environment	3 weeks
Module 5	Correlation with school curricula	2 weeks
Module 6	Design of product to develop	4 weeks
	Design Phase	
Module 7	Planning of activity	1 week

Considerable emphasis was given to practical work and inter-communication in each module: phases of individual and group work alternated with periods of interaction with other groups and tutors/experts (methods and contents).

At the outset of the course, the students were given a kit of materials that included a user guide, articles, videotapes, publications, and so on. Each module was based on individual study of the material, discussion about the content, activities proposed by the tutor in each local group, communication of results obtained by the local groups to other groups, and inter-group discussion.

Upon completion of MEDEA, the groups were to produce a final product, namely their EE project. A final face-to-face meeting was held at the end of the course to discuss the whole experience. After this experience, MEDEA was re-tuned and run again in 1996.

In 1998, a Europe-wide edition of MEDEA, called EuMedea, (Briano et al., 1998) was run. The EuMedea project was born from the idea of creating synergy between the European project T3 (Telematics for Teacher Training) (Davis and Prosser, 1999), and the experience developed at national level with MEDEA. EuMedea involved practising and student teachers from five European countries: Finland, Italy, The Netherlands, Portugal and UK. Besides seeking to overcome some of shortcomings of MEDEA, the design of EuMedea entailed a number of adaptations to the multinational and multicultural context of T3 The course also needed to strike a balance between the different organisational requirements in the various countries. In this context an ad hoc methodology to validate online courses was developed and used (Bocconi et al., 1999).

In the following, we briefly describe the differences and similarities between MEDEA and EuMedea, pointing out the reasons for the changes introduced.

3.1 Population

While MEDEA was addressed to local groups of practising teachers, EuMedea's local groups were composed of teachers and/or student teachers co-ordinated by a local tutor. Online courses rely on the ability of participants to build new knowledge based on the experience of each member. In EuMedea we studied the effectiveness of this kind of learning with student teachers who had little or no classroom experience. To increase the efficiency of each group, we suggested they each appoint a local tutor, and we sought to widen group knowledge by giving them online access via CMC to an in-service teacher.

Another important issue faced was language. We had been forced to choose a common language, English, which was the mother tongue of only one group. We studied how this influenced remote group communication and what could be done to minimise language-related problems. Finally, there was considerable variation in the contexts in which local groups operated. We studied the impact of this factor on the effectiveness of the course.

3.2 Timing

MEDEA lasted six mounts, while the EuMedea partners required a course duration of three months. As a consequence, we rearranged the content into three modules that covered the main points of the seven MEDEA modules.

3.3 Technology

Both MEDEA and EuMedea used a computer mediated communication system. However, since EuMedea took place in the context of a European project dealing with telematics, visibility through the web was an important requirement. On the other hand, course participation had to be limited to registered participants. These dual requirements meant that while there was a need for all Internet users to access EuMedea so as to observe it, an Intranet approach was called for to restrict communication to a given community. We chose to support EuMedea using the most recent release of *FirstClass,* because it allowed us to implement a system offering both possibilities.

Online courses usually start and end with face-to-face meetings, where participants familiarise with each other. In our experience these events are very useful for creating a friendly environment for course interaction. In the context of EuMedea, face-to-face meetings would have been too expensive so as an alternative we planned an initial and a final multi-point videoconference.

In 1999, MEDEA became an annual training program involving a set of parallel courses based on a revised version of the original.

Here, the key idea was to test two hypotheses:

1. tutors, other than the original course designers, are able to hold the MEDEA course;
2. a percentage of MEDEA alumni can become MEDEA tutors.

Confirmation would have meant that we had found a possible key to solving the problem of the great number of teachers to be trained. Three teams of tutors planned, organised and held three MEDEA courses in three different environmental education labs, (in Milan, Udine and Genoa) with excellent results. MEDEA99 verified the first hypothesis. However, it became clear that to ensure the "portability" of the course, some tools for future tutors had to be developed.

Late 1999 began MEDEA2000, which involves five courses, with 78 groups and 335 participants. MEDEA2000 tutors are both tutors and alumni of MEDEA99. The MEDEA2000 program started with a short two-day introductory course for the nine tutors. A tutor guide was developed to facilitate the tutors' work, and a conference area was opened to provide them with on-going assistance. The tutors were given tools for " real time" course validation, helping them to monitor the effectiveness of the course at any moment. MEDEA2000 is still in progress, but initial results have confirmed the second hypothesis.

4. LESSONS LEARNT

MEDEA shows how ICT can be used to develop quality mass teacher-training courses that deal with both an interdisciplinary content (EE in this case) and educational technology applied to that content. Below, some of the lessons learnt are briefly described.

1. MEDEA shows that it is possible to develop online courses that are effective and reusable for in-service teacher training. The MEDEA approach can be generalised to the development of online courses dealing with various curriculum areas, whose design involves both OLE and content experts. This should ensure the quality of these courses.
2. EuMedea has shown that adapting a well-designed online course to very different contexts is easy to accomplish and cheap as far as human and financial resources are concerned. Far from posing an obstacle, the differences arising in the different contexts may actually prove to be a source of wealth.
3. MEDEA99 has shown that tutors not involved in the development of an online course can run it successfully, with no significant lost of quality.
4. MEDEA99 has shown that instructional and support tools are useful for assisting new tutors to run courses designed by others.
5. In MEDEA2000 these tools consisted of a two-day course, a tutor guide and a conference area in the CMC system for posing questions and asking for help from more experienced tutors. These tools were effective in MEDEA2000 and may also prove effective for other kinds of online

courses. In any case, tools for helping tutors should be designed to ensure course portability.

6. Environmental education labs supported both MEDEA99 and MEDEA2000. These belong to a national network of EE labs called LABNET. ITD provided the CMC system and assisted the novice tutors while they were running the course. The lesson learnt is that in order to disseminate an online course, structures are required that can accomplish the tasks that in MEDEA were performed by the EE labs and ITD.
7. The described dissemination mechanism involves two apparently contrasting elements: a centralised element covering overall system planning matters, such as management of the whole program, administration of the CMC system, tutor assistance facilities etc.; and a local element entailing tasks like recruiting participants, localising the course, organising the local initial and final meetings, etc. The MEDEA experience has shown that this combination of centralism and localism can be very effective, provided that the quality of the whole system is continuously monitored.

5. CONCLUSIONS

The diffusion of computers and the Internet is comparable to that of telephone and television in the recent past. The scenario whereby every family has got one or more computers and Internet access is fast becoming a realistic one. These tools profoundly modify not only the ways of communicating, but also the ways of learning, co-operating and working. Schooling should change to accommodate this new situation and, in the process, the teacher's role should change. Teachers' competencies ought to be enriched to comprise ICT skills for both personal productivity and for use as a tool to facilitate children's learning. We cannot merely wait for a new generation of teachers to bring this change about; a great number of in-service teachers need to be retrained.

This paper has sought to help find possible solutions to the problem of how to train hundreds of thousands of in-service teachers. ICT and the outcomes of recent research in education technology can help us tackle this issue. MEDEA, an annual program of online courses that each year involves an every great number of participants, is an example of how ICT can be used for that purpose. Some of the lessons learnt have been discussed, but the main suggestion is that the solution to the problem of quality mass in-service teacher training can be found by connecting ICT, research and local educational structures, co-ordinated by means of central programs and structures.

REFERENCES

Bocconi, S., Midoro, V., and Sarti, L. (1999) *Valutazione della qualità nella formazione a distanza,* Tecnologie Didattiche, **1**, 24-40.

Briano, R., Midoro, V., and Trentin, G. (1997) *Computer mediated communication and on-line teacher training in environmental education,* Journal of Information Technology for Teacher Education, **6**, 127-145.

Briano, R., Midoro, V., Persico, D., Sarti, L., and Trentin, G. (1998) EuMedea, *a European online course to train European teachers in Environmental Education,* Proceedings of the XV IFIP World Computer Congress "Teleteaching '98", 31 August - 4 September, Vienna/Budapest.

Davis, N. (1998) *Developing telecommunications within European teacher education: progress, plans and policy,* Proceedings of the SITE (Society for Information Technology and Teacher Education) 98 International Conference, Washington, DC.

Davis, N. and Prosser, D. (1999) *T3 final report,* [http://telematics.ex.ac.uk/t3/deliver.htm].

Midoro, V. and Briano, R. (1996) *Learning by doing: Teachers and students working cooperatively to create hypermedia,* Proceedings of ED-MEDIA 96, Boston, 483-489.

Midoro, V. (1998) *Modelling online education,* Proceedings of ComnEd 99, Aulanko, Finland, 239-246.

BIOGRAPHY

Vittorio Midoro received his doctoral degree in 1972. He has been working in educational technology since 1974 and has been responsible for many research projects dealing with both methodological issues and theoretical issues. At present he is project manager of LABNET, a project funded by the Italian Ministry of Environment, aimed a developing a network of environmental education labs. His present activity involves online education, co-operative learning, and the use of telematics in environmental education.

Didactics, ICT and the teacher of the future

Bernard Cornu and Clara Danon
IUFM, 30 avenue Marcelin Berthelot, 38100 Grenoble, France.
bernard.cormu@grenoble.iufm.fr
Subdepartment of Educational technology and ICT, Ministry of Education,
110 rue de Grenelle, 75357 Paris 07, France.
clara.danon@education.gouv.fr

Abstract: France has several specialities, among which the development of didactical research, the way teachers are trained and the national public service characteristics of education. Research in didactics is developing in most countries, and especially in France. Application of such research leads to the elaboration of products, of tools for teaching and learning, of educational environments and of pedagogical strategies (such as co-operative work). The integration of ICT in the school of the future may lead to a uniform education around the world. How can we preserve the diversity and the local specialities? How can we take benefit of the positive aspects of the globalisation, while avoiding the negative ones? In many countries, education is a public service, and the state has the responsibility of equity in education, so that every pupil may have similar chances regarding education. Are we going towards a liberalisation of education? How can the fundamental values of education be preserved? The integration of ICT in education changes the knowledge and the way one can access the knowledge. Therefore, the role of the teacher is changing. What will be the future teaching profession?

Keywords: Didactical research, educational environments, cooperative working, knowledge, equity, teacher, teacher education

1. INTRODUCTION

We would like to take into account the reflections that are carried out in France and bring them as a contribution to the international reflection. Our country has several specialties: the way didactical research is developed and carried out, the way teachers are trained, and the national public service characteristics of education. In this paper we will examine how these specialties can influence the school of the future.

2. THE ROLE OF DIDACTICS IN THE DESIGN OF EDUCATIONAL ENVIRONMENTS

Research in didactics is developing in most countries, and especially in France. The French approach has produced theoretical frameworks, based on the relationships between the pupil, the teacher and the knowledge, and aiming at designing educational situations and didactical situations. This approach is more based on the pupil than on the teacher or the knowledge. But it is always linked with knowledge content. For example, there are lots of studies about epistemological obstacles and the way these obstacles occur for the pupils. There are lots of studies analyzing the errors pupils make as a consequence of the way the knowledge is organized and structured in their mind. Didactical research is also used in order to produce didactical environments. Many researchers apply didactical research for producing tools and resources for teaching and learning and pedagogical strategies.

Due to the simultaneous development of ICT and educational research, there is a fruitful convergence between these two fields. This leads to the design of pedagogical environments, integrating ICT, and to the elaboration of ICT-products based on a didactical approach. Cabri-Geometry, software for learning geometry, is a good example of such a convergence.

Didactical research will influence the school of the future. The teacher of the future will generally not be a researcher, but will have to be able to integrate and apply outputs of research and to put questions to researchers.

There is still a problem in France with didactical research, which is not considered with the same dignity as other fields, and many researchers in didactics feel neglected. There is a tendency to include didactical research in the field of educational sciences, rather than in the field of each discipline. But the strong link of didactical research with the contents of the knowledge make it necessary to keep the didactics of each discipline in the scientific community of this discipline.

3. DIVERSITY OR UNIFORMITY?

The integration of ICT in the school of the future may lead to a uniformed education around the world. The teacher of the future will have to preserve the diversity and the local specialties. But at the same time where there is a risk of uniformity, the access to other cultures, other knowledge and other educational systems is a huge enrichment and can be very fruitful for teachers. We are in a world of diversity. The teaching profession is a profession of diversity, and this diversity may be reinforced by ICT. This diversity can make the school of the future better adapted to each pupil and therefore may be a tool for more equity.

Globalization has many positive aspects. For example human rights have developed around the world not mainly as an effect of local cultures, but as a result of a global culture and philosophy. Similarly, future education can take benefit from the globalization. It enables schools to work together even at a long distance, and to cooperate with schools in developing countries.

In brief, ICT and education must integrate the positive aspects of diversity and the positive aspects of globalization.

4. THE SCHOOL OF TOMORROW AND THE PUBLIC SERVICE OF EDUCATION

In many countries education is a public service and the state has the responsibility of equity in education, so that every pupil may have similar chances regarding education. ICT brings many changes in the knowledge and the way the knowledge is accessible. Knowledge and pedagogy have become merchandise. Are we going towards a liberalization of education? What will we have to pay for in the school of the future? How can the fundamental values of education be preserved?

The state is the guarantor of accessing public services; it is the guarantor of equity in education. Many countries are thinking about decentralization and liberalization. ICT has an influence on the way educational systems are organized and structured. It has an influence on the way knowledge is accessible and is distributed. It makes necessary that a reflection on the role of the state in education is carried out, so that education remains a public service for all. This reflection is necessary for each teacher of the future.

5. THE KNOWLEDGE OF THE FUTURE

ICT changes the knowledge and the way one can access the knowledge. Knowledge is now over-abundant, knowledge is no longer stable but has become dynamic, evolving continuously (Spender, 1996). The knowledge which was printed was stable, could be learned and then taught in the same form. Digitized knowledge is now moving and interactive: everyone can act on the knowledge, interact with the knowledge. We have moved from the "chain" model to the network model: in a chain, there is a before and an after; the one who knows transmits to the one who doesn't. It implies a hierarchy in the distribution of knowledge, and therefore a hierarchy in the organization of educational systems. In the network model, everyone is a node, and the relationship between the nodes is not a hierarchical one. Every one is both a learner and a knowledge transmitter. And knowledge is no longer only in schools and in the teacher's head; it is now available in many places. This leads to the fundamental question of the specialty of schools in knowledge transmission. The school of the future will have to find its specialties. And the role of the teacher will be profoundly changed, from the one who knows and delivers the knowledge, to the one who helps and guides the pupil in accessing the knowledge, and helps the pupil sorting, making hierarchical structures, organizing the knowledge.

But the knowledge evolves in other ways. The strong link between knowledge and disciplines, the splitting of the knowledge into disciplines, is evolving. A French philosopher, Edgar Morin (1999), has proposed "the seven necessary kinds of knowledge for the education of the future". He says that rather than teaching disciplines according to classical curricula, the society needs new kinds of knowledge to be taught. His suggestions are:

- Teach the weaknesses of knowledge: what is human knowledge? Teach its errors, its illusions. Teach to know what to know is!
- Teach the principles of relevant knowledge. One must be able to take into account global and fundamental problems, in which partial and local knowledge will then be used. The knowledge cannot be split into disciplines. One must be able to consider the objects of knowledge in their context, in their complexity, in their whole.
- Teach the human condition. Teach the unity and the complexity of human nature. This needs input from biology, from human sciences, from literature, from philosophy. Teach the relationship between the unity and the diversity of what is human.
- Teach the world identity. Teach knowledge at a worldwide level. Teach the history of the planet and the solidarity between all parts of the world.

- Teach how to face the uncertainties. Sciences have established a lot of certainties, but they also have revealed many uncertainties. Teach the uncertainties in physics, in biology, in history.
- Teach understanding. Understanding in all its meanings, mutual understanding between human beings. Teach what misunderstanding is. It is a crucial basis for peace education.
- Teach the ethics of humanity preparing citizens of the world. Teach how democracy relates to the mutual control between society and individuals.

The teaching should not only be organized through disciplines, but also through topics. What will be the concept of a curriculum in the school of the future? More and more society and the economical world demand us to teach competencies rather than knowledge. Knowledge changes very quickly and one can obtain knowledge when needed. But fundamental competencies, in order to solve problems should be taught at school.

Working in the current society means acquire, transmit and produce knowledge. It is no longer the role of the teacher to transmit knowledge, the role of the pupil to acquire knowledge and the role of researchers to produce knowledge. Acquiring, transmitting and producing knowledge is an objective for teachers as well as for pupils. Therefore, the role of the teacher is changing.

6. THE NEW TEACHING PROFESSION : THE TEACHER OF THE FUTURE

In the report "Learning, the treasure within" (Jaques Delors, 1996) the UNESCO Commission for Education in the XXIst century proposed four pillars of education: learning to know, learning to do, learning to live together, learning to be. In implementing these four pillars the role of the teacher was underlined, as an agent for changes.

A working group of the French National Commission for UNESCO, produced a report based on Delors' work, called: "The new teaching profession" (Cornu, 1999). In this report it is shown that the expectations of society towards teachers have changed and increased. Democratisation of schools have made the pupils more numerous and more heterogeneous. Teachers are facing the increasing complexity of society. And globalisation, with the mixing of cultures, has made the role of the teacher more complex.

So teachers have two major roles: prepare and train citizens and make the pupils acquire knowledge. In order to prepare the citizens of the future, teachers have to help the pupils learn to live together. They have to transmit the fundamental values of society and the universal values of humanity. They must make pupils live according to these values inside the school.

These roles of the teachers have consequences on the way they work everyday, on their official duty, on the way they work in teams.

The evolutions of society and the development of ICT have added lots of new competencies for teachers. The teacher of tomorrow will have to access the knowledge, sort it, organise and give it hierarchical structure. He or she will have to master the teaching and learning processes, to be a guide and a tutor, to contribute to the production of knowledge, to be an agent for policy and equity. The teacher of tomorrow will have to be involved in a life long learning process. He or she will have to work in the future school with the pupils of tomorrow and to find a place in the virtual and global classroom. Listing all the competencies one can expect for teachers, it appears clearly that this is impossible: no one will have all the competencies required.

Therefore we must consider the concept of collective competency, rather than individual competency. In each school the team of teachers must have the required competencies, but not necessarily each of them.

Competency is not a definite acquisition for teachers. They must mainly have an ability to evolve and adapt during their career. In-service training must therefore be a normal component of the teaching profession. Finally, new professions start to appear in schools. ICT makes a lot of new activities emerge, and this leads to the need of new professions.

7. TEACHER EDUCATION

In France a reform of teacher education was set up in 1990. The IUFM's were created ("Instituts Universitaires de Formation des Maîtres). They have to train primary and secondary teachers in the same institution, for the same number of years (as a consequence, primary and secondary teachers are now paid the same salaries). Students who want to become teachers must first take three years at university (up to the "licence" degree). Then they apply for admission at IUFM; at the end of the first year at IUFM, they pass the competitive recruiting exam, through which the state recruits future teachers. If they succeed, they are admitted in the second year at IUFM, with the status (and the salary) of a civil servant. They get a second year of training and the year after they are given a job in a school. IUFM's also perform in-service training and they contribute to educational research.

After ten years some improvement is needed in teachers preparation and recruitment. A reflection about this is being carried out now. It aims at reinforcing the professional dimension in the recruitment exams, at better articulating theory and practice (the practice periods in schools and the more theoretical input at the institute) in teacher education, and at articulating pre- and in-service training. For this purpose it is proposed that new teachers, during their first year as full teachers, are given free time deduced from their duty for training activities. And it is proposed that every future teacher receives a training for integrating ICT in his or her professional activity (and is evaluated on this topic). The project of such an evolution has reactivated the debate about the balance between knowledge and pedagogy. The main objective in this evolution in to reinforce the professional dimension of teacher training.

Teacher education should take into account some basic principles:

- Do not train teachers as yesterday with today's tools: we are training teachers for tomorrow! ICT allows new strategies, new ways of learning and teaching, and it is not enough (and less efficient) just to implement the old methods with the new tools.
- The profession of a teacher is an intellectual profession, and a profession of freedom. This implies that there is no "official pedagogy", that the "best pedagogical method" does not exist, and that we must provide future teachers with a wide diversity of tools, resources and strategies, so that they can build their professional competency by themselves.
- Knowledge (disciplines to be taught), human and social sciences (psychology, sociology, philosophy), pedagogy and educational concerns, must be well balanced in teacher education. They must not only be juxtaposed, but must be put in interaction.
- Teacher education needs interaction between theory and practice. School practice periods are necessary in teacher education, but they are not efficient if they are not well prepared, accompanied and exploited. Tools for observation and analysis are necessary before going to school practice. Theoretical tools must be used in order to solve real problems encountered in practice. Thus, theory feeds practice and practice feeds theory, in a permanent go and return process.
- It is impossible to provide a future teacher with all the competencies and knowledge he or she needs, for an entire career. No "rucksack"! In-service training is an essential component of the profession of a teacher. Ability to evolve and adapt is an essential component of this profession.
- In teacher education, training methods are as important as content. Teachers will generally teach not the way they are told to do, but reproduce the way they were taught themselves. This "induction" process must be taken into account, both in the strategies and methods used for training, and in the diversity of pedagogical approaches. Regarding ICT, it implies that it is not enough to give courses about new technologies and their integration into education. ICT must be actually used in teacher education, in each subject, and in each component of the training.

The new competencies for preparing the teacher of the future make a need for renewed competencies for teacher trainers. So we must also think about the teacher trainer of the future, who will not have to deliver a fixed knowledge, but who actually practices what he or she teaches.

The school of the future has to be prepared today. This is a great challenge for teacher training institutions.

REFERENCES

Cornu B. (1999) *Le nouveau métier d'enseignant*, Commission Nationale Française pour l'UNESCO, Paris.

Delors J. (1996) *Learning, the treasure within*, UNESCO Publishing, Paris.

Morin E. (1999) *Les sept savoirs nécessaires à l'éducation du futur*, UNESCO, Paris.

Spender D. (1996) *Creativity and the Computer Education Industry*, IFIP-Congress, Canberra, Australia (available at www.acs.org.au/ifip96.html)

BIOGRAPHIES

Bernard Cornu is the Director of the IUFM (University Institute for Teacher Education) of Grenoble, France. He contributed to the French reform of initial teacher education, leading in 1990 to the creation of the IUFMs, in which all primary and secondary teachers, in all disciplines, are trained. Until 1994 he was chairman of the 29 IUFM's in France.

He studied the influence of computers and informatics on mathematics and its teaching, and also worked in the field of didactics of mathematics. He has been the Director of the Institute of Research on Mathematics Teaching (IREM) of Grenoble and the Head at the in-service teacher training office for the Academy of Grenoble. He is president of the French Commission for Mathematics Education, and a member of the Commission of the French Republic for UNESCO.

As a member of IFIP he chairman of Working Group 3.1 ("Informatics Education at the Secondary Education Level").

Clara Danon graduated at the Ecole Normale Superieure and the Ecole Nationale d'Administration. She has been the head of several sub-departments at the French ministry of education. She has been in charge of teacher education and she played a major role in the creation of IUFM's. At present she is head of the sub-department of Educational Technologies and ICT for all the levels of education (primary, secondary and university).

A taxonomy of ICT mediated future thinking skills

David Passig
School of Education, Bar-Ilan University, 52900 Ramat-Gan, Israel.
passig@mail.biu.ac.il

Abstract: Our future society will be different from that we have known in the last fifty years. Futurists foresee that in the near decades the world's community will traverse through a period of rapid technological innovations that will change the foundations of society as we used to know. Changes will engulf all aspects of life (Gleick, 1999). These changes will have great impact on society, work, culture and art. People will have to innovate or evaporate. They will have to adapt continuously to never-ending permutations and engage in a never-ending adaptation. It makes sense, therefore, to assume that the graduates of today's schooling will need a different set of cognitive and learning skills reflecting the profound change that they will encounter. This paper traces the basic nature of future society and proposes a relevant taxonomy of future cognitive skills that will provide our students with appropriate tools to succeed in the future. We have used Bloom's taxonomy as a working ground and expanded his categories to reflect the needs of the future. This paper suggests an additional cognitive category to add to our teaching procedures named *melioration*, which we believe, is not addressed in today's curriculum.

Keywords: ICT, future, taxonomy, learning skills, cognition, knowledge

1. INTRODUCTION

From time immemorial, every generation's role was to prepare its next generation to the future. However, the nature of the future we are facing today does not resemble futures that past generations have been confronted with. The nature of the social, economical, industrial, and technological passages that our generation is facing will present our students with challenges that no past generation has encountered (Schwartz, 1999; Gleick,

1999). This should bring us, at the turn of the century, towards examining the cognitive proficiencies that our children will need to succeed in their adulthood lives.

Dealing with such an issue in itself will probably raise substantial scepticism from various disciplines. How do you conduct such an examination? What are your research methodologies and do they insure the results indeed point to the skills that will be required from our graduates in the future?

It is unnecessary to point out that questions such as these are too convoluted to be treated in this framework. The methodological literature concerning future research methodologies is full with discussions of this nature (Kurian and Molitor, 1996).

We must emphasise that the research, which is partly reported here, does not suggest the results to be projections. We used *content analysis* as a methodology. We investigated how a variety of authors in various knowledge domains reckon, at present, what learning and cognitive skills will be required for our schools' graduates in future social, technological, industrial and economical environments.

For this purpose we have grounded our research on the tradition of cognitive taxonomies developed in the course of the recent half century. We have selected Bloom's taxonomy since it is a well-known taxonomy among educators world-wide. We have assumed to be able to modify it to reflect future thinking necessities of future adults.

Our research suggests that an additional cognitive proficiency should be reflected in today's curriculum. *Melioration* reflects a critical cognitive activity in future societies. In this paper we define this skill, and discuss its characteristics and importance.

Obviously the results of this research should be examined in light of the subjective perspective of the literature we have analysed to date. We do not aim to point out future cognitive skills. We do not have, in our present stage, the ability to estimate these skills accurately. All we can do is to estimate how we see future needs today. Thus, the goal of this study is to present these evaluations to those of us developing curricular materials.

2. THE KNOWLEDGE AGE

In the course of the 1990's, various cultures have already begun to experience a wave of changes characterised by a profound transition from the socio-economic state of trading information as a commodity into a global state of manufacturing knowledge (Perelman,1992; Kennedy, 1993). In this "knowledge-age" it is not sufficient to have skills of accessing information in order to achieve a relative advantage. The knowledge-age indicates that there is a need of unique cognitive skills in order to achieve a successful implementation of information in real time. Those who will have the skills of collecting information in real time, as well as the ability to analyse, classify and organise it, will be those to achieve a social, cultural and economical advantage.

Most of the intellectual activity will be to amplify the value of available information. Thus, education in this age will have to be focused on knowledge: a successful implementation of information under the right circumstances and at the right time. The knowledge-age acknowledges the fact that shifts at the information overflow will be accelerated, and that the main role of people will be to add value to the exchange of information (Harkins, 1992; O'Dell, 1998).

In past generations the insulated elite was requested to manage information of large complexity and capacity in order to guide humanity in its efforts to improve life conditions. These efforts took place in relatively small communities. On the other hand, in a knowledge-age could be available information in great quantity to many people who will globally compete for its use. In order for societies to succeed in guiding their efforts to improve conditions effectively, they will need a significant amount of working teams that will be able to generate personal and/or collective, ethnic, and cultural added value (Passig, 1996).

2.1 The nature of future knowledge

Knowledge is the product of information processing. Thus, future knowledge will have local and personal characterisation. Knowledge as a product will reflect where and when it has been processed. To produce knowledge, societies will have to develop procedures that filter information and blend it with religious values, tradition, customs and even cultural or political preferences. Successful future societies will have to alternate their focal efforts from negotiating information into negotiating exclusive and local values, and retail them among different cultures.

3. THE RESEARCH PROCEDURE

In preparing this study we have used *Content Analysis* as our research methodology. After deciding upon the research technique we faced an unsolved dilemma. We had to define the depth and range of the literature we were about to cover in order to guarantee a reasonable validity of our results. Eventually we did not rule out this question, since we believe that such a research has to be extensive and continuous. Thus, we intend to conduct this study in several stages. This paper summarises the results of the first stage of a continuous study in which we are engaged. In this first stage, we examined about 300 books from various future fields of interest as being categorised by the World Future Society (www.wfs.org). We selected from categories such as future technology, future economy, future life style, etc., a handful of representing recent publications (a complete list of publications can be found in Passig, 1998).

3.1 The theoretical framework

We assumed we would be able to find in the literature key words and phrases depicting future and most needed skills. In order to avoid formulation of lists concerning skills with no theoretical base, we had to choose a proper theoretical framework that will guide our efforts and consolidate our findings. Thus, we have examined various theories such as Bloom's taxonomy of cognitive skills (Bloom, 1956), Gardner's intelligences (Gardner, 1983, 1999), and Sterenberg's thinking styles (Sterenberg, 1997). We have decided that, in order to simplify the editing process of our findings, it would be better if we worked out from the most familiar theoretical framework: Bloom's cognitive taxonomy.

Many examined the nature of thinking in order to improve it and developed efficient learning strategies. During the years, different and various concepts were developed such as: high-thinking, productive thinking, interactive thinking, etc. However, Bloom and his colleagues were among the first to suggest a taxonomy of thinking constituents. Its essence was a layout of goals concerning fostering a type of thinking higher than remembering and understanding. Bloom suggested a hierarchy of six thinking levels/categories: *knowledge, comprehension, application, analysis, synthesis* and *evaluation.*

Over the years many researchers criticised Bloom's taxonomy (Nelson, 1981; Ennis, 1981; Seddon, 1978). Ennis for example claimed that the three highest levels in Bloom's taxonomy are thinking skills of a higher order. They supply a too thin guidance for training and they are not escorted with criteria for teaching evaluation. Many criticised the fact that there is an abundance of terms and definitions in the domains of psychology and education, and offered that instead of undertaking one term or another, it is better to adapt the use of the ultra-term "Higher Thinking Skills". This term is not exclusive to one type of thinking or another. It generally emphasises the contrast between lower order thinking skills (memorising, remembering, etc.) and thinking skills, which require more complex mental functions.

Nevertheless, since its publication (Bloom, 1956), the taxonomy has endured criticism and has developed in various directions. It was not feasible at the initial stage of this study to consider the variety of nuances that are attached to Bloom's taxonomy. However, a more comprehensive discussion in a wider framework is needed in the future.

3.2 Bloom's taxonomy of cognitive skills

Bloom's taxonomy was meant to achieve two main objectives: curricular planning and achievement tests. His taxonomy offered the possibility to examine achievements in organised teaching procedures with regard to their behavioural goals. Table 1 shows a short version of Bloom's taxonomy and its behavioural objectives.

Table 1: Bloom's Taxonomy: definitions and behavioural objectives

Categories	Definitions	Behavioural Objectives
Knowledge	Any teaching purpose that needs just memorisation	Defines, outlines, identifies, titles, classifies, notes, chooses, attaches, memorises
Comprehension	A thinking process in which a message is changing form	Reverses. defends, discerns, assesses, explains, inclusion, expands, exemplifies, concludes, rewrites, summarises, translates, changes, supplements
Application	The ability to implement rules, principles, information, assumptions, theories, or other abstractions for new and real situations	Calculates, demonstrates, discovers, comprehends, improves, activates, predicts, understands, produces, relates to, divides into sections, develops, includes, attributes
Analysis	A thorough study to comprehend the structure of the learned content, its formal and logic way of organisation, in order to detect the elements, outlooks and methods the content is based upon	Divides into sections, graphically describes, classifies, distinguishes, identifies, concludes, emphasises, connects, categorises, confronts, compares
Synthesis	Establishing a whole new creation by combination of ideas from different sources, in a way that formats and moulds will be created, and will stand at the basis of the new creation	Combines and adds, creates, prepares, plans, improves, organises, rearranges, restructures, replicates, offers, tells, develops
Evaluation	Judging the values in the ideas through use of standards of estimations, determining the accuracy level, purposefulness and practicality of the details	Evaluates, compares, concludes, criticises, separates, attributes, summarises, supports, judges, claims, confronts, sets a norm

4. FUTURE THINKING SKILLS

Using content analysis we have researched the list of publications assembled from the World Future Society and examined key words and phrases depicting the possible nature of future thinking and learning skills. We then consolidated the large amount of findings into sub-categories along side with examples from the literature being researched (Passig, 1998).

Table 2 shows a condensed version of our findings organised under the same categories developed by Bloom and his colleagues. The suggested thinking and learning skills can be derived from the various challenges that human society faces in the short-term (5-10 years) and the median term futures (10-25 years).

Table 2. Future cognitive learning taxonomy

Categories	Definitions	Behavioural Objectives	Key Words
Knowledge	Achieving successful application of information in real time	To know where to find details; to master search strategies; to develop new symbols in a super-symbolic society; to develop conventions	To locate; to know where to search; to filter; to be updated; to leave out; to develop
Comprehen-sion	Multi-facet comprehension of a certain information; setting up fragments of information in various ways, when each composition has a different meaning	To expand existing models of thinking; to set the way of thinking in a wider framework; to invent symbols for concrete elements and to trade in these symbols; to create inferences and analogies in various ways	To expand; to set up in a wider framework; to invent symbols; to relatively connect
Application	Producing new ideas out of an old idea, in order to implement relevant information in real time and in different variations; creating new meaning for new symbols, new meaning for existing symbols and a new symbol for an existing meaning	To use codes and symbols: new and old; to change old codes and symbols	To initiate change; to be flexible; to decide; to reorganise
Analysis	Dividing a unit of information into its components and structuring varied and different relationships, even opposed	To create relations; to distinguish between relations; to analyse pieces of information in various ways; to evaluate	To make a relevant choice, subtle in a personal perspective; to

	to the unit's components; choosing from the ocean of dynamic information, out of personal/cultural/ ethnic judgmental values; setting fragments of information up in a multi-dimensional spatial structure; simulating various implications to various relations and simulating various perspectives in the multi-dimensional space	reliability of information and set fragments of information up in different relations putting in mind that the relations will be given to the influences of time space and personal intuition	disassemble and structure relations between fragments of information
Synthesis	Creating various combinations with different meanings out of given units of information.	To locate a separate element out of the pieces of information that it was taken from, in order to grant it a new meaning	To identify; to connect
Evaluation	Knowing how to choose suitable criteria and developing new criteria for an evaluation that will be useful for the continuation of learning process; evaluating the concealed as well	To evaluate qualitatively and quantitatively; to focus and to connect between the overall relevant items	to disqualify; to process; to check; to confront

Amazingly, or not, the driving forces behind these challenges are mostly information and communication technologies. The literature we have examined is a fascinating evidence that there exists today a consensus across the board that ICT is the pivotal force behind most permutations we are about to encounter on most realms of future reality. Moreover, the depth and pace of connectivity that ICT is about to deliver, is in our belief what will make ICT to the primary driving force for societal upheaval.

We suppose however, that ICT itself is the key that can help us deliver to our students the skills needed to successfully ride the transitions ahead. However, even if everyone does not agree with this statement, surely we need to prepare our next generation to undertake the kind of challenges that ICT will introduce to society, by providing our students with metacognitive tools for using ICT. Therefore we suggest that the suggested skills will be considered at least as such. It is evident from the literature we have examined that people who will master these skills will have great advantages over others.

Nonetheless, the suggested list of skills can be considered as a reminder that intelligence itself is evolutionary, and that we cannot rely solely on the way we defined cognitive skills half a century ago. This list of skills however, cannot replace other lists or curricular objectives. It merely aims to enlarge existing definitions of thinking skills. It might be considered just as a proactive approach to the evolution of intelligence, since we really cannot predict where human cognition is heading.

5. MELIORATION

Summarising our findings we found that out of the literature stems a new category that could stand on its own. We struggled to choose a name that will support its independence, and chose the term "melioration." Finally, although the category could be a composition of several skills, it seemed that we should set it separately, mainly since it points to a type of cognitive skill with which we have not dealt in our curriculum so far. Especially since, according to the literature that we have examined, this skill is becoming increasingly important in future thinking procedures. See Table 3.

Table 3. Melioration: A future cognitive skill

Category	Definition	Behavioural Objectives	Key Words
Melioration	The skill to choose the suitable combination of information and implement it in problem solving in different situations, dependent on time and space, in order to meliorate the combination.	Consonance: to create an agreement; harmony; accord; personal new logical connection between two domains seemed distant from each other. Association: the mental notion of connection or relation between thoughts, feelings, ideas or sensations. A remembered or imagined feeling, emotion, idea or sensation linked to a person, object or idea	to adapt, to innovate simultaneously, to invent, to adjust

In order to meliorate information, one needs to embed in his/her thinking procedures ethnic, cultural, traditional and personal connotations. The following example can demonstrate what melioration is about: The president of one of the most successful high-tech companies in Israel, El-Rom, was once asked: Does El-Rom, in its way to success, imitates American technologies? What actually makes El-Rom unique and successful? He then answered:

"In many aspects, El-Rom adjusted American technologies and work procedures to the Israeli social and ethnic fabric. El-Rom has *adapted* manufacturing processes. That is, the company has innovated.

People from all over the world are coming to see and learn from that innovation. We also help them innovate in their own way."

At this point of time, we cannot predict with any certainty, what will be the hierarchy of skills that our graduates will be asked to master. However, it is certain that some of the skills we brought up to master are irrelevant to today's reality. Take for example memorisation. There are world-wide generations of students that attended schools in the 50s and 60s, who were forced to invest time and effort to master techniques for faster and efficient memorisation of poetry, mathematical tables and entire chapters of books. It was believed that by being able to recite prose by heart you would have some advantage in your adulthood life and in the work force. It was true then. It is not true anymore.

In this study, as opposed to the literature aimed at defining the core of intelligence, we searched for a different approach in defining the goals of education with regard to thinking skills. We embraced the proactive approach for a change and engaged to identify beforehand what might be the skills needed in the future of our students attending secondary education. These skills probably will become obsolete in the future. We need to be constantly proactive to identify the evolutionary nature of human intelligence.

6. CONCLUSIONS

Many people contend that ICT has not made a great difference in education, since it was introduced two decades ago into the classroom. Likewise, the body of literature reporting on the improvement of cognitive skills facilitated with computer assisted learning barely mounts to its expectations. The debate on this issue has taken ground in various scientific gatherings in recent years. However, it occurred to us the more we progressed with this study, that the reason for the poor results scientists are receiving worldwide from ICT performance in classes might be explained by another reason. It might be because we have been trying to teach a baby to crawl with skateboards. It might be that ICT could improve a different hierarchy of skills not listed in today's educational and cognitive goals. This study claims ICT is driving a much higher and sophisticated hierarchy of cognitive skills. ICT is challenging our broadly known hierarchy of skills. However, it is also providing us with ways to execute the potential embedded in it.

REFERENCES

Bloom, B. (1956) *Taxonomy of Educational Objectives,* Longmans, New York.
Ennis, R. (1981) *Eight fallacies in Bloom's Taxonomy,* in *Philosophy of Education* (ed C. Macmillan), Philosophy of Education Society, Bloomington, IN.
Gardner, H. (1983) *Frames of Mind: The Theory of Multiple Intelligences*, Basic Books.
Gardner, H. (1999) *Intelligence Reframed: Multiple Intelligences for the 21st Century*, Basic Books.
Gleick, J. (1999) *Faster: The Acceleration of Just about Everything*, Pantheon Books.
Harkins, A. (1992) *Knowledge Base Learning: Bridging Industrial Education to the Knowledge*, Saturn Institute, St. Paul, MN.
Kennedy, P. (1993) *Preparing for the 21st Century,* Random House, New York.
Kurian, G. and Molitor, G. (1996), *Encyclopedia of the Future,* Macmillan Library Reference.
Nelson, B. (1981) *Hierarchy, utility, and fallacy in Bloom's Taxonomy,* in *Philosophy of Education* (ed. C. Macmillan), Philosophy of Education Society. Bloomington, IN.
O'Dell, C. (1998) *If Only We Knew What We Know: The Transfer of Internal Knowledge and Best Practice*, Free Press.
Passig, D. (1996) *An Israeli model of a networked teachers' training center for implementation of information technology in curriculum development,* in *Information Technology: Supporting Change through Teacher Education* (eds. D. Benzie and Y. Katz), IFIP, Laxenburg, Austria.
Passig, D. (1998) *A Taxonomy of Future Cognitive Skills,* School of Education, Bar Ilan University. Israel (in Hebrew).
Perelman, L. (1992) *School's Out: Hyperlearning, The New Technology, and the End of Education*, W. Morrow, New York.
Schwartz, P. (1999) *The Long Boom: The Coming Age of Prosperity*, Perseus Books.
Seddon, G. (1978) *The properties of Bloom's Taxonomy of Educational Objectives domain,* in *Review of Educational Research,* 48, 303-323.
Sterenberg, R. (1997) *Thinking Styles,* Cambridge University Press, Cambridge, MA.

BIOGRAPHY

David Passig holds bachelors and masters' degrees in Education and a Ph.D. in Future Studies from the University of Minnesota, Minneapolis, USA. He is teaching graduate and undergraduate courses on Educational Futures, Future Technologies, Social Systems Theories, Futures' Methodologies, Multimedia and Virtual Reality. He is heading the Multimedia and Virtual Reality Laboratories and is conducting research on the Human User Learning Interface of Virtual Reality and Multimedia. A variety of the VR Worlds that have been developed for research can be accessed via his website at: http://faculty.biu.ac.il/~passig.

New literacies for connected learning in global classrooms

Toni Downes and Katina Zammit
University of Western Sydney, P.O. Box 555 Campbelltown, NSW 2560 Australia.
t.downes@uws.edu.au, k.zammit@uws.edu.au

Abstract: While much is being researched and written about the nature of new learning environments and the changing roles for teachers in the school of the future little serious attention is being paid to the new demands being placed upon students in secondary schools as they communicate, handle information and learn in global networked classrooms. In secondary schools, teachers expect to build on students' existing literacy skills and understandings. These skills and understandings are essentially built around the paper-based technologies of pen, paper, books and libraries. Learning processes in networked learning environments require substantially different literacies. The key differences relate to the changing nature of texts with which students will need to work. This paper will discuss the implications for secondary curricula and pedagogy of the challenges presented by the literacy demands these "new texts" place on secondary school students in networked learning environments. In particular it will argue for a redefinition of basic literacies and learning processes taught and used in secondary classrooms.

Keywords: Literacies, secondary, learning environments, networked classrooms

1. LITERACY AND LEARNING IN SCHOOL

Historically to be literate in Western society has meant that an individual has a capacity to read and write at a level that enables them to learn formally within educational institutions and to effectively participate as a worker and citizen. Within Australian schools while it has been accepted that learning about subject areas occurs through literacy, it has been assumed that secondary school teachers were working with literate individuals. Learning about the components of literacy was considered a task for primary schooling. In recent years, this has changed such that today most secondary school teachers believe that within the context of teaching their particular subject matter, they too are teachers of literacy.

Accompanying these changes have been developments in the theoretical framework surrounding literacy education. These relate to the addition of socio-cultural and critical aspects to the historical definition of literacy. The socio-cultural component expands the concept of literacy to include the social practices and conceptions that surround reading and writing. As such literacy has many forms according to different contexts, as readers engage with different types of written texts, such as newspapers, novels or instructions on food packaging. In this sense different literacies exist and they are inextricably connected to purposes and practicalities of use. This approach has led to a growing understanding of how and why various social groups have different and unequal access to literacy (and knowledge). Thus a further dimension has evolved, critical literacy. Critical literacy includes the skills and understandings needed to analyse and evaluate texts and the wider social practices made possible through the reading and writing of particular texts.

In the past two decades there have also been significant changes in practices associated with literacy learning in Australia. The early changes related to major shifts in teaching strategies. For example, there was a move away from drill and practice to whole language and now to genre-based approaches. The more recent changes reflect the broader understandings of the socio-cultural and critical components of literacy. Many educators now accept that literacy is not just a set of cognitive abilities or skills based on an identifiable technology, e.g. alphabetic script, but also a social activity embedded within larger social practices. Making meaning has as much to do with socio-cultural processes as with internal cognitive events (Lankshear, 1997). Hence the literacy demands and practices in secondary school are different in each subject area. The geography teacher and students learn about and work with a range of particular practices and texts types to develop and demonstrate skills and understandings central to the discipline of geography. The science and art teachers and students learn about and work with others.

The increasing understanding of the role of critical literacy has seen many of the practices associated with literary studies and media studies now being applied to other types of texts in the various subject areas. Students now attend to the way texts "talk about" people, places, events and phenomena and "talk to" the reader, whether they be literary or factual texts. For example, when working with historical texts which retell events of World War II students analyse the text not only for its content, but also for its purpose and audience, and the techniques it uses to position the people and events within particular ideological frameworks.

Significantly within these shifts to the socio-cultural and critical, the concept of literacies still refers to the reading and writing of paper-based texts within a particular culture. In this sense the notion of a literate person remains interconnected with the technologies of paper, pen, books and libraries and the social practices surrounding reading and writing within a particular cultural community. Essentially, the new ICT has been ignored as has the impact of globalisation and the issue of inter-cultural understandings. Consistent with this, literacy practices in secondary classrooms have been, and generally continue to be, based on competencies and social practices surrounding paper-based technologies in particular cultures. Today's global digital society demands a further re-definition of literacy and places significant stress on traditional practices in schooling.

New digital and network technologies have come into the workplace, home and school as major information and communication technologies. This ICT is placing new demands on students, workers and citizens who need to be able to communicate and handle information using these new media. The demands include the ability to handle an increasingly diverse and complex range of texts. The diversity stems from access to large numbers of written, visual and aural texts from many cultures and countries and the complexity from the convergence of media and text types and their interrelationship (Leu & Kinzer, in press). Learning environments in schools need to include both traditional environments as well as those characterised by the use of new technologies and more diverse and complex texts. Given the rate of social, cultural and technological change, new learning environments and text types will continue to emerge at an ever-increasing rate (Leu, in press). Within this framework it is essential that schools address how to provide students with the necessary skills and understandings to deal with new learning environments and the literacies needed to learn and work effectively within them.

2. NEW TEXTS AND SOCIAL PRACTICES

Text types, also known as genres, and social practices surrounding literacy are always evolving and changing. Key changes have occurred as society has moved from aural technologies to paper-based technologies, to analogue broadcast and communication technologies. Similarly, with the advent of the digital interactive technologies "new" or hybrid texts have emerged within the new environments created by these technologies. The new technologies have created a space for more creative and playful interactions with visual, spoken and written forms of making meaning, i.e. modes of representation. With the construction of these "new" texts come "new" ways of interacting with texts, as well as with people.

Some of the new texts are variations of "old" texts that use the new technologies as a medium to convey their messages. Hypertexts while similar in many ways to linear texts have non-linear structures. Multi-modal texts, combine and use the visual, aural and written modes in different ways. New texts are also being created within environments where the computer mediates communication, these texts seem to integrate features of written and aural texts. Similarly, some of the social practices have evolved from existing practices with traditional texts and others are significantly different. In the following sections, these new text types and practices will be discussed.

2.1 Hypertexts

Traditionally, paper-based texts are written on the basis that they are read in a particular sequence, from chapter one to the next chapter to the next, until the text is finished. They are linear texts. Hypertexts while similar in many ways to linear texts have non-linear structures (see Fig 1). They can have multiple pathways and multiple endpoints. The reader does not necessarily have a set beginning point, nor a set sequence of reading nor a set endpoint to the overall text.

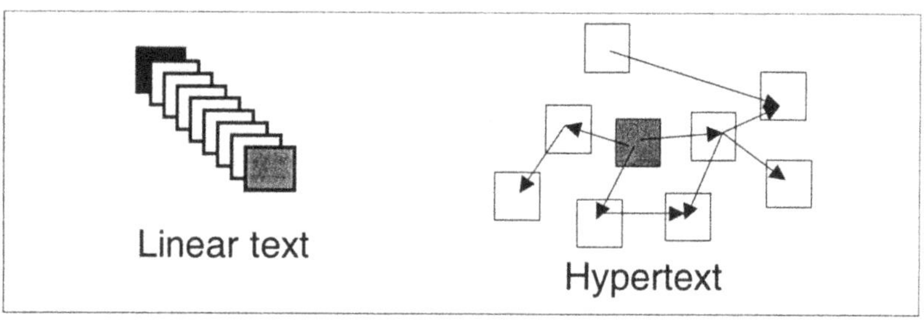

Figure 1. The structure of texts

Hot-linked words and navigation icons enable the reader to decide where to go, what screens and information sequence to engage with. The construction of meaning of the new text is influenced by the pathway the reader takes, the navigation icons and tools engaged with (Joyce, 1997), and ultimately the visual elements of each screen. The links and pathways that are provided are vital keys to tacit assumptions and values of the designer/author.

Access to the information within hypertext environments depends on an individual's information skills, the search strategies they use to locate information and to extract information. This can be quite challenging since the organisational structure is not obvious, nor easily discerned. Many of the strategies developed with linear texts do not apply, new strategies are needed to effectively negotiate the various pathways. One of these strategies, surface reading, has become a means by which students can efficiently access information. Surface reading is akin to the "surfing" of the Internet. It is also the reading necessary in this type of environment as it enables students to be more adept at rapid screening and parallel processing of different materials simultaneously. The user is less inclined to attend to one text for sustained periods of time (deep reading). Also the quickness associated with this form of reading tactic enables users to view or read a large number of sites of information and make decisions about which to revisit and engage with more deeply. In effect for users of networked environments, like the Internet, a sustained attention span may be less useful than successive attending (Joyce, 1997).

2.2 Multi-modal texts

Many of these new texts incorporate a range of modes, not just the written and static visual, but also sound, video and animation. In an electronic environment it is easy to combine different modes of representation. Multi-modal texts have become the norm within networked environments, such as the Internet. In the past, the different modes were managed by experts. Now technology allows individuals to create and control all modes, including sound, with only limited skills.

For most electronic texts, it is the visual elements that dominate the screen, "the look" is important to all (Kress, 1997). Both the words and the images are visual elements and their development can be more easily controlled, designed and changed than in a paper-based environment. These visual texts place further demands on the reader, particularly where the images have taken over some of the functions of the words. The result being that written language has become less complex and the images more complex as they act as highly abstract representations of objects and relationships (Kress, 1997).

The reading of visual texts has been presumed to be easy, with the meaning of the images being considered transparent to the reader. While in one sense it is correct to think that images are easier to "read" than words, strategies and techniques used to construct meaning, and to position the "reader" in relation to the message are complex and subtle. For example the layout, composition, components of an image and its placement on a page in relation to the written text, all influence the understanding of the message by the reader.

2.3 Computer Mediated Communication (CMC) texts

Computer mediated communication has also generated a range of new texts in homes, workplaces and classrooms. These include texts in both synchronous and asynchronous environments. Examples of synchronous environments are chat rooms and MUD Object Oriented environments (MOOs). Within these environments individuals of any age can "speak" with other people from around the world or with their friends. The text is written but the mode is spoken. The interaction is socially oriented, with the development of a punctuated written text similar to overlapping speech during a conversation.

Email is yet another "new" text type that exists within asynchronous environments. It has a whole new set of social practices emerging around its use. Similar to those in IRCs, texts generated by users of email vary along the mode continuum between spoken and written (Yates, 1996). However, the asynchronous nature of email allows for a time delay and more fully developed texts. This enables the writer to use the rules and conventions of print-based texts in the formation of their texts. But there are differences between email and paper-based texts. For example, spelling does not have to be perfect; metalinguistic cues such as emoticons and "visual" signatures made of key strokes are used; there is an assumption of immediacy and closeness in distance when a message is sent. In many ways email represents the digital equivalent to a telephone message.

2.4 The cultural dimension of new text types

Within the new texts English tends to be the *lingua franca*. Not only does English dominate the texts published as sites on networks but the production is predominantly based in the United States of America (Yates, 1996). This dominance of English can be seen as cultural imperialism, which is developing from the internationalisation and globalisation of the networked society based on traditional western print-based culture (Luke, 2000). There are increasing numbers of sites emerging in different languages and from different cultures. As these sites increase, the Internet will readily afford users access to sites, texts and languages from all over the world. But it remains to be seen if the environment continues to be based on western cultural texts.

As teachers and students learn about and work with new texts, the demand for inter-cultural understandings creates another layer of complexity surrounding the new literacies. Traditionally, textbooks provided sources of information within the student's cultural framework. While there has been growing attention to how such texts position students from minority cultural and linguistic backgrounds, to date there has been little need to pay attention to Australian students accessing information texts created in other cultures and languages. Readers of the new texts will require the critical skills to determine the cultural and ideological meanings being conveyed in the texts. Authors will need to consider the variety of sociocultural backgrounds their readers may come from or to whom they may be writing.

Making meaning from images is also situated within cultural and social practices and exploring the visual layout of the screen reflects these practices. As most of the Internet is based on western culture, the screen is presented reflecting western text development: reading from left to right, top to bottom, frames placed in particular relationship to the page. The matter of cultural differences in visual representations (Iedema, 1998) and the way other cultures read "English" visual representations should be addressed as they are important aspects of critical visual literacy, essential skills for readers of "new" texts.

2.5 Social practices surrounding new electronic environments

Broader social practices with the new electronic environments impact on the way that secondary students interact with digital texts. One social practice, in particular, is likely to impinge on the effective use of digital texts for learning in the various subject areas in the secondary schools. This relates to the way that young people first encounter these new technologies in their homes and in broader society within the framework of popular culture. Young people in Australia are most likely to have their first encounters with digital interactive texts in the home in the form of computer games (Australian Bureau of Statistics, 1996). Through their experience of game playing, they develop particular orientations to the use of computer technologies (Downes, 1998). Some of these orientations generate beneficial outcomes for new learning environments in classrooms. They develop a general proficiency with the technology; they learn to deal with complex and ambiguous interactive multi-modal texts such as games by employing a "playful" or exploratory mode of learning. Within these informal learning environments visual feedback dominates and young people are used to being "in charge" of their learning and performance. On the other hand, a number of authors (Birkerts,1996) argue that computer game playing can have negative effects. For example, they argue that playing games generates trivial attitudes towards all virtual environments and consolidates predispositions to high stimulus environments while reducing capacity to concentrate within less stimulating ones.

While these social practices relate more to the use of new texts within popular culture than within learning environments, they are part of the broader social framework within which students interact with the new technologies and texts. They generate attitudes and habits of thought that can be productively built upon or can create barriers to the effective use of these texts for learning. These issues need to be considered as part of the social practices surrounding the new digital texts.

2.6 Broadening our definition of literacy

It light of all the changes in the home, workplace as well as the school in relation to the nature of texts and the dominance of new text types, and the increasing volume and complexity of collections of texts it is important for educators to redefine literacy to encompass these "new" texts and the social, cultural and critical dimensions of their use.

To this end, a working definition has been devised to assist the development of new curriculum and pedagogical frameworks for both new and traditional learning environments in a global and digital world. This definition draws on elements from several different theoretical perspectives for example The New London Group (1995) and J.R. Martin (1992).

> *Literacy is the ability to locate, comprehend, use, create and be critical of a variety of texts and their accompanying social and cultural practices from diverse contexts, using a range of language modes, forms, features and structures.*

In this definition, the key terms: modes, form, features and structure are drawn from the current NSW English Stage 6 Syllabus (1999). Modes of language refer to listening, speaking, reading, writing, viewing and representing. These modes are often integrated and interdependent activities used to make meaning, especially when working with multi-modal texts. Language forms and features refers to the symbolic patterns and conventions that shape meaning in texts. Structures of texts refers to the relationship of different parts of a text to each other, and to the text as a complex whole. For example some texts are linear, others such as hypertexts can be hierarchical or networked.

3. AN EMERGING CURRICULUM FRAMEWORK

This broader definition of literacy provides a basis for developing a curriculum framework within which teachers in secondary schools can create new learning environments that use new technologies and new types of texts to support learning in their subject area. These new learning environments require the modification of existing practices and the generation of new practices. In particular it requires a re-evaluation of some common practices in paper-based learning environments in the light of their contribution to effective learning. For example, the practice of students independently completing "projects" is common in the junior years of secondary schooling. Yet, in Australia, it is generally done poorly with many students photocopying images, copying sections of written texts from books and sticking them on a piece of cardboard or in a folder. The students are re-presenting information on the topic without having engaged deeply with the concepts and understandings inherent in the topic. Simply transferring this practice into a digital environment, by having the students construct a website, and applauding it because "it looks great" does not address the pedagogical issues surrounding the efficacy of the practice itself. At all times, it is important for students to learn about and work with a range of texts in order to develop and demonstrate their understandings within the particular subject area.

Figure 2 presents the curriculum framework needed for the new learning environments. It addresses the demands placed on learners that use traditional and new types of texts for learning about and engaging with their global and digital world. The outcome is the development of a multiliterate individual, who is able to be literate in several modes of representation, and able to apply their skills and understandings to new learning environments and other modes of representation. The essential skills of the multiliterate individual are locating, comprehending, using, critiquing and creating texts within personal, social, educational, historical, cultural and workplace contexts. In particular for secondary school students, this is embedded within the context of the curriculum in the different subject areas.

The actual diagram presents the intersection of the texts, media and processes required within new learning environments, whatever the subject area. The inner circle is labelled "Developing and demonstrating understandings". This emphasises that all teachers and all classrooms are literacy classrooms, where the teaching of literacy is in the service of a deeper engagement with the content of the subject area.

The next two layers represent the range of texts and media with which students engage in these classrooms. They include visual, aural and multi-modal texts as well as the more traditional written texts. The media of these texts can be live (as in speeches and dramatic performances), paper-based or electronic. In addition, the framework recognises that these texts are part of social practices, that they may be part of a collection of texts, and not just individual items.

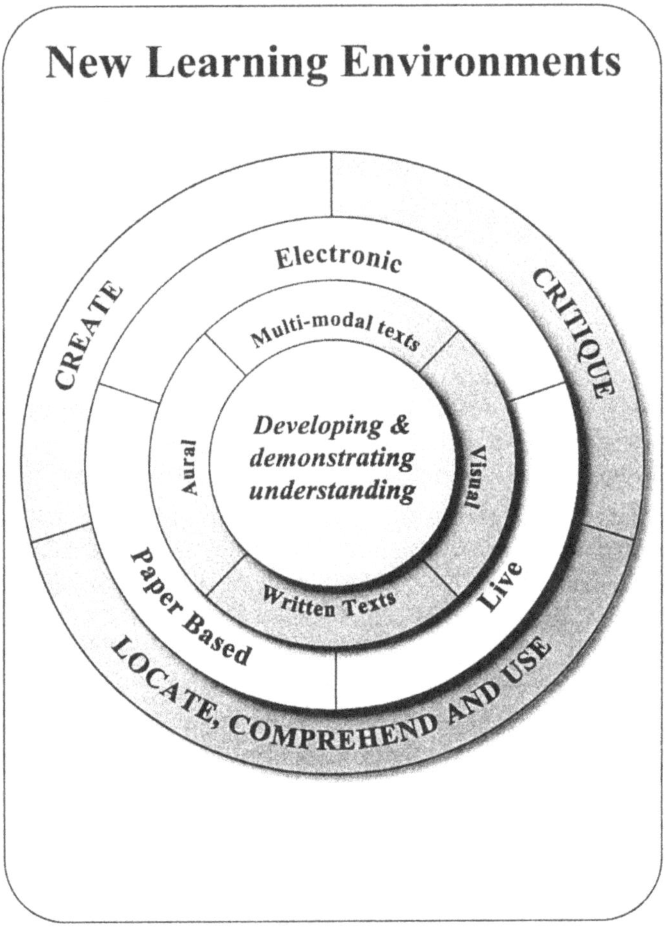

Figure 2. A curriculum model for new learning environments

The outer circle focuses on the processes of teaching and learning, within the class, as teachers and students work with texts. Equal emphasis is placed on three sets of processes: "locate, comprehend and use", "critique", and "create". For many years the emphasis has mainly been on the comprehension and use of texts. Locating texts has become a more strategic skill and is intertwined with "comprehending and using" as learners move from accessing limited, moderated and ordered collections such as those found in school libraries to accessing the chaotic, anarchic and almost boundless collection of texts in the Internet. Critiquing texts has been a common feature of literary and media studies for many years. However it is not a common practice in secondary curricula in relation to factual texts nor to the investigation of ideological stances within historical or scientific texts.

Similarly the creating of anything other than written texts has not been common in secondary classrooms. Students need to develop the skills to create texts in different modes and mediums. For example, students need to construct speeches, radio interviews, video, film, and multimedia texts such as web pages or hypertexts. They need to move beyond the viewing and critiquing of such texts and their production to the creation of their own texts for particular purposes and audiences. This takes for granted competence in the use of the media, and in the conventions and patterns used in these different types of texts. It also requires monitoring and evaluating the most appropriate media and text types for organising and presenting ideas and experiences in a variety of contexts.

To implement this framework for multi-literacies in new learning environments across the secondary school attention needs to be paid to both pedagogical practices and changes to curriculum. The key elements of these are:

- *The pedagogy* involves learning literacies, learning through literacies and learning about literacies. Learning literacies and learning about literacies will remain primarily the responsibility of the English, Art, Music, Drama and Design and Technology teachers. Learning through literacies is the responsibility of all teachers. All teachers need to engage in the explicit teaching of the various texts and processes within subject area classrooms to enhance the development and demonstration of subject matter understanding.
- *The curriculum* includes the teaching of metalanguages to provide the labels and tools with which teachers and students can explicitly describe and talk about the various texts. For example, students need a language to talk about visual (Callow, 1999) and aural texts as well as written texts. This requires co-operative planning so that English, Art, Music and Drama teachers who traditionally teach the metalanguages for the study of literary, aesthetic, and performed texts work in tandem with other subject matter teachers to develop ways of talking about factual texts in terms of their form, features and structures and their relationships to the cultural dimensions of the text.

Both of these present real challenges to teachers, many of whom have limited knowledge of the new technologies and who fear losing control over content delivery (Golman, Cole & Syer, 1999).

4. CLASSROOM EXAMPLES

In this section two examples are presented to highlight the nature of changes to the pedagogy and the curriculum that the new learning environments require. The first is an example from a History classroom and the second from a Geography classroom.

4.1 A history classroom

A class of modern history students (15-16 year olds) studied "The Cold War". Early in the unit of work the history teacher posed a series of questions to engage students in a critical reading of the written texts they were using to gather information about their topic from the school and local libraries: Whose history are they reading? Who wrote that history? What are the ideologies embedded in their accounts? How have they positioned East and West? Why have they positioned them in this way? What strategies have they used to position them?

In their English classroom, the students worked with selected written texts to critique how the form and features of these texts positioned the various events and people described in the text and how they positioned the reader in relation to the text. They wrote from particular perspectives, they read literature written by authors during the Cold War, about the Cold War and discussed the questions above and point of views. Similarly in the Art classroom, they worked with selected photos from texts about the topic to critique how the composition of elements, and the use of light portrayed the phenomena, events and people in particular ways.

Later in the unit of work the same critical questions were applied to a range of Internet sites found by the students during their search for information on the subject. Again the English and Art teachers provided support through critiquing the written and visual elements of these electronic texts. The teacher-librarian and history teacher reinforced the information skills necessary for searching, navigating and using the Internet. Students practised their surface reading skills, explicitly talking about where they went by printing out the history of their time on the computer.

As part of the assessment for the subject, students formed groups and produced a web page to link to the class history website. In the history classroom, they deconstructed and discussed the layout and visual design of web pages with similar purpose and content. Students were given different roles and tasks, to develop expertise and also content for their web page. The final product was a co-operative (joint) construction, a team effort. The key characteristic of the content of the web page was to present a variety of cultural and historical yet authoritative perspectives on the Cold War.

Scaffolding of the tasks was provided through contact with a range of "experts" and through explicit teaching and learning. The English and Art teachers provided explicit teaching about the form and features or particular texts. The Art and Design and Technology teachers became visiting experts for the production phase, offering advice on design and technical issues. Each student kept a journal about their experiences of producing the web page, including the ideological background of the site; whose position it was trying to give prominence to; why images, writing and sound texts were used; and reasons for the placement of texts in regards to supporting the message/s they were trying to convey to the reader.

4.2 A Geography classroom

A class of 12-13 year olds were studying deserts to deepen their understanding of the interactions between physical environments and their related human communities. As part of the assessment of this work, students worked in pairs to locate information about a particular desert and its human community and to create a multi-modal information report on their desert that would become part of a large hypertext on "Desert regions and their peoples".

A number of teachers worked co-operatively to improve the students' skills and understandings throughout the unit and to develop their literacy skills in the context of this work. The teacher librarian worked on the students' information handling skills in searching the library using the online catalogue, in searching the Internet using subject-based sites, and taking notes related to key questions generated in their Geography lessons. Also in these classes the issue of citing sources of information, and seeking permission from website owners to use images, sounds and graphics in their works were discussed and a model email was devised in the English classroom for students to use when writing for such permission.

The Design and Technology teacher, introduced all the students to the features of the "outline" view in word processing packages and its use for note taking and recording sources of ideas, images, and sound bites. As well, in the Design and Technology classroom the students looked at a range of multimedia factual texts and discussed design issues that made such texts easy to comprehend and use. A key issue to emerge was the function and relationship of the written and visual modes. As part of the design process the students discussed criteria for evaluating the design of their final information report. The students used computer lab time from both their

Design and Technology, English and Geography classes to work on their reports.

As part of the process the English teacher explicitly taught the students how to generate information reports that have particular forms and features that work in screen-based environments. The Geography teacher used one of the existing online project networks to generate communication between the class and students who lived in many of the world's desert communities being studied. Email communication with these students was used not only to collect further information but to seek feedback on the final report. Again, the English teacher worked with the students to learn about the form and features of email messages, so that students would feel confident in introducing themselves to students in other countries, outlining their project and asking questions.

The Geography teacher concentrated on working with the students to organise and analyse the information they collected in ways that lead them to further understand the interaction of the environment and the its peoples and to present their findings in ways that highlighted this interaction. As part of this work, the class had a discussion about the overall structure of the hypertext; its key organising features (would it be organised around regions of the world, types of deserts, or developing and developed communities?) and the ways links could be used to highlight the commonalties and differences within the physical elements of the environments, lifestyles of the communities and their apparent interaction. As part of these discussions, the teachers and students developed criteria for evaluating the content of each pair's work on a particular desert/community as well as the whole hypertext as put together.

The actual construction of the whole hypertext, was done by a group of interested students outside of normal class time. This was done under the guidance of the Design and Technology teacher, but based on a design brief developed by the whole class and the Geography teacher and with feedback from the whole group. This approach took account of the limited timeframe of the unit of work, and the general skill level of the students. Each pair of students created a simple hypertext that demonstrated their understandings while the design of the whole hypertext, with its more complex features, reinforced the broader inter-relationship of environments and their human communities.

5. CONCLUSION

Co-operation and teamwork are essential aspects of learning in the new electronic and global environments, for both teachers and students. A curriculum framework that draws on the expertise of relevant subject specialists, those with the metalanguages (the language to talk about how the text is created, its form, features and structure) and technical skills, and those with the knowledge of the content will provide students with the tools they need to locate, comprehend and use, critique and create new text types. With this approach to literacy, or multi-literacies, students will be well equipped to work with new, and future, learning environments.

REFERENCES

Australian Bureau of Statistics. (1996) *Household Use of Information Technology, Australia* Catalogue No 8128.0, Commonwealth of Australia, Canberra.

Birkerts, S. (1996) *The Gutenberg Elegies. The Fate of Reading in an Electronic Age,* Faber and Faber, London.

Board of Studies, NSW. (1999) *English, Stage 6 Syllabus,* Author, Sydney.

Burbules, N. (1997) *Rhetorics of the Web: Hyperreading & critical literacy,* in *From Page to Screen: Taking Literacy into the Electronic Era* (ed. I. Snyder), Allen & Unwin, Sydney, 102-122.

Callow, J. (1999) *Image Matters: Visual Texts in the Classroom,* Primary English Teaching Association, Sydney.

Christie, F. and Martin, J. (1997) *Genre and Institutions: Social Processes in the Workplace and School,* Caswell, London.

Downes, T. (1998) *Children's use of computers in their homes,* PhD Thesis, University of Western Sydney.

Goldman, S., Cole, K., and Syer, C. (1999) *The Technology/ Content Dilemma,* paper presented to the Secretary's Conference on Educational Technology, [*http://www.ed.gov/Technology/TechConf/1999/whitepapers/paper4.html*].

Iedema, R. (1998) *Culture-Specific Representations of Conflict: Bonnie & Clyde (USA) versus The Runner (Iran),* paper presented at the 25th International Systemic Functional Congress, Cardiff, U.K., 13-18 July.

Joyce, M. (1997) *New stories for new readers: Contour, coherence and constructive hypertext,* in *From Page to Screen: Taking Literacy into the Electronic Era* (ed. I. Snyder), Allen & Unwin, Sydney, 163-182.

Kress, G. (1997) *Visual and Verbal Modes of Representation in Electronically Mediated Communication: The Potentials of New Forms of Text,* in *From Page to Screen: Taking Literacy into the Electronic Era* (ed. I Snyder), Allen & Unwin, Sydney.

Lankshear, C. (1997), *Changing Literacies,* Open University Press, London.

Leu, D. and Kinzer, C. (in press) *The convergence of literacy instruction with networked technologies for information and communication,* in *Reading Research Quarterly,* **35** (1).

Luke, C. (2000) *Cyber-Schooling and Technological Change: Multiliteracies for New Times,* in *Multiliteracies: Literacy Learning and the Design of Social Futures* (eds. B. Cope and M. Kalantzis). Macmillan, Melbourne.

Martin, J. (1992) *English Text: System and Structure,* John Benjamin Publishing Co, Philadelphia.

The New London Group. (1995) *A Pedagogy of Multiliteracies: Designing Social Futures,* The NLLIA Centre for Workplace Communication and Culture, Sydney.

Yates, S. (1996) *English in Cyberspace*, in *Redesigning English: New Texts, New Identities* (eds. S. Goodman and D. Graddol). Open University Press, London, 69-91.

BIOGRAPHIES

Toni Downes is an Associate Professor in educational computing at the University of Western Sydney. Her teaching responsibilities include educational computing, leadership and technology, and research methodologies. Her current research projects and consultancies span from early childhood education to university education. They include the development of an online course in quality leadership and technology, the investigation of the educational use of the Internet with young children, the changing nature of literacy, and the use of computers for teaching and learning in educational settings.

Katina Zammit is a Lecturer in language and literacy at the University of Western Sydney. Her teaching focuses on the learning of language and literacy in the elementary years, educational linguistics, and the intersection of literacy and technology. Her research interests revolve around the analysis and use of multi-modal texts for literacy learning and teaching. These include the analysis of multimedia environments from a sociolinguistic perspective, information skills for young children using hypertext environments and the development and use of on-line learning environments for the teaching and learning of literacy.

Identifying educational core competencies for the Information Age

J. R. Isaac
Center for Research in Cognitive Systems (CRCS), 2nd Floor, Synergy Building, IIT-Delhi
Hauz Khas, New Delhi 110 016, India.
Jisaac@niit.com

Abstract: The Information Age cries out for education to be re-conceptualised, re-structured and re-vitalised from its Industrial Age model. Information has become a tacit, taken-for-granted entity, which education has ignored. If education is to capitalise on the opportunities offered by the Information Age, many bold steps have to be taken. A novel course titled *Information Search and Analysis Skills (ISAS)* was developed, based on a specially designed monthly publication *IT-Digest*, to train thousands of students in ICT. The course offers students a mechanism by which the very subtle transformation from data to information to knowledge can be clearly understood and practised. The paradigm shift from teacher-driven to learner- driven follows, as an obvious consequence of course objectives. The paper converts this experience into a full proposal for a core-competency course on information literacy and information skills. Such a course has very wide implications, as it could also be made independent of subject area, cultural and language issues.

Keywords: Information literacy, knowledge as a resource, social issues

1. INTRODUCTION

"Now, as never before, the prospects for a human future are exceptionally dismal." Konrad Lorenz (1989)

Lorenz sees great dangers and feels that the survival of any species is at risk, when sections of it compete for dominance. He sees one ray of hope and that is in education. And yet, it could not be the same education that has got humans into the present predicament in the first place. Many sages of education (led by Ivan Illich, 1973) warned that something was wrong ages ago, but somehow education seems to have a mind of its own.

The aim of this paper is to derive, formulate and propose an entirely new course, as a core course for all school curricula. This is felt necessary in view of the challenging Information Age paradigms that confront us. Present day school systems are deeply entrenched in traditional and established forms of education and training, and see no reason to change. However, what has been the result of these forms of education? Education was presumed to be the fundamental stepping stone towards progress and a better life. But are we any nearer towards humans achieving a better life?

And now education can make use of the advancing technologies beyond all expectations. What to do with what appeared to be a golden opportunity?

2. THE DAWN OF A NEW TECHNOLOGICAL ERA

The Industrial Age had assisted man in his manual or physical tasks only. The raw materials as input, the processing and the finished products were well-understood entities, often even by the general public. Such material production had little direct influence on fundamental education.

Computers and associated technologies now came to lead Man into the Information Age. Entirely new paradigms entered the scene. The fundamental clarity of purpose was no longer there. There was the headlong rush towards reaching out towards the unreachable. ICT seemed to expand that reach. Artificial Intelligence led to Intelligent Tutoring Systems and to Expert Systems in an effort to capture the essence of human understanding and expertise. Simulation seemed a more effective educational support than real live experience. The final triumph was to mimic life itself through the notion of Artificial Life. Human algorithms and heuristics seemed to be the order of the day, and even raised ethical issues.

It was then found that the new information thrust, brought about by these technologies, had much wider implications and ramifications than had been imagined. While Industrial Age technologies were designed to meet specific and well identified (closed) ends, such was not the case with ICT which deals essentially with open systems. These systems had built-in, and unexpected, potential for expansion and proliferation into society. The ultimate example of such an open information system is of course the Internet.

Let us consider a few well-known manifestations of ICT impacts on society, analysing the underlying concepts and issues in detail. In particular, we will monitor how these would have direct effects on educational needs.

2.1 The three computer ages

Any technology, using information, have serious consequences on humans and their inter-relationships. Let us consider some societal impacts of a simple telephone. Taken in the light of Marshal McCluhan's statements on the "global village" and the "media is the message", this indicated that it were not the actual messages (and their meanings) that were transferred over telephones that mattered. It was the societal fact of "intimate interconnectivity" that telephones had established. The same decomposition can be done for ICT. This results in three ages, see Table 1.

Table 1. The three ages

THE THREE AGES	INTERPRETATIONS
AUTOMATE	Computers are used to automate various processes (the Data Processing Era)
INFORMATE	Computers function as Information Systems , for example MIS (Management Information Systems)
TRANSFORMATE	As information capability percolated into society, it began to transform society (this results in the re-engineering of businesses to adapt to the information and knowledge environments).

The Industrial Age did not have such levels of influence, ranging from the machine to its applications and effect on society. The Industrial Age certainly affected the various aspects of life, for example, various forms of transportation, increased human connectivity. However, this was in a physical sense only. The Information Age however increases information connectivity, and information is man's powerful logical and decision-making tool, which ultimately leads to the enhancement of his knowledge.

This increase leads to the global village effect. It results in reduced distances between people, through instant communication across the globe. The Internet appears to be a source of unlimited information not only for being informed, but also for learning, publishing and so on. This opportunity offers the business community scope for very wide markets, and e-commerce has the potential to alter the face of business.

2.2 From material production into the productivity of the Information Age

The Agricultural and Industrial Ages were intimately linked to the production of physical or material goods. With the thrust towards achieving more efficiency and productivity, the paradigm of the factory system was established to achieve greater efficiency and productivity, leading to mass production. Associated was the concept of hierarchical management (the pyramid). With the focus on exploiting nature and the physical world, science and technology evolved, together with associated educational initiatives.

In the Information Age, with its emphasis on a service orientation, value systems had to be re-conceptualised. Though the central player was information, there was a problem. The word "information" had been absorbed into society and had become a tacit, taken-for-granted entity. This resulted in slogans such as "Information is Power". No one wondered how exactly information became an economic factor.

Numerous theories had evolved through the ages, invariably considering an environment of the Industrial Age. For example, leading learning theorists often based their studies on analogies between animals and humans. Obviously the emphasis was on the physical environment. How applicable would these theories be if we are to shift into an information environment? How would educational strategies and theories change? With the introduction of Cognitive Science, especially with regard to learning, one would have expected studies in information to play a leading role. However, somewhat analogous to Computer Science and Information Science, Cognitive Science also ignored information as a core subject of societal interest.

The disciplinary era was synonymous with the Industrial Age and mainly focussed on science, technology and the understanding of nature and the environment. However, the Information Age has networked people so effectively that the soft sciences play a significant role. Knowledge is now generated not in closeted libraries and research laboratories, but in "man-built" human environments. So the very nature of knowledge, which education reaches out to, has drifted from its traditional mould. This has resulted in a drift from discipline-based (depth-based) education to trans-disciplinary (breadth-based) approaches.

2.3 From data to information to knowledge

If students are to fit into the Information Age, they should be familiar with the fundamental terms: data, information and knowledge. Yet education chooses to ignore this aspect, almost consciously. But more important than just being familiar with the exact usage of these terms, is for students to know how they relate to the Information Age. And most importantly, how are data transformed into information and information into knowledge, and how are such transformations made possible and experienced (Isaac, 1997a).

While entities like knowledge management, data mining and virtual communities gain in prominence in the Information Society, students and the public have little awareness of what they signify. Just as in the Industrial Age, various educational mechanisms were applied to meet well-defined goals. However, there will be serious deviations. While industrial age educational goals were set on the basis of scientific content and stability, information age goals have to be set on the ability to meet competition and tackle variability. The information age will have to lay more stress on how information can be used to shape more innovative and creative work environments. Transformations between data, information and knowledge begin to gain significance (Liebowitz, 1999).

By enabling information and knowledge to be available at every street corner, the role of the teacher as a repository of knowledge is no longer valid. The teaching role turns into that of a facilitator in accessing information, and the teacher-driven world makes way for a learner-driven one. This calls for re-thinking on the very nature of educational systems.

2.4 From knowledge to skill emphasis

The Information Age may be thought of as a technology, thus going through 3 stages before being absorbed into society. This model indicates how the human needs, especially education and training, evolve through the stages. This also builds a case for information skills, see Table 2.

Table 2. Stages in education

TECHNOLOGIES:	Stage 1: CREATE	Stage 2: DEPLOY	Stage 3: USE
Technology requirements	Innovation and creativity	Deployment into society	Absorption and proliferation into society
Emphasis	Conceptualisation, development,	Deployment, awareness, marketing	Business promotion, towards building user communities.
Human need: knowledge to skills	Scientific knowledge	Marketing skills	Promotional skills business skills
"Education" versus "Training" needs	Education high training low	Transition stage	Education low skill high in large community of users
Human interaction	Individual	Transition	Inter-personnel

In the Industrial Age the connotation of "skills" was related to manual labour and low-level tasks. Hence, rarely did one compare skills with education, which remained on a pedestal. However, in the Information Age it is not manual skills that prevail, it is "information skills". This concept will be very fundamental to the course to be proposed. If one were to consider the Management Pyramid, manual skills would be restricted to the lowest rung of the pyramid in the operational level only. However, information skills are the tools of management at all levels of the hierarchy. While excellence in manual skills would bring little additional returns, the same cannot be said for information skills. In fact, in principle, information skills can get one to the very pinnacle of management pyramid.

2.5 How should education respond to these Information Age imperatives?

All major educational paradigms have been set by the Industrial Age, and most strategies remain based on them due to educational inertia. Yet from the above it can be seen that there have been dramatic upheavals and changes, from all points-of-view in educational needs, society and the business environment. The educational response has been to introduce numerous new initiatives and strategies: such as CBT, instruction design, distance education, flexible learning, linear/non-linear learning, learning styles, computer-based collaborative learning, learning-to-learn, technology facilitated learning, performance centred design, constructivism, Just-in-Time, Just-What-is-Needed, Just-Where-it-is-Needed, cognitive apprenticeship, learner modelling, adaptive authoring systems, and so on.

However, in practically all cases, it is the rate of change in educational needs, brought about by the Information Age, that is being catered to, not the root or core educational need of the Information Age itself. Also the attention seems to be on new and innovative methodologies and strategies and not on identifying the fundamental core "content" per se.

The purpose of this paper is to consider the complexities brought about by the Information Age and the potential opportunities that it offers. This then leads to the definition of "Information Literacy" as a core competency (see also Vockel and van Deusen, 1989 and Isaac, 1997b). We will outline an Information Literacy course, the ISAS course, which has been tried out on thousands of students in the domain of ICT education. However, the mechanisms and strategies used are applicable to school environments.

3. THE CORE COMPETENCY: INFORMATION LITERACY

With the critical issue being information and its understanding, Information Literacy is the core competency that we are searching for. It is the competency that enables one to understand the world of information and to acquire the necessary "information skills". These skills can be taught from the very early standards in schools. The crucial issues will be in getting students to understand the concepts of data, information and knowledge; and the possibility of conscious conversions from one to the other in project contexts. They will have to be provided with an "Information Laboratory" in which to experiment and hone up their information skills.

Interestingly, as will be seen, the projects assigned in this ISAS course not only require the student to consciously exercise information skills, but also acquire skills associated with several other holistic and integrative tasks associated with general education. Students first work as individuals (in the data and information phases) and then as teams (in knowledge or integrative stage). A major learning from this approach is that students gain experience in tackling open-ended real-life problems, and find their own answers to hitherto rarely discussed, or unanswered, issues and questions. Examples:

- Why are there so many subjects in a school curriculum? In what ways do they support or complement each other? Are there any relationships between e.g. history, geography, English and mathematics?
- What are the different functions of a social organisation and how do they serve society (or a, municipality or county council, club, etc.)?
- How would you perform a study on the functioning of a selected school body (the library, a sports body, a school club)?
- How would you provide a comparative study on media effectiveness for various media (radio, TV, Internet, conversation, books, newspapers)?

When confronted with questions of this open nature, most students would not know how to even start, there seem to be so many issues, and yet no specific issue! How can the problem be given a more meaningful "known" context, so that some constructive activity can be initiated? What information sources would be most relevant and where would they be found? What follows after all the information is collected? How does one proceed with individualised information, and how does one integrate findings from differnt sources? How can final conclusions be arrived at? How does one gain confidence and acquire proficiency, in such problem situations?

The aim of the course described in this paper is to train students through systematic information processes to acquire general competencies and experience in facing such open-ended questions. However, a crucial fall-out is that the information skills acquired are easily transferable to all other academic activities and studies. Each project will be an exercise in data acquisition from relevant sources, conversion to information (in their own contexts), and then to knowledge (as an add-on to world knowledge). Further, these skills are life-long assets in a world of change. Thus the Information Literacy course becomes a "Core Course", which enables students to acquire fundamental skills and methodologies which re-vitalise all forms of study and learning.

4. THE ISAS COURSE: INFORMATION SEARCH AND ANALYSIS

The ISAS course was designed for use in computer career programs of one of the world's largest organisations (NIIT Ltd.) dealing with computer education (annually over 100,000 students). ISAS, at different levels, is used in all four six-month semesters in which students are trained on various software systems and applications (including the Internet and Web-based applications). The objective of the course is to equip students with all tools required as a computer professional in addition to technical competence. Professionals need to be aware of government policies, industrial norms, companies, personalities, imports/exports, commercial needs and so on, tempered with technical know-how and competence. ISAS attempts to train students for this professional world. Obviously, while placed in the specialised area of ICT, the course will have to be adapted and fine-tuned for other contexts. As ISAS was for students of ICT, it necessarily has an ICT bias. To give a realistic feel for the course, the ICT bias will not be entirely removed when applied to other areas. The justification for this is that even general students do have to pick up a certain amount of computer and information awareness, which is imbedded in the ISAS course.

4.1 Tools used by ISAS

ISAS several support materials for instructors and students. Here only the essential items to understand the course will be given. The course has a detailed Student Guide (theoretical background and problem sets) and Instructor Guide (further inputs on the data-information-knowledge process) for each semester. The sources of information inputs play a key role, and in this case, we bring out a special "abstracting and indexing" service called "IT-Digest". This is a monthly publication that is brought out in hard copy format, and recently is also made available to students at some centres through the Intranet. Brief descriptions of these will be given, as they are essential to understanding the intent and modality of the course.

4.2 The Student Guide and Instructor Guide

Contents: A comparative study of the three ages: Agriculture, Industrial and Information, is given against numerous parameters (production processes, tools used, societal implications, educational impacts and so on). Questions and exercise assist deeper understanding. In particular the Information Age introduces radical departures from normal thought and understanding. The notions of data, information and knowledge are derived from the primary communication aspects of signal, sign and symbols.

4.2.1 Defining data, information and knowledge

Table 3 gives a first level simplified model, used in order to explain fundamental concepts.

Table 3. Data, information and knowledge

ITEM	DESCRIPTION/FUNCTION	EXAMPLES /USAGE
DATA	A Representation of facts, entities, ideas, a set of "raw" fields	The teacher writes "1011" on the board. Use: Has no meaning to user. At most can be reproduced later (memory).
INFORMATION	Data + a set of descriptions define its meaning to the user. Required for user "interpretation". HOW or in what form is the representation, and WHAT is being represented, i.e. the context to the user.	Again "1011" Let us convert this into information for the user: - It is a decimal number. - It is the number of students in a college. Use: The user can interpret and use this information in his/her own context.
KNOWLEDGE	Information + a set of rules, regulations or conventions, governing its application in a user context. Intelligence is problem-solving ability using information and knowledge.	Again "1011", but represents a "knowledge base" to the user. A knowledge base is a networked collection of information or knowledge nodes, related to each other by rules, etc. Use: The number is given as the "average" number of student in city colleges. It is assumed that the user is aware of the number of colleges and the rules by which averages are calculated.

Undoubtedly, there is a great deal of abstraction involved with the above, yet this may be expressed in simpler ways at lower classes. Similarly, the abstraction can be raised to higher levels also. For example, students can be told that the above is an example using numbers. Can a similar example be given using only alphabets? Or, symbols only? This of course has to be extended to words, sentences, and above, as understanding grows.

4.2.2 What is information? Why the Information Age?

A closer study of the above reveals that the data and knowledge are representational levels (can be captured in a computer and are not dependent on purely the user context). These two levels may be said to be "passive" (or "static") levels. However, information is the operational or active level, in which the user actually interprets the data or knowledge in his/her context for application in a specific context. Users can obviously have different contexts. So all three levels are externalised only through the information modality. Therefore it is information that plays the key role. The Information Level may be said to be active (or dynamic).

All three levels can also be split into two categories, implicit and explicit. The implicit or tacit part implies personalised or individualised aspects, which can not be codified or captured in a computer. The explicit part is not abstract, and is therefore easier to understand, explain and formalise, and will be the one used in most of our discussions.

Information comes at various context levels. Let us consider information, which has economic consequences, What exactly is the function or purpose of information? How is it used? Information is used in "a continuum of social choices" from "control" to "co-ordination".

4.2.3 Information usage: A continuum of social choices between co-ordination and control

CO-ORDINATION
Within same level of
management hierarchy
Synergism possible
between players.

CONTROL
Top down control between
layers of the hierarchy.
Synergism is not possible.

Though in principle co-ordination (group or team activities) would be the more productive due to the synergism possibility, usually control is used, as in say advertising. One lesson that students can learn is that society gains more by the identification of co-ordination, rather than control activities. The developed world has thrived on control activities, however, in the context of development, the developing world must turn more towards co-ordination.

4.2.4 Why are information and information goods/commodities so difficult to understand?

The Industrial Age paradigm made the understanding of material goods quite simple, particularly due to their tangible physical nature and the easy logic of barter as an economic tool. In fact, Man's notion of value was established in this context. However, when we arrive in the Information age, in which information and information goods are abstract intangible entities, problems arise. The notion of barter of information does not make sense, information given away is not lost to the sender (seller). The easy-to-understand concept of the gold standard is no longer valid. A new value system has to evolve, supported by abstract concepts such as Intellectual Property Rights (IPR). Such thoughts are totally shielded from present day school-going children. Yet they must be exposed to the fundamental concepts of how value gets ingrained into information, right from school days if they are to thrive. It is only through personal and group involvement with information studies that these abstract notions can evolve, and be better understood. As an information environment impacts on the individual, the group and society, education must bring about its awareness and implications at school level itself.

4.3 *IT-Digest*: The information source for ISAS

"IT-Digest" (ITD) is a monthly publication, specifically designed as an Information Laboratory to support ISAS. It is basically an abstracting and indexing service, which uses about 70 selected publications as information inputs. The diversity of publications makes it possible for students to have inputs from a variety of information sources and also to get familiar with their nature and intent. At present, the sources consist of 12 Indian newspapers, about 20 Indian IT magazines and journals, and some international publications. There is a diverse spread among newspapers, magazines and journals, as they will include not only commercial aspects, but also several levels of technical information. From these sources, articles are abstracted, indexed and also cross-indexed by information specialists. The emphasis for ISAS is now on ICT and related aspects.

The supportive role of ITD, as an information laboratory is essential to understand in the context of the core course to be proposed. A major aspect is that IT-Digest (ITD) is specifically designed for the course. For this, the essential human element exploited must be acknowledged. ITD is not just one vast source of information. It's course-supportive features, include:

- Only relevant articles are extracted and classified.
- The articles are carefully indexed in a uniform way, irrespective of their original source. There are 15 categories, each further split into 3 sub-categories, ranging from computers (hardware, software, etc.) to communications to societal impacts of information. This results in an information access matrix which enables the student to integrate information into logical groupings.
- There are special sections, some specifically designed to tame the information overload. Articles are filtered and condensed into themes and sub-themes. The very human aspect of perception is captured through a few selected articles. A bibliography section covers a wide range of objectives: simplified explanations for the beginner and hundreds of classified references for the specialist.
- The *Annual IT-Digest* (each December issue), gives the user an annual index which links all articles of the year together – under the various categories and sub-categories.

4.4 STRUCTURE OF THE ISAS COURSE

The structure of ISAS has been carefully derived in order to get students to consciously understand and practice the processes behind the conversion

Table 3. An example of a group project

Group Project Assigned: Derive India's global ICT potential through study of 5 Indian ICT companies			
Phase	**Mode**	**Main actions**	**Details**
Phase 0: Project allotment (Group uses own criteria for company selection – diverse contributory areas or partitioned focussed area)	Group uses ITD and selects say TCS, WIPRO, CMC, NIIT and IBM (India). Covering software, hardware, applications, manpower, etc.	Case of individual student: say company allotted TCS. Identify nature of company, products, services, management strategies, performance ratings.	Plan to collect and organise facts on TCS: How to compile actual data, to be collected through ITD and other sources - focus on software.
Phase 1: Presentation and Report 1	Individual (in this case, focus on TCS data)	All facts and figures on TCS data	The student begins to organise and interrelate data (Software Co. TCS)
Phase 2: Presentation and Report 2	Individual (personal interpretation of data)	Begins to "interpret" data (information)	Builds case for TCS. Uses more expressive title. (Flagship)
Phase 3: Group presentation, and executive summary	Group ("putting things together")	Combining all 5 conclusions into consolidated "findings"	Networking of information into a knowledge base (global player)

of data to information and then to knowledge. The normal grouping of students is 5 and the duration of a course is six months. A theme, topic or project is given to the group. This theme has been logically split into 5 sub-themes. Table 3 shows a probable project in the ICT area, and we see how it is decomposed, in order to enable systematic training in the exploitation of identified Information Skills in the general processes of problem solving.

4.4.1 Linking course structure with the data / information / knowledge process

This is a crucial aspect of the ISAS methodology, as it illustrates the conversion from data to information and then knowledge. See table 4.

Table 4. Project phases and associated information skills

Project Phase	Phase analogy	Information skills called into play	
		Main Skills	Sub-skills
Phase 1	DATA	Focusing Information gathering Remembering Organising	Defining problems, setting goals Observing, formulating questions Encoding, recalling Comparing, classifying, ordering, representing
Phase 2	INFOR-MATION	Analysing Generating	Identifying attributes and components Identifying relationships and patterns Identifying main ideas Identifying errors Inferring, predicting, elaborating
Phase 3	KNOWLEDGE	Integrating Evaluating	Summarising, restructuring Establishing criteria, verifying

4.4.2 On the identification of information skills

In table 4 the information skills derived by Vockel and van Deusen (1989) have been used. For the ISAS course developed, the aim was to select a model that could be used most effectively for both teacher and student understanding. The main categories and the sub-categories enable suitable adaptations to the range of situations encountered in the course. Also, the information-skill resolution allowed permits the full power of this model to be explained in simple terms. However, information skills have been classified or modelled in various ways, by various researchers. One model organises the information skills in a pyramid of five levels, identified with the mode of use of the information received. The lowest level is the passive level (receive, process, store, retrieve, circulate), then the reactive level, the pro-active level, the initiative and finally the causative (create demand). The model of Table 5 gives the progression from data to information, knowledge, education and finally wisdom.

Table 5. Model from data to wisdom

Entity	Information or thinking skill
DATA	Researching, Accessing, comprehending
INFORMATION	Critical and creative thinking
KNOWLEDGE	Linking, conceptualising, synthesising
EDUCATION	Application, judging, philosophising
WISDOM	Goal attainment

In general, specific meanings and functions assigned may vary slightly between researchers. However, the general import and intent remain substantially constant. It should make an interesting study to attempt to match these levels with the levels of Bloom's Taxonomy of Education - which has established itself as a standard. The lowest level in that model is knowledge, then comprehension, application, followed by analysis, synthesis and evaluation.

4.5 ISAS in summary

As students take up their successive semesters of 6 months each, the project levels are raised. They start with a data-orientation and gradually shift to a knowledge orientation. With experience, students devise their own stratagems for the data to knowledge conversion process. Such a process from data to wisdom is illustrated in table 6 below for a military context, using only a "So What" mechanism for eliciting information at each stage.

Table 6. From data to wisdom

Input Statement	*It rained heavily last night.*
Question to elicit more information	Responses to pro-active, but simple, queries
So What?	The ground will be wet
So What?	It will turn into mud quickly
So What?	If many troops and vehicles pass over the same ground, movement will be progressively slower and more difficult, as the ground get muddier and more difficult.
So What?	Where possible stick to metalled roads or expect movement to be slower than normal.

ISAS is a special course for ICT students intending to turn into ICT professionals. Hence, the Information Laboratory used *IT-Digest* and other support materials that were ICT-related. Students are not restricted to using only *IT-Digest*, but are encouraged to widen their input information sources. However, the process ensures that the student, after four successive semesters, has gained considerable knowledge that is expected to be possessed by an ICT professional. Such knowledge would include not only the technical content of the program, but also professional knowledge gained through ISAS. Such knowledge enhances the confidence of the potential employer, and the purpose of the course is served.

It was noticed that ISAS was also able to meet interesting side issues. Due to healthy competition between individuals and groups to excel, motivation was aroused automatically. The individual responsibilities in the first two phases and then the final group responsibility encapsulated some of the fundamental learning initiatives. Constructivism in student and group learning was built-in. The third phase enforced the formation of co-operative learning groups. The open-ended learning and involvement with an Information Laboratory often gave rise to serendipitous findings, a feature lacking in traditional learning, and yet, an essential component of learning in the Information Age.

5. DEFINING INFORMATION LITERACY

Information Literacy was first defined by Zurkowski in 1974 as the ability to use techniques and skills "for utilising the wide range of information tools as well as primary sources in moulding information-solutions to ... problems" (Kuhlthau, 1987). This definition still remains current and valid. However, the definition should take into account the totally changed information environment from the 1970s.

A more recent (1985) definition of the term, is provided by the American Library Association, Presidential Committee on Information Literacy, which states:

> "To be information literate, a person must be able to recognise when information is needed and have the ability to locate, evaluate and use effectively the needed information. Producing such a citizenry will require that schools and colleges appreciate and integrate the concept of information literacy into their learning programs and that they play a leadership role in equipping individuals and institutions to take advantage of the opportunities inherent within the information society."

However, the information environment has taken a totally new context since the proliferation of ICT, and the definition of information literacy should be suitably adapted. Particularly the advent of the Internet and its radically new paradigms had not been fully envisaged. Apart from the information onslaught, the student's major educational hurdle is change, particularly the rate of change. The smug complacency of Industrial Age educational paradigms will have to be shed. But then, what are the educational implications, as far as the student is concerned?

5.1 The educational paradigm shift: From teacher-driven to learner-driven

The aftermath of the Internet, virtual environments and the Information Age has resulted in a major shift of emphasis from the teacher to the learner. Educational systems, known for their inertia, have to respond to this call. As mentioned earlier, the response of educators has been to devise a series of new methodologies and strategies. However, none of these confront the educational challenge head on. The ISAS course fully supports the learner-driven paradigm, in which instructors essentially play the roles of facilitators.

5.2 Towards an information environment

With the merger of ICT, there was a major thrust towards the enhancement and aggregation of an information environment. Falling computer costs resulted in a wide proliferation into society. Even developing countries in which computers were still comparatively expensive found proliferation taking place. This was due to government initiatives usually taken on the grounds that the introduction of ICT would expedite developmental processes. Besides, the Internet was a powerful lure, as a cure-all for all information ills.

It may be recalled that the evolution of information usage first started as a conversation. Then scientific discovery and the printing press brought about an Age of Enlightenment in the form of the Guttenburg revolution. This was a period of hope for the growth of science and education. Then one started to realise that something was wrong, when the Internet seemed to arrive as a saviour. However, it must be realised that the US courts branded the Internet as a "giant conversation between people", which, if censored, would be tantamount to banning free speech. So society had gone full cycle from conversation to a return to conversation! It does not take much thought to realise that a conversation cannot give rise to an educational base.

5.3 Putting things together again

Just as in the case of the first conversation expanding into an intellectual explosion, so also it is expected that this second conversation will ultimately explode into an intellectual asset. However, at the moment, not only from a legal point of view, but also from an academic, the Internet is in a primitive stage and is an enigma with respect to extracting hard-core education. However, attempts are in progress to put things together again in the form of virtual universities, educational portals, and so on.

6. SCHOOLS OF THE FUTURE

With the current rapid-change environment and the full potential of the Internet yet to be achieved, planning for schools of the future presents numerous problems. The only solution seems to lie in identifying educational core entities, which could have lasting utility, despite the rapid change. Also there is no doubt that the proposed plan should be Internet-ready. While Internet may not at present have direct and crucial educational relevance, there is no doubt that it will be an important player.

It is in this context that it is felt that school courses can be modelled on the ISAS experience, as the emphasis is on information literacy and the acquisition of information skills. These initiatives are fundamental to the Information Age, and hence would have lasting value. They are particularly relevant to the change from one-time to life-long education.

We must not forget that in talking of the schools of the future, we can not ignore the schools in the developing world, which are highly significant in sheer numbers. What is being planned for them, considering that most of them do not have a computer or information environment at present? In the context of developing countries, there is a significant difference. A proposal that has been submitted calls for the introduction of information literacy in schools that do not as yet have computers. This is to get them to be information savvy, so that they prepare the ground for computer acceptance. However, it must be noted that through the process of co-ordination, developing countries could benefit greatly. Imagine for instance the implementation of a program to simultaneously teach six million primary teachers all over India (and that too in various languages!).

6.1 School core courses: Modelled on the ISAS experience

In many ways the school course could resemble the ISAS course in structure and intent, with appropriate minor modifications and extensions. As in the case of ISAS, it would be desirable to have a Student Guide and an Instructor/Co-ordinator Guide. These can vary their contents, depending on the level of the classes that they are intended for. However, the three phases of the individual/group project must be retained. The idea would be to get the students to gradually acquire an understanding of the conscious data to information to knowledge transformation process. This will be briefly illustrated with one of the sample problems stated earlier.

6.1.1 Case study

Let us assume a student group of five. The Group Assignment Project is: "Why are there so many subjects in a school curriculum?" The course duration for ISAS is six months. However, depending on the level, an appropriate number of months should be allotted. Individual Sub-Projects: This could be done in two ways: 1) The teacher assigns the subjects, say English, Mathematics, History, Geography and Physical Education, or 2) The five students could be asked to come up with five subjects that they would like to take up.

Table 7. A case study

Phase 1	Each student of the group begins a data search in class and school library, public library, magazines and books, the Internet, discussions with peers and teachers. It is the students' responsibility to systematically record all the data collected. All information skills, related to this level, should be consciously exercised. The data should be condensed, correlated and structured. The student should submit a written report and, if possible, present a short talk on his/her findings. An appropriate "data" level title should be used (example: Why should English be part of the curriculum?). This would be the data level of activity.
Phase 2	The student seeks more data if possible, and then begins to order and interpret the data collected. What does it all mean in my context? The student should plan how he/she will most effectively sell the study made to others. (The information title: "English: The Educational Foundation or The Stepping-Stone to Education".)
Phase 3	The five students have to present their cases to each other in open debate and then negotiate on the principle factors to be included in the Executive Summary Report (restricted to, say one or two pages only). This is the knowledge conversion stage in which the information items are networked in a logical manner, to publish the final group finding. (Possible knowledge title: "The Five Pillars of Education".)

Initially, the instructor assigns the project in either of the two forms above, after ensuring that information fundamentals have been studied from the Student Guide. Assume that the teacher has allotted the sub-projects. The group must initially evolve an appropriate strategy to carry out the project, with a view towards arriving at a logical conclusion to the project. Students should be familiar with information skills and their use. In Table 7 we explore the different phases of this case.

6.2 The one hurdle to this process

The success of the ISAS course was ensured due to the Information Laboratory environment provided to the student by the *IT-Digest*. The *IT-Digest* was most effective due to the human effort that went into it in the context of ICT only. How could this be substituted in the school scenario? The school learning can be in focussed areas at certain levels or may be totally open-ended. When it is focussed it should be possible to give a similar human support, but for the open-ended case there would be a problem. However, this problem is not insurmountable, after all, we are moving into an information environment.

At each level of the course, an appropriate level of an Information Laboratory would have to be created in order to enable a more focussed and educationally-guided search. In other words there should be a project list together with references to selected magazines, journals and books in the library and with supportive web-sites. The Internet effectiveness could increase at higher levels by having course supportive "information portals".

In fact, even in the *IT-Digest*/ISAS combination, we are planning to expose students to more and more of Internet, as the competence builds. Obviously, if students can transfer their data-information-knowledge transformation skills into Internet, it would potentially be ideal.

7. CONCLUSIONS

In view of the dramatic shift from Industrial Age to the needs of the Information Age, and the rate of change, it is argued that a sustainable educational core competency has to be identified for schools of the future. From a study of the effects of the Information Age, information literacy has been derived as the core competency. Information literacy is vitalised by the acquisition of core information skills, which will serve as growing life-long assets in an expanding world of information. Information skills go a long way towards putting things together again, as they search for holistic solutions.

The course structure proposed is applicable both to developed and developing countries, as information literacy is a universal concept. Further it is not language or culture dependent. It is also a tool towards levelling the field between the "haves" and "have nots", because above all information literacy is human, and not technology, dependent. Understanding information literacy should drive ICT and not visa-versa.

REFERENCES

Illich, I. (1973) *Deschooling Society*, Penguin Books.

Lorenz, K. (1989) *The Waning of Humaneness*, Unwin Paperbacks.

Liebowitz, J. (1999) *Knowledge Management Handbook*, CRC Press.

Isaac, J. (1997a) *Information Systems: Changing Paradigms in Society, Management, Education & Training*, Proceedings of ISAS'97, World Conference on Systemics, Cybernetics and Informatics, Editor: Nagib Callaos, Caracas, Venezuela, July 7-11.

Isaac, J. (1997b) *Information Literacy - The Missing Link in Education: With Special Reference to Developing Countries*, Proceedings of CapBIT'97, IFIP Working Groups 3.1,3.4 and 3.5 Working Conference, Harare, Zimbabwe, August 25-29.

Vockell, E. and van Deusen, R. (1989) *The Computer and Higher-Order Thinking Skills*, (McGraw-Hill) Mitchell Publishing Inc.

Kuhlthau, C. (1987) *Information Skills for an Information Society: A Review of Research*, Syracuse, NY.

BIOGRAPHY

J.R.Isaac completed his engineering studies in Bangalore, India and at the Carnegie Institute of Technology (now Carnegie Mellon Institute in Pittsburgh, PA, USA). He worked for two years at the IBM Research and Product Development Labs in Poughkeepsie, NY. From 1958 until 1990 he taught electronics and computer science courses, the last 29 years at the Indian Institute of technology (IIT) in Bombay, India. On retirement from IIT-B in 1990, he joined NIIT (National Institute of Information Technology) Ltd., New Delhi, as a senior advisor and he is also director of the Institute for Research in Information Sciences (IRIS), a division of NIIT.

Students teach students

A German-Japanese school education project based on a real time audio-visual distance learning environment

Klaus-D Graf and Kiyoshi Yokochi

Freie Universitaet Berlin, Takustr. 9, 14195 Berlin, Germany.

graf@inf.fu-berlin.de

4 of 8, 2-chome, Matsugaoka, Nakano-ku, Tokyo165 Japan.

Tokai University, Japan (professor emeritus) and

Beijing Normal University, China (visiting professor).

yokochi@blue.ocn.ne.jp

Abstract: Distance learning experiments in mathematics and science education as well as in art education in Japan have initiated considerable increase in creativity of pupils, improvement of scholarship, and growth in understanding cultural characteristics of different regions. Based on these experiments, an environment for German-Japanese school education projects using real time interactive audio-visual distance learning between remote classrooms has been established. This has been done with elementary school children speaking in their native languages, translated by interpreters on the topics of symmetries in rectangles and stripes. It has been done with lower secondary students speaking in English on topics related to discovering, proving, and applying the Pythagorean Theorem. Another project is underway now with four pairs of Berlin and Tokyo schools, co-operating in environmental education, Japanese language education, literature (haiku), and music education. In these experiments, the pupils take over the teaching, a method that will be more and more important in the future of learning. Initiated and supervised by their teachers, the pupils select problems from some subject matter, they explore the Internet, and in groups of 2 or 3 they prepare teaching clips for their peers in the foreign country. This technique brings about both progress in personal learning as well as deep mutual understanding in difficulties and aptitudes of the learning partners.

Keywords: Collaborative learning, distance learning, videoconferencing, culture, creativity

1. BACKGROUND FOR THE PROJECT

There were two rather different observations about new objectives of education at the beginning of work on our joint project: Yokochi was concerned with the growing demand for an improvement of the quality of mathematics education, naming intentions like originality, creativity, comprehensive uses, mathematical scholarship, etc. In this context appreciation and exploitation of different cultural characteristics as well as interdisciplinary components (mathematics and arts) played highly influential roles.

Reflecting activities for more general intentions like interdisciplinary and intercultural context within subject matter education, Graf had pointed out that decision makers in education agree that modern societies rely increasingly on larger numbers of individuals with high-level knowledge and skills at their disposal (Graf 1995, referring to Ruiz, 1993). This means, in addition to elementary cultural techniques such as reading, writing and calculating, school has to teach other skills such as analysing, abstracting and modelling. Conceptual and communication skills are also required, in the fields of production and service. For example, an increasing range of jobs depend on individuals who know about their responsibilities in a wide context. Often many of these people must be able to work in multi-disciplinary teams.

When exchanging these observations, we agreed that in Japan and in Germany as well as in other countries there are challenges to societies by universal problems such as the world economy or environment. These problems are of extreme complexity and require immense international interaction. Any success is dependent on mutual understanding and acknowledgement of different traditions and attitudes related with problems like mass production, environmental protection, political, and social structures. Readiness and goodwill have to be developed in young people growing into these societies, so more attention has to be given to interdisciplinary and intercultural intentions in education. There are avenues in many subjects in school to pursue directions such as the ones discussed above and every school subject could contribute. In particular, information and communication technologies form a rich source for contributing to such mutual understanding, linked with subjects like mathematics or social science which carry the high-level knowledge and skills mentioned above.

2. BASIC STRUCTURE OF THE LEARNING AND TEACHING EXPERIMENTS

Several distance learning experiments of Yokochi's research group, including pairs of classes from distant provinces in Japan had shown that mathematics education as well as science and art education could profit considerably from theses activities. This encouraged us to plan practical work growing out of the very general considerations extended above. In a series of distance learning experiments between school classes in Japan and Germany, it could be demonstrated that these activities form an excellent platform to promote objectives like the ones mentioned above in school education. Each experiment consisted of different activities of two partner school classes and their teachers, together with researchers in didactics at universities, extending over six to twelve weeks. The activities started with preparation of a project by researchers and teachers, contacts running via mutual visits in Germany and Japan or via e-mail, Internet homepages or airmail. After this, teachers in the two countries started working with their classes concurrently on the same topic, mostly taken from mathematics, social science (environmental problems) or arts.

Besides learning about the topic in different ways the students, in more or less co-operation with their teachers, started to prepare demonstrations for their peers about their findings and results. These were executed in several videoconferences, integrated in the total activity of 6 – 12 weeks. Material was also forwarded by e-mail or fax or put in the respective homepages in the Internet. Some conferences consisted of teaching of the teachers about the mathematical background of some products generated (tiles with patterns e.g.), and sometimes groups of students did the teaching.

In addition to concentration on special subject matter, which was essential in our design of the learning units, there were passages in the activities, per e-mail or in the video conferences, where the students tried to find out more personal information about each other concerning pets, grading systems, views on the other countries or people, including the students themselves.

3. FINDINGS FOR GENERAL AND SUBJECT MATTER EDUCATION

It should be mentioned that our experiments did not only effect the learning and understanding of the students. At the same time, the researchers from teacher education as well as the teachers active in the preparation, execution, and evaluation of the distance learning experiments profited a lot. They had to reflect deeply on the educational theories they were relying on, so that they could be understood by their partners in the other country. Considerable feedback had to be given to make sure that the others' intentions had been understood. It became clear that understanding went far beyond the language problems. Still, using English to explain activities based on German or Japanese language was a problem in itself. The teachers had extra work to invest since they had to explain their project in their environment, for example to colleagues, school administrators and parents. They experienced that both sides were very ambitious to "perform" good presentations and they had to control these tendencies for the sake of allowing genuine learning processes.

Before we give detailed descriptions of students, contents, methods, media and other topics determining our learning units, we want to list some general findings.

- The students' interest in each project was great and held on for the whole period of the learning units and afterwards
- The students were planning with great zeal how to explain their results to the pupils in the other country
- They were very interested in learning and understanding what they were told by the other students and how others solved their problems
- They picked up their ideas and adapted them when doing their own work
- They developed a very general interest in the other environment and country, also in individual peers
- They discussed the project with other students and teachers from their schools, and with their parents and families
- In the sessions they were extremely attentive and ready to perform
- They were competing in a friendly way; when they put questions they reinforced good answers by cheering.
- Without problems in using the new technology they put direct questions to their peers in the other countries, forgetting about the distance
- They patiently waited for translations or – when English was the joint language of communication – for repetitions of statements and questions

We also had positive findings about special intentions and goals related to the subject matter chosen. In most cases it was geometry. Learning progress in some specific matter was always the main purpose of the experiments. We took great care that neither just general intentions like discussed above dominated the activities nor mere use of technology.

Especially for mathematics education we had put up a list with aims for the reorganisation of this subject:

- Initiating mathematical originality and creativity of students

- Learning comprehensive uses of mathematics with other subjects through solving real problems
- Improving the mathematical scholarship of students
- Appreciating and acknowledging the mathematical cultural characteristics of each district or country in problem solving
- Cultural exchanges related to science and technique between students of two classes
- Interaction with peers from different regions in mathematical problem solving.

Interviews with the students as well as their behaviour and performance have shown that many elements of these purposes were attained through the intercultural learning units of our experiments. This confirms with the results reported by Yokochi and his project group about internal Japanese distance learning activities. Students took up contents as well as methods from their partners and used them when solving problems or creating art objects.

4. AGE LEVELS AND CONTENT OF EXPERIMENTS

The following partnerships and learning units between German and Japanese classes have been realised so far:

a) **Peter-Witte-Primary-School in Berlin and Primary School attached to Yamanashi University in Kofu**. The students came from grades 5 and 6, there were 20 in Berlin and 40 in Japan. Their subject matter was stripe patterns and rectangular patterns, seen under aspects of mathematics and arts. There were four video conferences of one hour each included, two dominated by students presentations and discussions, two by teaching of the teachers to remote classes. Two German teachers performed team-teaching for some periods.

b) **Hildegard-Wegscheider-Secondary-School in Berlin and Irihirose High School in Niigata.** The students came from grade 10 in Berlin and grades 8 and 9 in Japan. Subject matter was the Theorem of Pythagoras. Groups of German students explained proofs on different levels: experimental work, visualisation by graphics and logical proofing based on constructions at the blackboard. This took about one hour.

c) **Hildegard-Wegscheider-Secondary-School in Berlin and Secondary School attached to Yamagata University in Yamagata.** The students came from grade 10 in Berlin and grade 9 in Japan. The subject matter was the sundial and its mathematical background from the geometry of the globe. Like in b) groups of Japanese students taught the German students using models and logical explanations at the blackboard. They put forward excellent questions to the German students and they showed great excitement on good answers.

The partners in subprojects d) to f) were secondary schools in Berlin and Tokyo. They had a common videoconference on one day, open to the public in Tokyo. The contributions were co-ordinated and prepared in a period of about five weeks.

d) **Hildegard-Wegscheider-Schule and Mukogaoka School.** Seven Japanese students gave a presentation of the City of Tokyo. 15 German students answered with singing a popular Japanese song and some of them then presented some facts and pictures from Berlin in the Japanese Language.

e) **Canisius-College and Koyamadai School**. Seven Japanese students gave a presentation about 'cleaning of the classroom by students', five German students answered about the same topic, followed by a lively discussion.

f) **Camille-Claudel-Schule and Kokusai High School**. Subject matter was "saving energy in school". Both groups of five students each presented explorations about the topic; the Germans reported about an investigation in their school. A lively discussion followed, including questions about how the students experience each other and what they think about the other country, respectively.

g) **An experiment at university level was performed between a research lab of Mitsubishi Electric and Freie Universitaet Berlin.** German students from mathematics, computer science and physics were instructed by researcher Dr. Toshio Ito about using computer simulation when designing kites, including video simulation using a computer. The conference was interactive so that students could ask each other questions.

5. TEACHING AND LEARNING METHODS

Different methods were applied and experienced. In the primary school experiment both sides followed a rather conservative mode of teachers on both sides controlling the performance of the classes and asking most of the questions. The pupils were given opportunities to present their works by prepared statements. Students and teachers spoke in their mothers' languages; they were translated consecutively by interpreters in both classrooms.

The Pythagoras experiment was characterised by independent teaching of German groups of students to the other side. They had explored the topic on the Internet and evaluated the results together with their teacher. The effect of learning was considerable on both sides, since there was a high motivation to good teaching and understanding. This experiment was also characterised by both classes speaking English. This caused many misunderstandings and repetitions. Using figures and visualisations helped relieve this situation.

The sundial experiment was also conducted in English with the Japanese students doing most of the teaching in small groups. This was an outstanding event in a Japanese classroom.

In the Berlin – Tokyo experiments all activities came from the students after having communicated before via electronic means. As to language there was a special situation since all of the German students had taken Japanese language courses in their schools. So they had prepared their statements in Japanese language which was happily accepted by their peers in Japan. Japanese students gave their contributions in their own language and the Germans tried to understand. Interpreters in both classrooms translated consecutively, if necessary.

After we had noticed that the teaching could be done very well by small groups of students, co-operating carefully in structuring subject matter and applying different methods (informal, formal), we started planning to organise bilingual groups to prepare elements of teaching. So far, however, this has turned out to be too difficult and could not yet be realised. The main reason was the great amount of communication in English via e-mail, which needs constant assistance by the teachers.

This brings us to some general remark about the role of teachers in our special learning setting. We started our experiments with teachers organising most of the planning and the execution of work in the classes. The students' roles were mostly to demonstrate what they had learned. Elder students then took over some of the teaching. This was still organised or "filtered" by the teachers. With growing experience, the students' demand grew to erase the filters totally, including the activities of preparing to teach and so to replace their own learning by preparing to teach. This, of course, causes a gain in active learning, but at the same time a loss in efficient learning.

6. SCHOOL ENVIRONMENT AND MEDIA

Experiments such as those described in this paper can only be performed in a very friendly environment. It certainly became clear from the descriptions above that many questions about the "how" and "why" of such experiments will arise. To accept the answers, decision makers in education, responsible for the schools, teachers, parents, and sponsors have to be very far-sighted and open-minded.

Students and teachers will have to invest very much time for such projects, and they have to be very patient. Intercultural understanding and co-operation is very rewarding, but it is hard work at the same time. Language is one problem; different thinking and planning styles are others.

Cost for equipment is considerable and so is the telecommunication. The minimal equipment is a computer, a beamer plus a standard teleconferencing unit (about 2,000 $US). If a computer and beamer are not available, a total of $US 10,000 will do. Communication needs 2 ISDN lines carrying 64 kilobytes per second each. Considering the development in telephone cost, a price of one dollar per minute can be expected, even between continents.

The equipment that we used in Germany and Japan was sponsored by Mitsubishi Electric. The company had expanded the structure of a standard teleconferencing system considerably to meet the demands from two school classes "conferring" (Koizumi and others, 1999). So the systems used a 42-inch monitor in the German classroom (about 20 people) or a LC-projector on an 80-inch screen in a Japanese classroom (about 40 people).

There was a panorama camera and a motorised camera zooming and following individual persons or groups in each room. Video recorders recorded incoming and outgoing pictures and sound for later evaluation. A camera projector (stand camera) was used to transport any pictures and graphics to the remote monitors. Besides controlling the system, the PC could be used to create and transport computer screen images. For good sound transport a complicated system of ceiling microphones was installed. Besides a basic readiness to use such equipment for distance learning as indicated above the system demands technical and didactical or methodological knowledge about the best use from teachers and students. This implies in-service teacher training and better pre-service teacher education.

7. CONCLUSIONS AND VISIONS

Neither the cost of the equipment and communication nor the extra amount of work related to the new media for distance learning should discourage us from integrating these media into the teaching and learning processes. This situation is comparable to the days when computers first entered schools and appeared uneconomical and unusable for education.

Teleconferencing systems or what will be developed from them will be a standard medium in schools within several years. They will not only be used for communication with peers, which we consider a very fruitful application, but also for communication with any point on the globe and anybody on the globe who can contribute to the demands of students to get information in an interactive way. Teachers will have to become advisers and supervisors for this learning by exploring. They have to prevent students from wasting too much time by unqualified exploring.

Distance learning is originated from the problem of physical distance in time and/or space between a class and a teacher, or, more general, between learners and knowledge bases including intelligence to interact – real or artificial. The more this intelligence and its means to interact (through multimedia) grow, the less the physical distance will matter. Instead, cultural distance as we used it in our experiments will become important for the learning process between learners and an intelligent source of knowledge. This distance can cause the learners to get more provoked to learn from a distant source, be it a group of peers or a knowledge base, to learn more through competing, or just through imitation and variation.

Putting individuals into school classes for learning may have economical reasons. But – each student coming from a different environment (the "culture of a family", e.g.) – it also means to initiate some kind of distance learning. This idea can be forwarded to the family of man.

REFERENCES

Downes, T. and Zammit, K. (2000) New literacies for connected learning in global classrooms, in Taylor, H. and Hogenbirk, P. (Eds.) The Bookmark of the School of the Future. Boston/Dordrecht/London: Kluwer Academic Publishers.

Graf, K-D. (1995) Promoting interdisciplinary and intercultural intentions through the history of informatics, in D. Watson and D. Tinsley (eds.) Integrating Information Technology into Education. London: Chapman & Hall, 139-150.

Graf, K-D. and Yokochi, K. (1998) Educational experiments of distance learning and reorganisation of mathematics education, in D. Tinsley and D. C. Johnson (eds.) Information and Communication Technologies in School Mathematics. London: Chapman & Hall, 265-274.

Koizumi, K., Dasai, T., and Moriya, S. (1997) Proposal of interactive distance learning with CCV educational system and verification experiments. In Proceedings of the Int. Conference for Computer Communications (ICCC'97), 107-114,

Koizumi, H., Dasai, T., Yokochi, K., Graf, K-D, and Moriya, S. (1999) An interactive distance learning system and verification experiments between Japan and Germany, in D. Watson and T. Downes (eds.) Communications and Networking in Education. Boston/ Dordrecht/ London: Kluwer Academic Publishers, 39-50

Ruiz i Tarrago, F. (1993) Integration of information technology into secondary education: Main issues and perspectives, in Van Weert (ed.) Guidelines for Good Practice, IFIP Working Group 3.1, Geneva.

Wibe, J. and others (1999) Projects in Networked Learning: European experiences, in Watson, D. and Downes, T. [eds] Communications and Networking in Education. Boston/ Dordrecht/ London: Kluwer Academic Publishers, 101-126

BIOGRAPHIES

Klaus-D Graf studied mathematics, physics and education in Erlangen, Berlin, Muenchen, Tuebingen and Mainz between 1957 and 1996. He was a research assistant at the University of Illinois and the California Institute of Technology in 1963'64 before taking his PhD in Mathematics at the University of Mainz and becoming Assistant Professor in Cybernetics. He became Professor in mathematics and mathematics education in 1971, and subsequently in cybernetics, computer science, and computer science education at Freie Universitaet Berlin. In 1987 he was visiting professor at the National Central University at Taiwan. He specialises in applications of information and communication technologies in mathematics education, history of computer science, and international and intercultural Cupertino. He is an active member of IFIP working groups and ICMI activities.

Kiyoshi Yokochi has held professional posts at Wako University, Yamanashi and Tokai Universities before becoming guest professor at Beijing Normal University in 1985. He has been president of the Mathematical Education Society of Japan since 1986, organiser of the Five Nations Conference on Mathematics Education since 1986 and organiser of the International Conference on Cultural History of Mathematics since 1991. His special fields include mathematics, mathematics education, informatics, cultural history of mathematics, and kindergarten education.

Developing home-school links: Implications for learners, learning, and learning support

Don Passey
Senior Research Fellow, Department of Educational Research,
Lancaster University, Lancaster LA1 4YF, United Kingdom.
d.passey@lancaster.ac.uk

Abstract: It is a fact that school-home links can be developed now by utilising a range of possible communications and information technologies. Yet there has been rather limited exploration of the implications of developing such links. It appears often to be a commonly held view that creating mere physical links will create positive outcomes. This paper will draw on the outcomes of a range of current and recent evaluation and research studies that have focused on home-school links, will explore the limitations of establishing technological links, and examine further educational and social factors which should be considered and integrated into successful models of home-school practice. The paper will show that learning expectations shift when home-school links are successful, but that learners in the traditional sense are not then necessarily learners in the same.

Keywords: Home-school links, school culture, learning environments, partnerships for learning

1. INTRODUCTION

The importance of home-school links, which lead to positive parental support for educational endeavour, should not be underestimated. An article in a recent daily newspaper describes how a head teacher of an inner city primary school is striving to create an environment where parents positively support their children, let alone the school. A headline calls parents: "The real enemy in the classroom", it says how: "This heroic teacher believes passionately in her pupils. Yet the shocking truth is that it is the parents who are often holding them back. Some can't even be bothered to get up in the morning to send their children to school...". The article also, however, offers a rather different perspective, by quoting one parent as saying about her child: "Our Perry wouldn't dream of going to university. He's already in a category where that doesn't happen. You have to be a certain type of person to go to university. Our Perry doesn't even want to go to school some days." (Daily Mail, 11 December 1999). The limited vision and low expectations that are summed up by this parent are not uncommon, and are not newly arising. The evidence of research studies such as those of Jackson and Marsden (1966) identified exactly parallel concerns decades ago.

2. EFFECTIVE HOME-SCHOOL LINKS

The issue for teacher practitioners, school managers, and policy makers alike, is how to provide an educational experience which offers pupils the potential to succeed, and involves parents so that they are empathetic with, and supportive of, the processes. Some schools, and some policy makers, are currently considering information and communications technologies (ICT) as a means to develop these positive educational experiences. This paper will show that creating physical links and offering the potential will not in itself be sufficient to gain the called-for result. Home-school links need to consider overall (but not in any priority order): physical infrastructure linking schools with homes; accessing technologies enabling access by those involved at times and places appropriate to learning; content provision enabling learning activities and interactions to be undertaken; activity development providing opportunities for creation and amendment, according to the involvement of those guiding the educational processes, as well as those creating the educational outcomes; and criteria to assess the success of outcomes, and who hold and use these criteria for what purpose.

It is essential for those developing home-school practice that the factors affecting, and leading to, potential successes in this domain are understood and used to frame those developments. This paper explores a range of these factors, and some of the implications, through instances of practices already under development.

3. EXISTING HOME-SCHOOL LINKS

Discussions with teachers and head teachers show that schools continue to place a significant emphasis upon developing home-school links, to achieve shared educational vision and purpose, and to create the means which enable pupils to develop educational outcomes in both school and home environments. Schools often develop:

- parent and teacher associations (where parents and teachers can discuss joint endeavours to support educational needs, and put on wider social events to enable interchanges of ideas whilst at the same time generating additional funds);
- parent meetings (where parents can discuss their children's progress, and whether particular emphasis or support might help them further);
- parent newsletters (to keep parents informed of school wide developments, and the achievements and expectations of the school and individual pupils or groups of pupils);
- parent workshops or courses (where parents can attend during the day, or at weekends, to focus on specific interests or skills, and perhaps gain forms of qualification or accreditation);
- homework (tasks in subject or curriculum areas to do outside school);
- homework diaries (where parents are made aware of homework set each day, where they may need to be involved in supporting this homework actively, or perhaps signing it off when completed);
- open days (where parents are able to see a range of activities their children experience in the school, and where they can gain ideas of the wider scope and intentions of the curriculum);
- in-school parental support (where parents are encouraged to come into school, to support pupils in lessons or in a wider resource capacity); and
- prospectuses or brochures (in which parents are given often detailed information about school organisation, management and intentions over a year long period).

An analysis, of characteristics of each of these forms, which might be considered to be more 'traditional' types of home-school links, suggests that:

- many home-school links are focused at an institutional level on the school, with very few focused on the home;
- provision only implicitly offers ways for parents to become involved in setting a longer term vision and higher expectations for their pupils;
- few methods involve parents and pupils directly in mutual activities;
- links between short term provision, and medium and longer term provision is loosely linked, if at all; and
- interactions depend largely upon formal written information or communication flow, or infrequent formal social interactions.

Overall, this traditional range of home-school provision can be considered through a number of features. Individual characterisation of each form through a number of features is offered in Table 1 below.

Table 1. Features of home-school provision of various types

Type of provision	Form and type of interaction	Key recipients	Institutional focus, and period of focus
parent and teacher associations	discussion, social, face-to-face, two-way exchange	parents, and teachers	school, largely, over long term, at least one year usually
parent evening meetings	information, social, face-to-face, can be two-way exchange	parents, pupils, and perhaps teachers	non-institutionally based, over medium term, usually up to one year
parent newsletters	information, written, one-way directional	parents	non-institutionally based, over medium term, but usually post-event reflective
parent workshops or courses	support, social, usually face-to-face, one-way directional	parents	non-institutionally based, over medium term, often up to one term or one year
homework	task-driven, written, one-way directional	pupils	non-institutionally based, over short term, usually up to one week
homework diaries	information and support, written, two-way directional	parents, and pupils, also teachers	school and home, over short term, usually one day or one week
open days	information, social, observation, can be two-way exchange	parents	school, over long term, at least one year
in-school parental support	support, social, largely one-way directional	pupils, or teachers	school, over medium term, usually one or more terms
prospectuses or brochures	information, written, one-way directional	parents	school, over long term, usually one year

4. LEARNING CONCERNS, OF PUPILS, OF TEACHERS, AND OF PARENTS

The outcomes of current home-school links identified and listed above, suggest a number of immediate weaknesses:

- if home effect on pupil learning is so important (and many sources suggest it is), then more institutionally focused effort on the home should be encouraged;

- if parental expectations for children are low, then mechanisms should enable longer term vision by parents to be developed;
- if parents are to develop long or medium term vision, their involvement in mutual activities with their children may be one way in which they are likely to gain a greater understanding of intention, and a greater interest in what is being offered to their children;
- if parents are to become more concerned with longer term vision, the links between short term tasks and longer term vision should be made much more explicit;
- if parents are to become involved to greater extents, more ad-hoc, more frequent, and more informal means to communicate need to become available to them.

The lack of opportunity for parents to develop longer term vision and expectations painted by this analysis is potentially exacerbated by two major factors. Firstly, differences in time frames operated by varying socio-economic or employment groups. For example, a company director is likely to work on time horizons of at least one year, if not five to ten years. A self-employed painter and decorator is likely to work on time horizons of at least one month, if not one year. A shop floor worker is likely to work on time horizons of perhaps one week. Secondly, differences in learning concerns that are held by pupils, teachers and parents. Pupils are concerned with completing tasks that are often contained within a single school class period, or rarely longer than a term of project or coursework. Teachers are concerned with planning at a variety of levels, but usually for a one-year period with a scheme of work, over a term-long period, and for lesson plans over a weekly period. Parents are concerned with supporting outcomes on a short-term basis (with homework), or in response to parent evenings or information received (often no more frequently than once each school term).

These differences suggest that positive educational vision, intentions and purposes would be likely to be supported by:

- offering parents access to material which gives examples of long term vision and effects;
- providing tasks and educational practices which involve parents and pupils in longer term projects and coursework;
- giving ways for pupils and parents to link short term work outcomes to longer term intentions; and
- involving parents in less formal activity, but on a more frequent basis, in considering educational practice, directions, and outcomes.

An issue for this paper is to ask whether ICT can support any of the needs listed above in any ways more effectively than more traditional media. Some evidence already points towards a positive potential in these respects. Cox (1997), for example, in looking at the impacts of ICT on pupil motivation, indicated that ICT can have positive effects on the long term concerns of pupils; pupils believe that ICT is offering them skills to support the potential for long term employment and employability status. Downes (1994), Scrimshaw (1997), Rockman et al (1997), and Passey et al (1997) indicated that home computer, broadband and laptop technologies could have beneficial effects at a social, as well as at an educational, level. An issue for the future, therefore, is how to effectively focus development in order to gain significant and beneficial outcomes.

5. POSITIVE PRACTICES AND APPROACHES

In identifying the positive practices and approaches that have been adopted and implemented in schools and within homes to date, it is necessary first, perhaps, to dispel some myths, which may be held about developments in this domain. The concept of ICT being able to be used to offer some form of panacea to positively support educational outcomes arising from use in the school-home domain is likely to be a myth. If it were true, then almost certainly the effects of radio, television and video tapes on supporting educational practices in the school and home would have been far greater than they have been. The number of households with televisions is very large, and covers the wide socio-economic spectrum. Yet little effect appears to have been made by this broadcast medium upon offering either wider views of educational intention, or wider developments of educational practice (see Sanger et al, 1997, for example). Broadcast media methods, in the traditional forms in which they exist, are not likely to offer wide interactions involving parents and pupils (as shown in Passey et al, 1997, when they looked at the effects of a video-on-demand ATM system).

Positive effects upon parents are identified when parents are involved from the outset in educational technology developments. Positive outcomes can arise when parents are involved in a positive financial outlay at some level, and when parents share one or more common social or educational concerns for developing educational interactivity (as shown in Passey et al, 1997; Passey et al, 1999; Passey et al, 2000). The systems, which lead to positive educational or social outcomes currently, rely upon access via the Internet at home and at school on a common Intranet, or upon laptops being carried between home and school (perhaps coupled with Internet access at home and at school). When parents have become involved in such ICT practices, the evidence shows that parents feel, as a consequence, that they are more aware of what is happening in schools, and are more interested in educational practices and in what the school is doing.

One research study (Passey et al, 1997) reported on the form of positive social outcomes from a home-school development in a school, which had developed an Intranet (called the Hub) to which homes were linked via modems and desktop PCs. The report stated that:

> "Most parents (13 out of 17 reporting) indicate that they believe that the use of the system has been of particular benefit to them. For example, parents have reported:
> - e-mail has increased social and business links;
> - that the Hub keeps them up to date with school work, as it gains more pages;
> - children can work at school and home on the same document."

> "Most parents (13 out of 17) report that they feel that the Hub has helped their needs as parents. Only two report that this is not the case. When asked in what ways parents felt it had helped, they indicated some significant outcomes, for example:
> - using the Hub had helped their relationship with their children, as they assisted each other on the system;
> - access to common data had improved their relationship with other parents;
> - the Hub had brought them into closer contact with their children's school, increasing understanding of materials and methods of teaching, and improving personal acquaintance with staff, etc.;
> - they now felt they had a role in their children's education, both specifically and in general."

One of the limitations recognised by those who developed the Highdown School Information Hub was the access limitation provided by desktop computers. In 1998, a pilot programme in 28 schools in the UK and the States of Jersey, supported by Microsoft UK, trialled the use of laptops in schools and homes (which addressed these limitations). Social outcomes were identified in a research study which looked at a range of implementation issues (Passey et al, 2000), and benefits reported by parents are indicated in Table 2 below.

Table 2. Benefits noticed when laptops are used at home (n=108)

Forms of benefit	**Frequency**
IT/operational skills	19
Work task related	16
Motivation	14
Family/social involvement	4

Portability for use	4
Monitoring easier	1
Specific learning outcomes	1
Family awareness	1

In this pilot programme, certain schools managed and developed the home-school interface to greater extents than did others. One school in the programme, Sawtry Community College, devoted considerable efforts to managing the relationship with parents. An extract from a case study report on the school follows.

> "In an evening meeting for parents in October 1998, seventeen parents were present. The parents raised at the meeting a wide range of issues, including whether the school had any plans to scan in books, and whether pupils would in future not pick up 'real' books. Expectations from those parents in the evening meeting were clearly high. One parent asked whether IR would be used for printing out, for example, while another asked about what could be expected of the teachers involved. Some parents were indicating that pupils had high expectations of teachers, and that they could 'pick up on hesitancy', for example.
>
> Parents were already at that stage asking about signs of improvement, and whether teaching approaches were meeting learning needs. The school AAL project manager had indicated to parents the possibility of running sessions on learning. One parent suggested that a guide to expected skills and presentation outcomes reached at certain times in certain subjects would be a useful resource to have. The school clearly wished to maintain high levels of communication with parents, and was putting mechanisms in place to ensure that they were kept fully informed of what was happening in each subject area."

In essence the positive practices and approaches studied incorporate one or more of the following key features:

- technological links are created after educational and social reasons for links are considered, to suit educational or social purpose and intention;
- partnership motives, needs, and management implications address parent, pupil, and business involvement;
- enhanced demands and expectations for parents and pupils are anticipated by teachers and schools;

- shifts in how learners treat and use ICT are identified as integration occurs;
- teachers focus upon the learning skills that ICT does not address;
- the input and output media of ICT are utilised fully; and
- tasks and educational work is developed as a more continuous activity (including use of ICT in both the home and out-of-school contexts).

6. ICT ENVIRONMENTS AT HOME AND SCHOOL

Typical ICT environments in both the home and the school are dramatically shifting at this current point in time. Recent indicators of typical ICT environments show increases in the range of ICT technologies, their communications capacities, and their sophistication levels. In part this is due to commercial and social interest, and in part due to implicit support within UK government initiatives that have sought to develop active community-wide implementation strategies and policies (DfEE, 1997; DfEE, 1998; BECTa, 1999). An indicator of typical home environments in 1995 is given by the results of a pupil-completed survey. Of 2,260 Year 7 pupils (aged 11 to 12 years) replying, 2,122 indicated some form of access at home. Details of access are given in Table 3 below.

Table 3. Home access to ICT reported by 2,260 Year 7 pupils (aged 11 to 12 years) in 1995

Form of access	Number reporting	Percentage (%)
Some level of access	2,122	94
Personally owned	1,610	71
Games machine	1,569	69
Floppy disk-drive	811	36
Mouse	1,024	45
Printer	809	36
CD-ROM	186	8
Modem	145	6

In 1998, a survey of Year 7 pupils undertaken by the Cornwallis School, for example, showed, in terms of more recent home access, that:

- all had used a computer before;
- computers in school were used about once a month;
- 70% had a home computer (of some form);
- 45% used the home computer for school work;
- 25% used the home computer for playing games;

- 15% had access to the Internet at home.

This pattern of outcome suggested that at least some pupils were using ICT at home to greater extents than they were using ICT at school. It also showed, if the comparison with results in Table 3 is reasonable, that numbers of home computers for educational work has risen, while numbers of home games computers have decreased. There is also an increase in the number of pupils gaining access to the Internet at home.

7. RELEVANCE TO SECONDARY EDUCATION

Given the access to ICT in the home-school domain, the roles that ICT can play in supporting educational endeavour in the home-school domain needs to consider:

- the places where educational activities can take place;
- the actors who can be involved; and
- the purposes and values of those involved.

The scope of those who can be involved in school-based educational practice commonly considers two interactants - the pupil, and one teacher. However, for the purposes of developing a consideration of the home-school domain, and an exploration of pedagogic processes involved, five interactants are considered in this section of the paper:

- the pupil (who can be considered, for the purposes of interactivity, to be an active recipient);
- the teacher (who can be considered to be an active provider);
- the parent or significant other (who can be considered to be an active reflector or supporter);
- the resource manager (who can be considered an active supporter); and
- the ICT itself (which can be considered to be an active reflector).

This categorisation of interactants makes some assumptions about the roles of those involved. It assumes that:

- interactivity has direction (that essentially purpose determines a flow from provision to recipient);
- interactivity is not dynamic (that the flow is not affected by feedback following any interactive event); and
- interactivity has positive intentions and fulfils expectations already set and agreed.

Clearly this is not true in every situation. Any model which attempts to show interactivity needs to be able to be viewed as dynamic, enabling feedback to occur, and for intentions, beliefs and expectations to be considered as factors in its working dynamic. Interactivity clearly has, in the accepted form, some social basis (whether it is through external chat, or internal 'talk'). For the purposes of this exploration, a model will be used which enables these features to be integrated (illustrated in Figure 1).

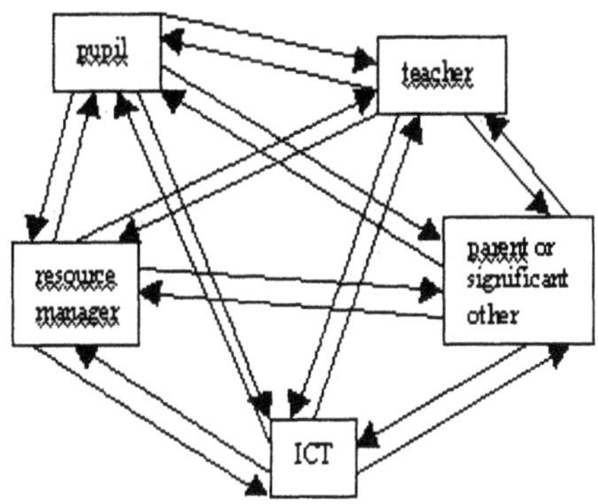

Figure 1. Model to characterise actors and sequences in pedagogic interactivities

8. ROLE OF ICT IN LEARNING APPROACHES AND SUPPORT FOR LEARNING

In a classroom situation where a teacher is standing in front of the class, and is explaining the causes and effects of the Napoleonic Wars, the interactivity is a one-way interaction - the learning is essentially internal, and dependent upon the pupil's ability to engage, assimilate, reconstruct, and reprioritise the outcomes of the interaction. The teacher describes verbally, while the pupil reconstructs in a form to suit existing understanding and memorisation, learning assimilation approaches and recall. If the teacher asks the pupil a question, then the interactivity is a sequential pedagogical interaction.

In temporal terms, the interactive teacher-to-pupil element pre-dates the interactive pupil-to-teacher element. If a discussion ensues, then a temporal sequence is set up. Such concepts of temporal sequencing of learning interactions are tied also with notions of incremental learning, and progressive learning, where learning is broken down into elements of a particular size and quality, and sequenced to build into a progressive experience. Such interactions also usually assume that both actors are present at the same time and in the same place.

This type of temporal sequencing is at the heart of interactivity when integrated learning systems (ILS) are involved, for example - pupils interact with the ICT. The ICT offers a task, the pupil responds, and the ICT responds. When an ILS is being used in a classroom, the teacher often does not become involved in any level of direct interaction, but may be, for the duration of all, or some, of the pupil-ICT interaction time, an observer. The strength of interactivity, therefore, may be perceived as lying with the pupil and the ICT, so that the strength of interactivity for the teacher is at a much lower level. Also the likelihood is that the interactivity by the teacher is with the ICT, at what the pupil is being successful with or being challenged by. Some teachers may find the lack of interaction with the pupils to be a disadvantage (this pattern is illustrated in Figure 2 below).

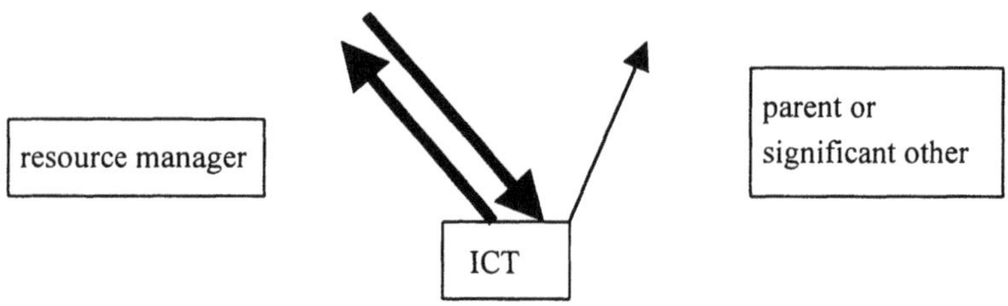

Figure 2. Model to characterise a sequence of ICT-related interactions of varying strength

This example of interactivity (which may be an extreme example) illustrates two important points. Firstly, ICT can create a temporal sequencing of activity, and secondly, ICT can support a strong level of interactivity with pupils. Pedagogically there are clearly implications for teachers:

- understanding the temporal nature of the sequences of interactivity; and
- engaging with interactivities which are stronger between pupils and ICT than between the teacher and the ICT, or the teacher and the pupil.

Is this different in any way from that when a non-ICT medium is involved? In some ways it is. Firstly, pupils are often engaged at stronger levels of interactivity with ICT than they are with non-ICT materials. Secondly, ICT often offers its own sequential interactivity, which may or may not relate to that offered by teachers. Thirdly, parents and significant others can be involved at an interactive level to greater extents with ICT. ICT enables work to be developed, using interactive and iterative experiences with teachers, parents and significant others, over longer periods of time, enabling more detail to be incorporated, and more amendment to be involved (explored in Passey, 2000). This clearly affects potentially, when and where work can be undertaken, the duration of the working process, the nature of the working process, and the outcomes (as well as their assessment). Pedagogically, there are clearly implications:

- learning interactions can occur in places outside classrooms, which can have a direct impact upon learning outcomes;
- learning interactivities can occur at a range of times other than those when classes are held;
- learning outcomes can be developed over longer, or more continuous, periods of time;
- learning patterns can rely much more upon extensive synthesis and periods of high-level engagement;
- outcomes being assessed may be much more in the process of being created than in the process of having been completed.

This brief exploration indicates that ICT can have a 'shift' function on:

- the scope of those who can be involved in educational practice (for example, resource managers are playing a much more significant role, in their capacity as Internet web site seekers;
- the roles of those involved (for example, the significant roles that ICT can itself assume, for example, as a portable tutor assisting in the checking of spelling and grammar accuracy);
- the outcomes for those involved (for example, the creation of work including enhanced details and ideas from wider sources, and in other forms, such as multi-media forms);
- the position and places when these are involved (for example, the development of a piece of work which captures digital camera imagery from a visit, but where the work is started before the visit, due to use of internet resources, perhaps, and completed after the visit); and
- the values for all involved (for example, the value of synthesising material over a period of time, rather than synthesising ideas in a limited time period, which might occur in a single lesson, or when writing an essay under examination conditions).

9. FUTURE NEED FOR ICT SYSTEMS WHICH SUPPORT HOME-SCHOOL ACTIVITIES

The need for a more widespread development and use of ICT systems to support educational endeavour in the home-school domain can be argued (as it was, for example, for integrating ICT practice into education, by Hawkridge, 1983), on the basis of present and future economic need, social need, educational need, and employment need. In economic terms, if educational endeavour can be supported more in the home-school domain, then the economic reliance placed on the entirety of a school-based system could be shifted. In social terms, the positive impacts that could be gained from society are considerable. Educationally, the need to maximise effectiveness of interactions when the curriculum is ever expanding is more crucial than ever before. For educational practices to match employment needs, where employees use ICT to increasing extents, is also clearly a significant need (see, for example, recent reviews of UK syllabuses of qualifications at ages of 16 to 19 years, in terms of GNVQ and Key Skills). An increasing future emphasis on the use of web-based technologies, and the need of employers to employ those who can develop and maintain web-shared information and communication systems, will require educational practices to adopt learning and assessment practices to endorse longer-term creativity rather than summative creativity. Educational activities will then need to be epitomised through production and outcomes of web-based documents rather than being epitomised through completed book and paper-based document forms (including timed completion of hand written examination questions following short-term in-mind synthesis of recalled ideas).

But the need for use of ICT systems can also be argued on the basis of desires to:

- enhance or improve involvement and interest, by parents as well as pupils (and some secondary schools are reporting that increasingly parents in lower socio-economic groups are purchasing computers for home use);
- develop an increasing number of individuals to higher levels in terms of educational attainment;
- match the practices which will be used in employment contexts (such as abilities of employees to develop web-based materials and resources);
- develop the social basis of education worldwide (where local links and interactivity are supported by networks and mechanisms operating nationally and internationally).

10. DEVELOPMENT OF HOME-SCHOOL LINKS AND A VISION FOR FUTURE EDUCATION

A number of successful developments, which have built educational pursuits across the home-school domain, enable a range of conclusions to be drawn (in the form of recommendations for future development). Without these key features, home-school links are likely to achieve little more than traditional home-school links have offered. Schools and those supporting schools should, when developing home-school practice, consider a range of key needs:

- school managers and teachers need to be prepared to develop relationships with parents, an ethos concerned with a greater sharing by parents, pupils and teachers, and consider a partnership means in this context, and what possibilities it offers;

- a strategic lead must be taken by the head teacher or a senior manager in the school, and the use of a management group should be considered – and whether to include library, technical staff, governors and parents;
- opportunities for pupils and parents to share is equally important, so schools need to offer joint parent, pupil, teacher activities, time to spend in personally talking to parents (including being prepared to address financial questions from parents), and the offering of advice, and how to support their children;
- setting up internal monitoring to identify successes and weaknesses is valuable, but feedback time is also needed, and in project aims, clear statements should be made about the specific learning benefits that are being sought (mechanisms should be in place to identify these, with evidence of outcomes gathered from teachers, pupils and parents);
- where access technologies vary from individual to individual, teachers need to be prepared to address questions of equity, and technical support;
- schools should be ready to respond to higher levels of parental demands, and expectations, and should expect parents to feel more involved and more knowledgeable.

A number of authors (e.g. Wood, undated; Heppell, 1993) have made reference to educational practice operating in circumstances where schools no longer have the same centralist roles. If this is to be the case, then clearly what those who require educational development regard, as centralist roles, will either need to be displaced or replaced. The role of social interaction to develop understanding is still as crucial as it has always been. Futuristic visions of education will therefore need to take account of this requirement. Within the UK, the role of examinations and assessment mechanisms is still a crucial one in shaping the practice in schools. Economic needs could well determine that Internet-based educational practice is a requirement currently, or at some point in the future. If this requirement then outstrips largely the need for paper-based practice (or shifts the balance significantly), then the future of classrooms will be likely to need to shift as a consequence.

The shifts which are likely to be seen in secondary schools are:

- some schools will take lead roles in developing school-home links, and some parent groups will become more heavily involved directly and indirectly in educational practices;
- on-line support systems (independently of schools, or with school collaboration) will be developed to encourage and match their needs;

- school management will devote more time to the school-home interface, and parents will become more demanding on teachers and schools when they do not respond to their parental values;
- schools will offer more information on-line for parents;
- some schools will offer more courses and workshops in which parents can become involved, and some teachers will develop more continuous, interactive and iterative forms of work (including working on-line increasing extents to support improvement of written work);
- some teachers will have higher expectations of pupils, and some teachers will use class time more for considering higher order skills and needs;
- the limitations to further development of school-home practice will be seen to be determined by demands imposed by current examination and assessment practice, and any new balances in examination practice will determine ultimately in-class and out-of-class practices.

While home-school practice is worthwhile from an educational perspective, the main driving forces for change are likely to be employment and economic need. The concept of changing the system or structure from a school-based institutional model will only happen if appropriate educational practice, and social concern, are included in any change mechanisms employed. If home-school practice is deemed to be worthwhile, then there is a need to focus on the educational practices and activities to make this a reality. However, doing so without involving parents and society more widely will be unlikely to enable a whole-scale shift from the system that exists currently. But, a 'new' system, offered by enterprising individuals, using social interaction and intervention via video-conferencing, for example, coupled with textual, sound and image communication, could provide an interesting competitive alternative, attractive to the life-styles and needs of some parents and their children. Fundamentally, however, from an educational and social perspective, the constant need for social intervention in shaping higher order educational outcomes, is likely to limit wide shifts (even from an access technology viewpoint). Systems that enable teachers to operate at a distance may work for some pupils and systems that enable parents or significant others to provide the educationally necessary social interactions may work for others. In many instances, however, the evidence suggests currently that these systems are likely to provide support systems within an educational system still based on schools.

REFERENCES

BECTa (1999) *Connecting Schools, Networking People* 2000, BECTa, Coventry.

Cox, M. (1997) *The Effects of Information Technology on Students' Motivation: Final Report*, NCET and Kings's College London, Coventry and London.
DfEE (1997) *Connecting the Learning Society: National Grid for Learning - the Government's Consultation Paper*, DfEE, London.
DfEE (1998) *Open for Learning. Open for Business: the Government's National Grid for Learning Challenge*, DfEE, London.
Downes, T. (1994) Children and electronic media in the home, in *Exploring a New Partnership: Children, Teachers and Technology* (eds. J. Wright and D. Benzie), Elsevier, Amsterdam.
Fowler, R. (1999) The real enemy in the classroom, in the Daily Mail, 11 December 1999.
Hawkridge, D. (1983) *New Information Technology in Education*, Croom Helm, Windsor.
Heppell, S. (1993) *The Technologies of the Future, in The Future Curriculum with I.T.: Seminar Report*, NCET, Coventry.
Jackson, B. and Marsden, D. (1966) *Education and the Working Class*, ARK Paperbacks, London.
Passey, D. (2000) Developing teaching strategies for distance (out-of-school) learning in primary and secondary schools. *Educational Media International*, March 2000.
Passey, D., Forsyth, K., Hutchison, D., Scott, A. and Steadman, S. (1999) *Anytime Anywhere Learning Pilot Programme: A Microsoft UK Supported Programme in 28 Pilot Schools - Overview Report*, Microsoft, Reading.
Passey, D., Forsyth, K., Hutchison, D., Scott, A. and Steadman, S. (2000) *Anytime Anywhere Learning Pilot Programme: End of First Phase Implementation* (September 1998 – December 1999) Summary Report, Microsoft, Reading.
Passey, D., Forsyth, K., Hutchison, D., Scott, A. and Williams, N. (1997) *Group D - Home-School Links: Final Report*, NCET, Coventry.
Rockman, S. et al (1997) *Report of a Laptop Program Pilot - A Project for Anytime Anywhere Learning by Microsoft Corporation: Notebook for Schools by Toshiba America Information Systems*, Rockman et al, San Francisco, CA.
Sanger, J., Wilson, J., Davies, B. and Whittaker, R. (1997) *Young Children, Videos and Computer Games: Issues for Teachers and Parents*, Falmer Press, London.
Scrimshaw, P. (1997). *Preparing for the Information Age: Synoptic Report of the Education Departments' Superhighways Initiative*, Welsh Office, Cardiff, Department of Education for Northern Ireland, Belfast, The Scottish Office, Edinburgh, and Department for Education and Employment, London.
Wood, D. (undated) *Classroom of 2015*, NCE, London.

BIOGRAPHY

Don Passey is a Senior Research Fellow in the Department of Educational Research at Lancaster University. He is currently leading evaluation teams investigating the management of broadband developments in Pathfinder LEAs, laptop use in schools and homes, and use of ICT in coursework. He was a member of the IT Task Group involved in the review of the National Curriculum. Within the last four years he has led an evaluation on home-school links, the commercial evaluation of a new ILS to support early years' mathematics development, and evaluations concerned with distant support of education and home education via fax tutoring and teletutoring. He has worked as a consultant in a number of individual schools, in LEAs, with government agencies, and for commercial companies.

Edunetmatics – education assisted by a world telematic net

Antonio Saldaño and Miguel Reyes
Universidad Metropolitana de Ciencias de la Educación, Santiago, Chile.
csaldano@entelchile.net / asaldano@umce.cl
Universidad de Playa de Ancha Ciencias de la Educación, Valparaíso, Chile.
converge@entelchile.net/mreyest@upa.cl

Abstract: Traditional education is developed by building up connections between specific ideas and related skills through repeated practice and positive reinforcement. All that has no sense in virtual learning environments because the new information and communication technologies, NICT, have induced a new space concept in society and a new dimension space for the culture. Thus the traditional learning environment must be changed and its meaning translated to a virtual learning environment. This new learning space must be constructed over an innovative educational paradigm, which is determined by a new concept, named edunetmatics (education assisted by telematic net). The edunetmatic process has a dynamics inspired on an uncertainty principle. The outcome is a learning cybernetic cave. Some evaluation has been done over the Chilean national educational net, Enlaces. A Virtualisation of Experiments on Science and Technology Project is being developed and implemented on the national educational net, according to the Chilean Educational Reform.

Keywords: Virtual learning environment, edunetmatics, collective intelligence, educational navigation, educational network

1. INTRODUCTION

The Internet, the computer world net, is one of the inventions having the most impact in the past century. As with many new inventions, it has been integrated into daily affairs. It has been also used in education, but as an invention which has not been created specifically for education, it has been applied without doing a thorough study to obtain a natural projection above all the real dimensions.

This work is the result of research to understand the meaning of the Internet and to derive a projection of how education could be achieved. This same path has been followed with the educational robotics (Saldaño, 1989) obtaining an educational model which has been applied on one side to the pupil knowledge construction (Vega, 1991) and on the other hand to scientific research. Thus, significant results have been obtained.

Naturally, there are big differences between these research studies, because for the Internet application, it was found that the generated subayacent space was far more complex, overcoming in a broad way the system, communication, information treatment, space globalization and time contraction models. From what has been already stated about this new hyperspace which has been created by the Internet, a good projection on education has been derived.

The first aspect considered was education as a dialogue process and the possible types of educational communication, as relation, friendship, and communion (common – union), over telematic (telecommunication and informatics) nets (Reyes & Sandaño, 1995), and then an edunetmatic (education assisted by telematic net) process conceptualization has been developed (Reyes & Saldaño, 1994). Then participation levels or educational telematic net participation (Reyes, Saldaño, Mendez, & Garay, 1995; Reyes, Saldaño, Garay, & Mendez, 1997) were recorded, and finally procedural dynamic principles on edunetmatics were developed (Reyes & Saldaño, 1998a; 1998b). Innovative and educational underlying foundational paradigm components will be treated in this work.

2. CONCEPTUAL FRAMEWORK

2.1 Edunetmatic foundational space

The new learning space must be constructed over an innovative educational paradigm, named edunetmatics which is determined by a new space concept, that is:

i) an inner space described by a topology, semiotics and valuation.

Topology means the space conformed by all the computers interconnected among them. Semiotics is the integration result of the oral, musical, text, hypertext, image, hyperimage and animation meanings. And valuation is interpreted as the valuation result of the all semiotic meanings.

This is very important because it will handle impulse and orientation to the navigation dynamics in the Internet hyperspace.

ii) an outer space composed by subjects, messages, communication means and reach

Subjects. They can interact as one-by-one (1-1), one-by-n (1-n), n-by-one (n-1) and n-by-n (n-n). So, they can be monopole or multipole, that is, not only one is emitting, but many of them can be emitting at the same time too. Then each subject, when it is emitting, is the center of the net. The net is multicentered. The subject may be collective and have life. Over the Internet the subject has life only when it is emitting. Otherwise it is latent, if it is plugged-in. Thus it is possible to say that there is a collective intelligence. This intelligence is independent of subjects belonging to the collective, but always dependent of one of them. It changes with the time but it is stable for the virtual space. The collective intelligence emerges from the direction and the action of subjects but it is absorbed by the reflection. Another characteristic of the subject is the educability, that is, to uninform and to exclude. Uninform has two meanings: to create criteria for the change and the permanency and to determine axiological and operative filter systems. Exclude includes managing codes and meanings in a critical, active and creative way.

Message. It is the integration result of oral, musical, text, hypertext, image, hyperimage and animation codes.

Communication means. These are defined by:

1. technological convergence: the integration of phone, radio, TV, computer, e-mail, chat, newsgroups and websites.(Dominique, 1999)
2. structure: as a cobweb.
3. space contiguity: in any place. time contiguity: in any time.
4. interactivity: 1-1, 1-n, n-1 and n-n. To any person, from any person.
5. navigation on World Wide Web net.

Reach. It is all the earth. A global village or globality.

2.2 Edunetmatic process

A new learning process is to be determined over the edunetmatic space just defined.

- Final or initial objective?

The traditional educational objectives are determined by the final goal of the process: "the student must be able to ...". In the edunetmatic learning process, only the initial conditions are known, such as in the seed situation, from which a plant is produced, because it is not possible to know the netway process. A statement begins as "student is going to be able to ...".

- Categoric or integral thinking?

The development work for the traditional thinking is done under a structured disciplinary frame. The thinking development network is constructed by an integral interdisciplinary knowledge.

- Competitive or cooperative methodology?

The present educational methodology is based on an individual paradigm (competitive) instead of community paradigm (cooperative), where students authenticaly grow up.

- Context or educational process?

Consider an uncertainty principle, the product of the context by the process is finite. This is an analogy to the Heisenberg physical principle. In other words, "the road is made by walking ...". A. Machado. So, in the traditional educational process if the process is more important than the context, the learning is unmeaningful. Inversely, if the context is more important than the process, the educational product is insignificant. In the edunetmatic process the result of navigating (walking) in a network-like way (road) is self-constructed knowledge.

- Actual or virtual learning purpose?

The traditional learning purpose emphasizes to have a transcendental life, to be someone in the world. A virtual learning in any netway point is achieved when one is able to cease to exist and then exist again.

2.3 Edunetmatic dynamics

The following are some characteristics of edunetmatic dynamics:

1. It is determined by the classic systemic notion (in, process, out and feedback)
2. It is impulsed and oriented by the semiotic and the valuation
3. It is organized by a self reference logics (like the evolution of a seed)
4. It is defined by the continuous motion of its kinematic center
5. It is supported by
   - the synergy - total energy is greater than the energy of the parts.
   - the recursivity - the final point is the initial point of the next step.

- the fractality - the structure of the total motion is similar to the motion structure of any part.

3. EDUNETMATIC PARADIGM

This paradigm will be derived, taking into account the integration result (14) of the telematic net framework in the context of the Chilean Educational Reform, defined by the Chilean Ministry of Education (1996), and the Chickering and Gamson (1991) seven principles as guides of a quality education.

From the conceptual framework and from its main features an educational paradigm is possible to draw out.

1. The Internet hyperspace is a cobweb kind of structure and multi-centred. A semiotic comprehension is the basis for doing a good valuation. The best valuation will give a good impulse and a clear motivation to obtain a good navigation dynamics in the Internet hyperspace. Internet work is for any space, in any time, in any place and by any person.
2. Subject educability is obtained by uninform and exclude process. Each subject must learn to share the knowledge, try to be a valid collector and be able to contrast other knowledge with his self-knowledge. The net knowledge (collective intelligence) is neither static nor trivial. Furthermore it is linked to a place and to a person who creates it. It is global. It is shared with anyone. It is universal with respect to belonging, language and location aspects. Each Internet user participates in a collective intelligence. The better the Internet work the better the navigation on the World Wide Web. Collective intelligence emerges from each action and direction subject. A collective intelligence must manage many unpredicted and unpredicted events.
3. Communications messages depend on the component codes and on the integration methods used for them. The better the technological convergence of communication means, the better the quality of messages will be.
4. The life and social holistic thinking are privileged over the bias of professional thinking. Entropic and distributed learning let persons grow up intellectually, affectively and socially. The learning purpose may be convergent or changeable, induced or emergent, deterministic or entropic.
5. In edunetmatics only initial learning objectives are known. An operative learning objective is to be able to construct new knowledge

and to develop critical, creative and metacognitive thinking and emotions (Reyes, Montes & Saldano, 1999).

6. The dynamical process is characterized by a one way motion - from the objective to the subjective, from the competitive to the cooperative, from the categorized to the integrated and from the actual to the virtual. The dynamical process is based on the self construction of integral transdisciplinary knowledge and on a community paradigm. The dynamical process results will be achieved as a self constructed knowledge through a navigation in a network-like way.
7. Finally it is necessary to consider the teacher role as an motivator, a guide, an animator and a facilitator (IGAF).

This educational paradigm must be picture-framed on the Chilean Educational Reform. The main features proposed are: a pedagogical activity centered on students, a cooperative work, a project methodology, probem solving and transversal objectives, and content about personal growth and self-formation, thinking development, ethical formation and personal environment (Chilean Ministry of Education, 1996).

Chickering and Gamson's (1991) seven principles serve as guides of a quality education. These seven principles have been applied many times and in different contexts. Moreover they define a picture-frame in which actors, learning activities and methods, and systems approach are integrated.

4. EDUNETMATIC PROJECT

Some evaluation has been done over the Chilean national net, Enlaces. But what has been done has not had a basic substantive framework which would let one obtain solid comparative results. The set of ideas can be exemplified by a project about the collection and information exchange about typical national dishes of five Latin American countries.

1. Project contextualization must be done to determine each one of the participants, individualizing them, organizing the communication system and defining in detail the compromises.
2. An interactive website must be designed and uploaded to the net. Integration, interaction, database definition, link and hyperlink, and assistance variables must be defined in an operative manner.
3. Topology and semiotic of codes and component meanings must be defined according to the project contents. The technological convergence of communication means level must be decided.
4. Dynamic space must be allocated with typical dishes list of each participanting country along with the local ingredients for each dish and

recipes for cooking each one. This is done so that groups from the other countries can cook them and interchange information about them.
5. Relations among the typical dishes, ecology, customs, costs, and impact from each country must be collected.
6. Student participation patterns must be set up to evaluate the results.

5. CONCLUSIONS

The net of connections of our planet minds, assisted by a computer net, is as a sum of intellects and emotions which have generated a cybernetic cave (Luker, 1999). Those primitive men who live there, now have a collective intelligence and "in net emotions" (Reyes, Montes & Saldaño, 1999). All that is a product of a virtualisation dynamics of their cognitive and affection potentialities through a navigation across a world telematic net. These issues and principles must be considered when designing the networked schools of the future for all citizens.

REFERENCES

Chilean Ministry of Education. Decrees 40/96 and 220/98. Santiago. Chile.

Chickering, A. and Gamson, A., (Eds.). (1991). New Directions in Teaching and Learning: Applying The Seven Principles for Good Practice in Undergraduate Education. San Francisco, CA: Jossey-Bass. USA.

Dominique, J. (1999). Tecnologías de los Medios del Conocimiento para integrar el trabajo y el Aprendizaje. IV Seminario Internacional: Las Nuevas Tecnologías y la Educación Superior. Consejo de Educación Superior. MINEDUC. Santiago. Chile.

Luker, M. (1999). Avances en el desarrollo de una Internet más efectiva para la educación superior por medio de la alianza entre universidades, industria y gobierno. IV Seminario Internacional: Las Nuevas Tecnologías y la Educación Superior. Consejo de Educación Superior. MINEDUC. Santiago. Chile.

Reyes, M., Montes, M. and Saldaño, A. (1999). Redes telemáticas para el desarrollo de personas. Emociones en Internet. III Jornadas de Educación a Distancia del Mercosur. Osorno. Chile.

Reyes, M. and Saldaño, A. (1998b). Educação a Distância e Avaliação. Edurredmatica. II Workshop Internacional "Formação de Profesores via Telematica. Unicamp. Campinas SP. Brasil.

Reyes, M. and Saldaño, A. (1994). Educación asistida por Red computacional. Edurredmática. VII Encuentro Nacional de Informática y Computación Educacional. Universidad de Concepción. Concepción. Chile.

Reyes, M. and Saldaño, A. (1998a). Inteligencia Colectiva sobre Redes Telemáticas. Congreso Internacional de Informática Educativa. Memorias Académicas '98. Fundaustral. Buenos Aires. Argentina.

Reyes, M. and Saldaño, A. (1995). La Comunicación como Espacio y el Espacio para la Comunicación. Vinculación, Tecnología y Valores en Procesos Educativos. Seminario de

Ciencia y Tecnología.. Ministerio de Educación, Consejo de Rectores y Universidad Técnica Federico Santa María. Quilpué. Chile.

Reyes, M., Saldaño, A., Mendez, A. M. and Garay, V. (1995). Niveles de participación de los estudiantes en su autoaprendizaje, asistido por red computacional, en experiencias que se desarrollan actualmente en Chile. Informe Final de Proyecto de Investigación. Dirección General de Investigación. Universidad de Playa Ancha de Ciencias de la Educación. Valparaíso. Chile.

Reyes, M., Saldaño, A., Garay, V. and Mendez, A. M. (1997). Student Participation, Educational Network Assisted. Multimedia/Hypermedia and Telecomunications. World Conference on Educational Multimedia/Hypermedia. Volumen I. Association for the Advancement of Computing in Education. Calgary. USA.

Saldaño, A. (1989). Robótica Educativa. Unidad de Medios Educativos. Area de Computación. Universidad Metropolitana de Ciencias de la Educación. Santiago. Chile.

Vega, V. (1991). Robótica Educativa. Memoria para optar al título de Profesor de Física y Ciencias Naturales. Universidad Metropolitana de Ciencias de la Educación. Santiago.

BIOGRAPHIES

Antonio Saldaño is a professor at Universidad Metropolitana de Ciencias de la Educación. His formal education includes: Teacher of Mathematics and Physics, Universidad Católica de Chile, 1969; Diplôme d'Etudes Approfondies en Physique Mathématique, Université Pierre et Marie Curie. Paris,1976; and Docteur en Physique-Mathématique. Université Pierre et Marie Curie, Paris, 1997. His areas of research are educational informatics, educational robotics, education assisted by telematic net - edunetmatics, artificial intelligence in education, and educational technology. He has served as visiting professor in more than 20 national and international universities. He is currently co-ordinator of a Master in Educational Informatics at UMCE. He is the winner of the Pioneer in Educational Informatics award, Chile Siglo XXI.

Miguel Reyes is a professor at the Universidad de Playa Ancha de Ciencias de la Educacion in Valpariso Chile and Director of the Centre of Research of Media Education (CIME). His formal education includes Teacher of Philosophy (U. Catolica de Valpariso, 1972), Master in Educational Sciences (U. Catolica de Chile, 1977), and Doctor in Educational Sciences (U. Pontificia Salesiana, Rome, 1999). His areas of research are educational communications, media education, collaborative learning, education assisted on telematic nets, and emotional intelligence over networks. As Director of CIME he has led more than 15 research projects. He has developed educational models such as the Dialogical Model (1979), Men/computer axiological model of educator (1982), and edunetmatic (1994). He has been invited as an expert in the last year to more than 10 countries in Latin America and Europe.

European Schoolnet – bringing the world into the classroom

Jan Hylén
Executive Secretary, Committee of European Schoolnet, Ministry of Education and Science, SE-103 33 Stockholm, Sweden.
jan.hylen@education.ministry.se

Abstract: The paper will deal with the two most important challenges facing education today: the increasing globalisation and permeation of ICT of our society. To meet these two challenges eighteen Ministries of Education in Europe joined forces in 1997 to create a common Internet platform, called the European Schoolnet. The objectives were to find synergies between national initiatives, to promote the use of ICT in education and to facilitate co-operation between schools in Europe.

Now the time has come to ask not only what ICT can do for schools, but also what ICT does to schools? How does the influence of ICT on society change the role of the school and the teacher? Two scenarios will be outlined: 1. the diminishing school - a reduction of the schools and the role of the teacher and a growth in home schooling; 2. the expanding school - where the need for lifelong learning puts the school in the centre of the development and changes the role of the teacher to become a guide to learning in schools and companies.

To help to transform the second scenario into reality, the European Schoolnet must in the coming year focus its attention on four areas: collaboration, communities, content and commerce. These four "c's" and their implication for the development of the European Schoolnet and the European schools using the Internet will be further elaborated in the paper.

Keywords: Communications, innovation, networks, policy

1. INTRODUCTION

The information and communications technology (ICT) society emerging today is a change as great as the transition to an industrial society. It influences all areas in society, and we are in the very middle of this process. No one can know with certainty what central development routes will become apparent. Perhaps it is possible to compare the importance of ICT today with the role of electricity in industrial society. From being a knowledge area for technicians, ICT has now become an everyday tool in an ever-increasing number of areas.

This technology has already to a great extent invaded many work places, and now it is beginning to penetrate education and commerce, and soon in cars and homes as well.

The growth of the ICT society is characterised by three things:

Knowledge: The value of knowledge and competence is continuously increasing. "The knowledge society" is in many respects a reality. New jobs in working life put much higher demands on education than earlier.

The old division between white and blue-collar work is no longer relevant. Today, all citizens need knowledge and skills in general subjects such as reading and writing, mathematics, foreign languages and social studies.

Networks: Networks are becoming increasingly prominent as the central organisational structure in and ICT-rich society. This is impacting industry and working life, as well as other areas. For example, in public administration we can see "mergers" in combination with decentralised activities and partnerships.

In schools, the traditional industrial way of organising teaching confronts new challenges, which create a need for change and development of approaches to teaching. The ICT society does not lead to a situation where all young persons need to become programmers. However, it does mean that all persons need to be prepared and have the ICT competencies needed to reprogram themselves in a constantly evolving working life.

For the European economy to develop positively and new jobs to be created, flexibility on the labour market is important. This can be achieved if many, preferably all, have the ability to adjust and develop in order to confront the new challenges posed by a working life that is rapidly changing. This, in turn, imposes high demands on basic education, lifelong learning and self-confidence.

Essentially, the school is confronted by a number of new and much more difficult tasks than ever before. Pupils should acquire more knowledge and more advanced knowledge than before. They should be familiar with the emerging technologies. They should learn to work both independently and together with others. They should develop self-confidence and lay the foundations for lifelong learning.

2. THE EUROPEAN SCHOOLNET

Paramount among the many challenges facing education today is the need for schools to prepare young people for the emerging information society. This has been realised throughout the European educational sector. This understanding was also the background for the informal meeting of European Council of Education Ministers in March 1997, to endorse the initiative to set up a network of networks, comprised of national, regional and other Web-based schoolnets, as a framework for co-operation and mutual support, called the European Schoolnet.

The European Schoolnet (EUN) was given four main goals:

1. to facilitate collaboration between schools in Europe,
2. to offer a range of high quality educational content and teaching services representing a European added-value,
3. to provide opportunities for professional development for teachers, and
4. to enhance co-operation at a European level among national education authorities, universities and industry to develop ICT in schools.

The EUN is much more than a website. It is an online campus where all those concerned with education in Europe will find information, locate resources, and meet people in a comprehensive service for schools and colleges. It is a human network and not just a technical one.

Currently 20 Ministries of Education in Europe take part in this joint venture. It is a framework for collaboration between the Ministries. There are separate arrangements for editors responsible for content in the national networks and for those providing the technical infrastructure. There are networks for school managers, for subject matter teachers, and for innovative schools.

Every country in the EUN Consortium has nominated a national network on the Internet, and there are direct links to each of these from the European Schoolnet website. These "Partner Networks" also deliver content with an added European value. The national networks are responsible for the translation of many sections of the website into their own languages.

Through its multi-lingual website the European Schoolnet provides high quality tools, content, and services. These assist teachers and learners to work together and to benefit from the Europe-wide range of resources and contacts which ICT brings within reach for every school. At the same time, the development of ICT capability among teachers and learners is actively encouraged.

The EUN has a simple intuitive structure. The four main areas of the network's activity (resources, innovation, school collaboration, and teacher development) are easy to locate from any point of the site. Pages aimed at teachers and pupils provide links to relevant updated content each week. There are weekly updates of relevant news and information in 10 different languages as well as free electronic newsletters. The framework and tools needed to run an international school project can be found, enabling any teacher to undertake a project supported by ICT.

3. EUN WEBSITE

Although the website is still very much under construction, it is widely used and appreciated by schools. According to statistics available so far, the number of visitors and downloaded pages has increased by 7.5 times from the fall 1998 to the fall 1999. On the peak month so far, almost 880,000 pages were downloaded. The five countries using the EUN the most so far are Sweden, Italy, Spain, Denmark and the United Kingdom.

Four evaluations with a more qualitative approach have been launched. These include an overall evaluation of the EUN website, a technical evaluation of the platform, a user requirement evaluation by schools, and an in-depth interview of national networks. Both external and internal reviewers are used. An interim evaluation report from September 1999 points out challenges such as creating a coherent vision to develop bottom-up projects with the many partners. The report also notes that the initiative has a huge potential and holds many promises that still have to be exploited.

4. RESULTS

It is fair to say that the European Schoolnet initiative has been successful so far. Together with national initiatives in almost every European country to develop the use of ICT in education, the EUN has stimulated European collaboration and the enhanced and enriched the utilisation of ICT in schools.

As is very clearly shown from the massive introduction of ICT in education, schools always operate within a context. The school is always a part of and affected by the surrounding society. From time to time it is important to try to have a view on how this larger context in the more long term might effect the schools. The time has come to ask not only what ICT can do for schools, but also how does the influence of ICT on society change the role of the school and the teacher?

Two different scenarios will very briefly be outlined:

1. the diminishing school - a reduction of the schools and the role of the teacher and a growth in home schooling; and
2. the expanding school - where the need for lifelong learning puts the school in the centre of the development and changes the role of the teacher to become a guide to learning in schools.

Two factors are of importance. One is, of course, the rapid development in ICT and particularly better and faster connections to the Internet. Soon we will have high-speed connections or information highways both in our homes and in our workplaces. At least in Sweden this will be the case in a 5-7 year perspective as a result of massive governmental investments in the years to come.

The other factor is the probable raise in demand for education and training, both from individuals, companies and public administration, as a result from the new economy and society that is emerging. The need for lifelong learning is more and more evident.

Most probably both the demand and supply of what so far has been called "distance education" will grow rapidly - i.e., online courses, self-instructive teaching material, "edutainment", etc. The formal education system will find itself placed in a much more competitive situation than ever before. This challenge to the educational system can be handled in two ways:

Method 1: If the formal education system fails to meet the competition and adapt itself to the new situation, we might end up with much more of private supply and demand for education where both companies and families buy education on the Internet from the best and cheapest supplier, private or public, domestic or international. This is already happening to schools in some countries and in the higher education sector in many nations.

If more and more parents believe that on-line education at home is a better alternative than the formal school system, such a development would drastically change and reduce the role of the school. Even if the politicians try to keep the mandatory school, the formal education system would be reduced in importance in the eyes of parents and pupils, and soon also in the eyes of policy makers and teachers. It would be reduced to a second best alternative.

Method 2: On the other hand, if the education system manages to adapt accordingly and succeed in transforming itself to a centre for learning not only for students but also for companies, the opposite development could take place. The role of the school in the community could be that of a centre for lifelong learning.

For this to happen a lot of changes have to come about, also in the role of the teacher, but foremost in the philosophy and understanding of what a school is or could be. Policy makers, school managers and teachers must start to look at the school as a resource centre in the community where it is situated. Schools should start to work together with distance education suppliers and local companies, with local teachers as tutors and facilitators for learning. The policy makers should encourage schools to develop, to be prepared for a new era and to try to be pro-active instead of looking at themselves as victims in an immovable process.

So far many have talked about the changing role of the teacher in the "information age", but it is ample time to start thinking of the role of the policy makers and school managers in this new era. How can they promote and facilitate the necessary changes? What new ways of managing and perhaps also financing schools do we need? What role do we want the formal education system to have in our future society? Also more concrete questions, as how to recognise skills learned outside school, need to be raised. How should we monitor learning for students engaged in virtual schooling both in school and out of school? These are the kind of questions those of us who still believe that the formal education system could be a guarantee for quality and equity in learning also in the future must start to ask ourselves.

Of course these questions are the responsibility and privilege for every country to deal with in the way they believe is the best. But 20 of the European countries have chosen to work together within the framework of the European Schoolnet as one way to develop ICT in their national education systems. The European Schoolnet is not only a web service for schools, but also a framework for co-operation between ministries. Seminars on national ICT strategies, workshops and exchange of experiences between ministers and key players from each country are also an important parts of the EUN. Therefore also the EUN has to develop a strategy to deal with this coming situation.

5. NECESSARY CONDITIONS

What is needed in order to give a contribution to transformation of the second scenario into reality is to create services, frameworks for development on an individual level for the teacher and for schools, and possibilities to explore the opportunities for new ways of teaching and learning created by the rapid technological development. The European Schoolnet must in the coming year focus its attention on four areas: collaboration, content, communities and commerce. These four "c's" and their implications could be a first step in the right direction. They all constitute services that are best provided by public authorities and not commercial providers.

Collaboration - School collaboration have from the very start been an important part of EUN. Collaboration between pupils and teachers, in subject related or cross curricula projects, to learn from each other, to make use of each other strengths, to support the use of foreign languages. The EUN should continue to provide content and services which enables teachers with varying experiences to plan, launch and complete projects using ICT. The services should be as automated as much as possible, with users adding content themselves, like forums, partner-finding tools and publishing tools.

Content - Throughout Europe there are many networks and projects funded by national Ministries of Education and the EU Commission. The EUN should make it easy to locate the information and resources which these initiatives have produced. They should be free, relevant, of good quality, easily accessible and easy to find. A search engine should allow pupils and teachers to make multilingual searches across websites exclusively selected by the EUN partners for their relevant educational and cultural content.

Communities - Collaboration activities should be encouraged to develop into learning communities. They could involve individual teachers, schools, researchers and teacher trainers, and officials and policy makers. The most promising development would be teachers working together, developing their skills, their contacts with colleagues in their subject field or area of interest. Schools should be encouraged to form communities centred around local strategies for organisational and pedagogical development with ICT. Schools could work with teacher training institutions involving both teachers, teacher trainers, teacher students and researchers.

Commerce - The EUN could make a unique contribution by offering a possibility for teacher-to-teacher e-commerce, were products developed by teachers for teachers are marketed and sold. The focus should not be to earn big money, rather to stimulate teachers to exchange material they have already developed, to get recognition of the value of their work, but also to encourage them to explore the opportunities offered by ICT. Such a service could also function as a test pilot in e-commerce in the education sector for national agencies and ministries.

The role of the European Schoolnet could not only be to develop these services on a European level but also to stimulate and act as a test case for national developments. The ultimate value of the EUN lies in offering services and a framework to create added value to the national networks and to help them to establish the public school networks as a competitive alternative to commercial products. If this could be done within the four areas briefly outlined above, the European Schoolnet would continue to be a very valuable contribution to the development of the schools in Europe in the years to come.

BIOGRAPHY

Jan Hylén is currently the Executive Secretary for the Committee on European Schoolnet within the Swedish Ministry of Education and Science. He received his Bachelor of Arts from University of Stockholm 1984 in Political Science, Philosophy and Economics and his Ph.D. from University of Stockholm in 1991 in Political Science. In 1986-87 Jan Hylén acted as secretary to the Nordic UNESCO Commissions in their evaluation of Minespol UNESCO research policy conferences. Dr Hylén was the head of the Research Department of the National Agency for Education in Sweden until 1995. The National Agency for Education is responsible for supervising and evaluating the Swedish school system. During1995-1998 he served as special advisor to the Minister of Schools and Adult Education.

Institutional perspectives for online learning: Policy and return-on-investment

Jef Moonen
Faculty of Educational Science and Technology, University of Twente, P.O. Box 217, 7500 AE Enschede, The Netherlands.
Moonen@edte.utwente.nl

Abstract: An analysis will be presented about why, at the institutional level and in particular at the university level, online learning is being introduced. This will be done in the context of a general design approach to steer innovation in education. Costs and financial-benefit issues will be explored, including costing models, measurement of productivity increases and return-on-investment. Although the article focuses on the university context, it can be predicted that similar issues will soon confront secondary schools.

Keywords: Costing, distance learning, flexible learning, management

1. INTRODUCTION

Most Western universities are currently introducing online learning facilities, primarily via use of Web-functionalities. When asked why, the most common answer is that they cannot *not* do it, as everybody else is doing it. Although specifics of their particular situations influence their decision making, a common reason seems to be not to loose (distance learning) students as those students' expectations include having online facilities. In addition most universities want to open new markets for (distance learning) students who did not consider taking courses before. Thus, economic reasons are a prime reason for the introduction of online learning. In addition quality and efficiency reasons are mentioned as well, although there is a general understanding that there is a long way to go before this improvement will show up. From a pure economic or return-on-investment (ROI) perspective, the equation still has to be worked out. It is generally agreed that investments in online learning are necessary. ROI will (hopefully) come later. However, decision makers balance project budgets with potential benefits. Instructors balance costs in terms of energy and time with possible payoff. ROI guides decision making even if the actors involved do not identify it as such.

2. INNOVATION AND DESIGN

Introducing an institution-wide online learning approach is an innovative activity as well as a (re)design of the teaching-learning environment.

There is a vast amount of literature about educational innovation and change. Major success factors in educational innovation and change processes are the positive involvement and support of the management of an institution, an already existing innovative culture within an institution and the fact that each innovation takes time in order to grow, find its anchors and flourish. Environmental pressures, technological and educational developments, institutional conditions, cost reduction/cost-effectiveness and support facilities are initiators for institutional change (Fisser, 1999).

Identifying change factors is one element of the change process. Influencing and controlling them are much more difficult issues. It is unlikely to expect that it is possible to handle all of the potential change issues at the same time. Construction of an implementation strategy with identifiable phases as well as an assessment of influential factors for each of the phases will improve the control and the understanding of the change process. Policy to support this implementation process is critical.

A perspective to understand a change process is to look at it from a design-oriented point of view. A design approach can focus on the major results of the change activity: the new products (including new kinds of learning and instructional material) and the new instructional and learning processes. Design is a very generic process. A design activity can be described referring to three so-called *activity spaces*: (a) the consensus space, (b) the task space, and (c) the implementation space (Moonen, 2000a). In the consensus space stakeholders negotiate the specifications of what has to be designed. The context, history, culture and what is already available as experiences and as products and processes, are determining factors. As soon as a consensus is reached and global specifications are agreed upon, these specifications form the starting point for the development of the products and processes in the task space. According to what has to be developed and the available expertise, particular methods will be used. The result of the activities in the task space will be products and processes, preferably in a format that can be further adapted in the implementation space. The adaptable products and processes will then be implemented in a real situation taking into account particular specifics determined by its implementation context.

A major aspect in such an approach is to determine the major stakeholders in each space, as well as the crucial decision makers and their criteria. In the following section, we focus upon crucial decisions in the consensus stage.

3. FACTORS TO STIMULATE THE INTRODUCTION OF ONLINE LEARNING

The introduction of online learning has been happening for more than a decade, most often on the basis of an individual decision made by a faculty member. Now online learning is becoming more popular, especially within the management of university institutions. In a detailed analysis three kind of reasons, with a different emphasis, can be extracted (Collis & Moonen, 2000): (a) not to loose students (economic argument), (b) improve the quality of the instructional environment (quality argument) and (c) improve the efficiency of the institutional environment (efficiency argument). The emphasis on each of these reasons is different with respect to the function of the person interviewed. Managers of institutions emphasise the economic argument, while instructors and students emphasise the quality argument. All actors in the online learning situation (including the students) are interested in the efficiency argument: managers for improving the financial basis of the institutions, instructors for reducing their workload and students for reducing their throughput time.

The main criterion of success will be the eventual incentive for the actor involved. For an institution the incentive will be (at least) a stabilisation and preferably an improvement of the financial basis. The incentive for the average instructor to be fully engaged will be a confirmation and strengthening of his faculty position, a potential reduction of the workload and an improved quality of his tasks. The student will expect improved quality of the teaching-learning process and efficiency gains in terms of flexibility in time and place. Each of the main actors wants the incentive to be tangible. The instructors and students want it in a short time, the institution will accept a longer-term perspective.

A discussion about the introduction of online learning should take into account a number of dimensions: (a) the 'spaces' in the design activity, (b) the decision-making arguments and criteria and (c) the main categories of actors. Each dimension has a number of components. There are three design spaces: consensus space, task space and implementation space. There are three main arguments: economic argument, quality argument and efficiency argument. Finally, there are (at least) three actors: institution, instructors and students. Thus, a 3x3x3 matrix constitutes the framework for our analysis. In this framework each combination of components should be analysed in terms of actions to improve the introduction and use of online learning (the design component), be related to the potential incentives (the argument component), for each category of actors (the actors component).

To simplify such an analysis, one can argue that the major involvement of the different actors will each be concentrated. The influence of the institutional management will be maximised in the consensus space of the design process, when the decision about the introduction of online learning has to be made. The contribution of the instructors (and the instructional designers) will be maximised in the task space when the specifics of the materials and processes have to be determined and worked out into products. The involvement of the instructors and the students will be maximum in the implementation space as the products and processes produced have to be used in practice.

4. ACTIVITIES IN THE CONSENSUS SPACE

As the focus of this article is on the institutional perspective, we will discuss now main activities in the consensus space. Such activities concentrate around discussions among the decision makers and result in a satisfactory answer to the 'why online learning?' question, in criteria to eventually measure its successful implementation and in functional specifications about how to work out the necessary steps, processes and products.

Most institutions have a consensus and explicit statements about their overall vision and mission. Visions are, almost by definition, nicely phrased but at the same indicate the central commitment of an organisation. Mission statements are further worked out in a strategic plan. It is noticeable that, in particular in newly published strategic plans, institutions are giving explicit references to the use of new technologies in their educational approach. Examples are the Edith Cowan University (1998) and Southern Cross University (1999), both Australia.

But visions and strategic plans have to be worked out and specific objectives and criteria for the assessment thereof have to appear. As indicated before there are many issues for which explicit criteria and methods have to be formulated. As an example, a discussion document for the reshaping of the University of Western Sydney mentions explicitly objectives "to improve the quality of services and educational experiences" and "to provide these services in a co-ordinated and cost efficient way, building on all elements of best practice" (Reid, 1999).

5. COST AND FINANCIAL BENEFIT ISSUES

As most universities are (partly) funded on the basis of the number of students, universities are competing to maintain or enlarge their student enrolment. Most universities are organised according to a projected minimal number of students. When that number of students goes down each institution reacts, striving for stability, predictability and legitimacy, and in particular, institutional survival. In addition, in many Western countries governmental funding for universities is in a slow but steady decline. Finally in some countries, for example Japan, the university system expects the overall student enrolment to be reduced dramatically in the near future.

In that context universities are looking for new markets, in particular to attract student populations that were not focussing on or not able to attend university education before. The need for lifelong learning and retraining feeds this potential. The Hyogo University for Teacher Education (Japan) is expanding its regular program with distance education "in order to survive". The University of Twente, and in particular the Faculty of Educational Science and Technology, has introduced online learning through its innovative TeleTOP Web-based course-management system, making its regular program also available for part-time and distance learning students. And in Australia, with the exception of the so-called *sandstone* universities, most universities are introducing online learning to expand the student population.

Another new market for universities is that of foreign students. In the English speaking world (UK, USA, Australia) universities have been very active in this market segment. Perth's Curtin University grew 15,4 per cent from 1997 to 1998 in foreign students enrolment. Other countries, in Europe and Japan, are also discovering this market, thereby responding to the growing need in developing countries for an enhancement of their educational systems and further economic development (Jongbloed, Maassen, & Neuve, 1999).

Another reaction, particularly from smaller or less prestigious universities, is the formation of strategic alliances. The University of Twente has formed a strategic alliance with other European partners in what is called a consortium of 'Entrepreneurial Universities'. In the Kyoto area of Japan 35 universities have formed a joint committee in order to discuss how to strengthen their positions. Even prestigious American Universities such as

MIT, University of Berkeley, University of Stanford, University of British Columbia and 22 others promote their distance learning courses in a single online catalogue.

The basic issue of all of these activities is to enlarge the student population in order to balance budgets and avoid major restructuring, or even closing down institutions. More careful monitoring of spending and costs have become a very important issue. Explicit awareness about the cost of providing instruction at the university level is a well known issue in the university distance education sector (Rumble, 1998). Researchers and course designers are much less aware of explicit costs of specific courses. As many are now starting to provide dual or mixed mode facilities, the financial consequences are unexplored territory. An interesting study in this respect is presented by Taylor and White (1991). They describe the transition from single to mixed mode, starting from a distance learning situation. Their analysis shows that "cost controls are in the hands of the teaching institution which can vary costs by producing different standards of instructional materials, just as they can vary face-to-face teaching costs by altering the contact time". They conclude that "the crucial point is that mixed-mode teaching is not readily available on a cost-effective basis for non-distance education institutions". In a recent report about the costs of networked learning (Bacsich, Ash, Boniwell and Kaplan, 1999) the authors indicate that "the key comes from the earlier (and still ongoing) debates about finance and planning for ICT. It is for educators (not planners or finance staff) to imbue and enliven financial and planning tools with a modern educational viewpoint". Not only a careful cost analysis of the new situation is necessary, but also an adequate positioning of the expected details of such an analysis in the broader context of educational and managerial decision making.

In the past, print material was the most important carrier of the instructional message. This situation has dramatically changed over the last decade in two perspectives: (a) a broad range of information and communication technologies (ICT) are being used as carriers for the instructional messages and (b) teaching for students off-campus is no longer the unique task of distance learning institutions; many traditional universities now are providing on- as well as off-campus instructional and learning facilities. In The Netherlands the Minister of Education has announced that as regular institutions for higher education are increasingly dealing with providing distributed learning facilities using technology, the typical open and distance learning task of the Dutch Open University has to be reconsidered. At Edith Cowan University 11,000 students are full-time, while 9,000 students are part-time or external students. At Charles Sturt

University (Australia) two-thirds of their 27,000 students are distance education students.

A crucial question in this new situation, with (partially) on- and off-campus students, is if these two or three cohorts of students, in their instructional approach, should be dealt with separately or in a combined way. Many approaches are possible. At the Faculty of Educational Science and Technology of the University of Twente for instance, three cohorts of students (full-time and on-campus, part-time, and external) exist. The policy is to offer those students a free choice of the modality (on-campus and very active, on-campus during a limited number of fixed days, or off-campus) through which they want to follow the courses.

Whatever the organisational context in which online learning will be introduced, the need for a thorough insight in the costs of different delivery methods is growing. This requires some form of costing model.

6. COSTING MODELS

Many costing models have been developed in order to measure the costs of educational delivery in relation to the use of ICT (for example De Vries, 1999, Jewett and Young, 1998, Shepherd, 1999 and Bacsich, Ash, Boniwell and Kaplan, 1999). It is found that there is a significant difference between a strong rational for costing models and the applicability of such models in practice.

In addition, the cost issue is only one side of the story: the other side represents the benefits when using online learning. Measuring the benefits of using networked learning is an even more difficult task than measuring costs. Arguments about benefits relate to the discussion about the productivity paradox when introducing information technology in industry. This topic will be more explicitly discussed in the next section.

When making a decision about a major change in an organisation, such as the introduction of online learning, explicit criteria should be used to measure the likelihood of success. At the management level those criteria relate to the cost and the benefits, and in particular to the perspective of a positive return-on-investment. However it is seen that there are no realistic cost or benefit data available to back up such a decision (Moonen, 1999).

So the management will have to decide to go on with online learning mainly based on positive speculation. However, is there serious ground for such speculation?

7. PRODUCTIVITY

There has been a constant discussion in the corporate world about the productivity gains as a result of investments in ICT. One argument is that such gains are unclear, certainly when compared to other major changes in industrial activity such as the introduction of steam machines or electricity. This phenomena has been called the 'productivity paradox' (e.g. Brynjolfsson and Yang, 1996). Nevertheless, industry is still investing huge amounts of money incorporating ICT for appropriate functionalities. Economists came up with four explanations to explain this strange behaviour. The first points to a measurement problem. As computers are often being used to offer faster, more personal and more varied services; those advantages are not taken into account in the traditional data collection and statistical overviews. The second explanation is that in industry only a small percentage of the total operational budget is used to introduce ICT. As a consequence, often a critical mass to create a clearly visible productivity gain is not reached. A third explanation is the fact that each change needs a long incubation time before it will lead to a productive exploitation of the new situation. Finally, one has to acknowledge that many of the current applications probably only provide us with products that are in fact still a kind of interim development; the real breakthrough will only be realised when computers and applications really are adapted to the task for which one wants to use them.

However, at this moment the relationship between productivity gains and ICT investment in business seems to have become more obvious. Economists are reviewing their opinions. Probably aspects of each of the reasons given above contribute to that change op opinion. One explanation could relate to changes in measurement, in particular with respect to the costs and intangible advantages. In the new economy business spending on software is now being considered as an investment. Previously, it was considered as a cost.

Critical mass and incubation time are also related. The continuing investment in ICT advances the chance of having a critical mass of ICT investments. As PCs were introduced in the beginning of the 1980s, the incubation time is now 15-20 years. 15-20 years is also comparable to the time span for a new generation of employees to enter the workforce. This new generation has grown up with computers around them and is much more familiar with them then the previous generation. Finally, the computer and its software have escaped their previous image of (mainly incomprehensible) mainframe applications, as ICT is becoming more powerful almost each day, allowing substantial improvements in the area of the human-computer interface and user friendliness.

Developments in education follow, at a certain time distance, developments in society. Therefore ICT has been introduced in education as well. With respect to the impact of ICT on education, introducing ICT in education seems to follow the same pattern as the introduction of ICT in industry. Past and current results about productivity gains in education because of ICT are not that obvious (Moonen, 1994). On the other hand, governments all over the world continue to invest huge amounts of money into ICT in education. To explain this paradox for the educational sector the same four arguments used in industry can be used: measurement problems, lack of critical mass, long incubation time and finding the right applications. To begin the analogy, indeed there is a severe measurement problem in education, especially when new instructional approaches such as a constructivist approach, supported by ICT are introduced. Educators believe that by following such an approach higher cognitive skills and even metacognitive skills will be stimulated. However, how do we measure those skills? Current test techniques have difficulties dealing with such outcomes. One can also assume that many of the positive results of using ICT in education, for instance to be better prepared for the current society and a more competitive commercial world, only will show up after many years.

A second problem is the need for a critical mass. Certainly in education the critical mass problem relates to the technical infrastructure, but also to the human (teacher/instructor) infrastructure needed to teach about and integrate ICT in existing curricula. That critical mass for technical infrastructure is already there in many educational institutions, certainly in the Western world. However, the needed critical mass of well-trained and knowledgeable instructors is another matter. Many efforts in the teacher-training area may be the only solution, producing a new generation of teachers, educated in another era, familiar with using ICT as a common commodity. So the incubation time for the introduction and productive implementation of ICT in education probably also needs 10-15 years. The last of the four explanations relates to the kind of ICT applications. Until now, many of the ICT applications in education can be referred to as tutorial-type educational software or courseware. Courseware, however, is not popular in education, nor does the use of it improve student performance in a significant way (with the exception of certain drill-and-practice programs in certain situations). In addition, educational publishers are not eager to invest in the development and production of educational software as there is, so they claim, no real market for it. However, the Internet and the WWW are now creating a wealth of new application areas for ICT. Maybe this will create the momentum for educational ICT applications to escape from a still existing 'antiquated' paradigm about how to apply ICT for educational purposes.

In summary one could ask: “Is there a new economy in education?” (Moonen, 2000b). One could argue that as education is going through a comparable cycle as has happened in industry, a future prospect of productivity gains as a result of using ICT in education is a reasonable one. As in industry, there are two conditions in order to reach that point: (a) traditional measurement methods must adapt to the new technologically supported approaches so that potential gains can be made visible and measurable and (b) ICT has to find its productive niche, probably through applications that make adequate use of the Internet. In the next section, such a measurement method based on return on investment is examined.

8. RETURN ON INVESTMENT

What are the consequences of the reasoning in the previous section with respect to the activities in the consensus space of the 3-Space Design Strategy introduced in Section 2? A major item is to agree upon the major functional specifications of what has to be designed, in our case an online learning system for an educational institution. Another crucial part of the decision-making process in the consensus space is to decide upon the criteria that will eventually determine if the chosen strategy is successful. In Section 4 it was argued that the main criterion for the management of an educational institution with respect to a decision about change and investments will be related to the return-on-investment (ROI) ratio.

Return-on-investment is a well-known concept in the business world and is used for decision-making criteria within industrial and corporate activities. However ROI is often used as a criterion for decision making in training situations (Shepherd, 1999), it is not common as an explicit concept in education, although there are some indications of a renewed interest (Gustafson and Watkins, 1998).

Conceptually, ROI is very simple. In order to measure the ROI of an activity one has to compute the benefits of the activity and compare (by dividing or subtracting) them by the costs. Both aspects have to be expressed in monetary terms in classic ROI. The simplicity of the concept immediately disappears however, as soon as one want to calculate both items. As has been argued in Section 6, benefits or results in education are not so easy to measure. Education is intended to result in benefits, but often benefits will be hidden, implicit or only show up after a long time. But even when the benefits are explicit and overt, it is often difficult to transform them into a number let alone converting that number into a monetary value. A comparable problem arises when calculating the costs. Although there are many items of which the cost can immediately be expressed in monetary terms, there also many other costs which have to be accounted for, in particular costs which are hidden or not explicitly available, such as the frustration costs of an instructor when working with crashing technology or the huge amount of extra time an instructor has to put into answering continuously incoming e-mail from students. In addition, arguments about the calculation of a ROI are only relevant after a change has been introduced and data about how the change is evolving become available. Using costs and benefits as a criterion at the start of the decision-making, when no reliable data are available at all, is a much more difficult issue.

There are a number of ways to deal with these problems. First of all one has to agree that collecting *exact* costs and benefits data at the start of a process is impossible. An alternative is to rely on data of comparable situations. However, comparable situations can only give global indications. Such data can be used as estimates, maybe even weighted by a certain probability, and put in the ROI equation. Manipulating the entries of the data and probabilities offers an output for decision support. A major issue in order to be able to carry out this process is that for the costs as well as for the benefits the relevant items have to be identified, estimated and put in the ROI equation. When a complete set of data for comparable situations are not available, another way to solve the ROI in education problem is to abandon the idea of a ROI calculation in a 'absolute' way, and concentrate on a more intuitive calculation that emphasises the relative comparison of ROI in one situation with another situation. We call this a simplified ROI.

9. SIMPLIFIED ROI

A simplified ROI approach is to replace the 'absolute' ROI calculation with a more 'relative' or 'simplified' ROI calculation. To reduce the complexity of the data gathering and calculation, a simplified ROI only takes those (positive and negative) items into account that are substantially different in a traditional versus a new situation. The result of the calculation gives an indication of the 'gain' in ROI if a situation is changed from A to B. It is not the absolute ROI of an educational approach that is being calculated, but how much positive (or negative) change in ROI will occur when changing situation A to B. This change can be expressed intuitively when concrete data are not available. A first and major task is to identify these 'substantially' different items. As such identification is dependent upon a specific situation, the example given in the following subsections can only be worked out in a generic way and should be interpreted as only an hypothetical example.

9.1 Cost issues in a simplified ROI

When introducing ICT in a teaching-learning situation, major tangible differences in cost items when compared with a traditional situation will be: (a) additional specialised personnel; (b) acquiring and depreciation of hard- and software; (c) new physical facilities; and (d) the production, distribution and maintenance costs of digital learning material.

Besides such tangible costs, other more implicit, hidden, or intangible costs will occur such as: (e) necessary training for staff to be able to handle the ICT; (f) time spent by teaching and help-desk staff accommodating the requests for online help and communication by students; (g) hidden and intangible non-monetary costs such as the frustration of students and teaching staff as a result of malfunctioning of the technology and the time spend to identify the problem and repair it; (h) opportunity costs, relating to the time that staff spend on technology which they could have spent on other things; and so on. Again this list is only meant as an example. In a specific situation much care is necessary to identify those items that really make a difference.

9.2 Benefit issues in a simplified ROI

A comparable approach can be worked out with respect to the benefits, whereby one should concentrate on those benefits that are potentially different in a situation with and without the use of ICT. Such a list could be based upon the literature about the effects of ICT and media. The most commonly expected benefit in addition to maintaining or increasing the number of students will be in the area of (a) performance. However, many research reports about the effects on performance when using ICT in education indicate that there is no significant improvement of the performance of students (Russell, 1999). Other potential benefits such as (b) attitude; (c) motivation, (d) completion and dropout rates and (e) throughput time are more likely to be positively related to IT use.

Besides the tangible effects mentioned, one can also think about a number of intangible benefits such as: (f) flexibility; (g) time-place independence; (h) communication facilities; (i) marketing value; (j) impact of working with ICT on future professional career, and so on. This list of benefit items is also only meant as an example. In a specific situation much care is necessary to identify those items that really make a difference.

9.3 Simplified ROI matrix

After identifying cost and benefit items that are substantially different in an ICT-based situation versus an traditional situation, a calculation method has to be used in order to come up with some numbers that can be interpreted. What is considered as a 'substantial difference' will have to be defined by the user of the method. In addition a measurement method will have to be designed in order to quantify the substantial differences.

A first issue to deal with, also with reference to the analysis proposal in Section 3, is that a simplified ROI calculation should distinguish between the different arguments (economic, quality and efficiency) and between the different actors (institution, instructor, student). Another issue is to distinguish between tangible (or easily measurable) costs and benefits, and intangible or hidden (and difficult to measure) costs and benefits. For the measurable items, one could use monetary data (if available) indicating the difference in costs and benefits when moving from situation A to situation B. For items that cannot be measured precisely, one can use estimates on a scale (+5 to –5) indicating the 'expected' differences in costs and benefits when moving from situation A to situation B. Similarly, for intangible costs and benefits relating to quality and efficiency, this sort of predictive and relative assessment can be elicited from the user. The purpose of the activity is not to calculate a specific metric, as such a calculation is not possible or feasible, but rather to give the decision maker a easy-to-use type of metric to increase systematic awareness of important factors related to return on investment.

9.4 Some examples

Assume that in an institution the management considers moving from a traditional learning-teaching situation (regular lectures + computer laboratories) towards a situation whereby each instructor and each student will instead of being provided with the use of a computer laboratory will be provided with a portable computer, to be used at home and at the institution. In both home and institution, connection to the university network will be available. In addition the number of lectures will be reduced to a minimum and activities will mainly be focussed on online learning activities.

In order to support decision making about this approach the management can make a simplified ROI calculation. According to the suggestion in Section 3, such a calculation could be split up with respect to the different design spaces (consensus space, task space and implementation space), as the costs and benefits in each of the spaces will be different. Eventually however, the combination of the results of activities in those spaces is of major importance.

Tables 1 and 2 illustrate some of the results of such a calculation. For each of the possibilities only a limited number of items is chosen as an illustration.

Table 1. Economic arguments, simplified ROI (in units of US$ 1,000)

Actors:	**Institution**		**Instructor**		**Student**	
Items:	Costs	Benefits	Costs	Benefits	Costs	Benefits
Extra hard- and software	+110	-	-	+5	-	+50
Reduction in hard- and software	-	+20	-	-	-	-
Completion and dropout	-	+12	-	-	-	-
Total	+110	+32	-	+5	-	+50
ROI (benefits–costs)	-68		+5		+50	

9.4.1 Assumptions in this example

- The institution is providing the hard- and software equipment out of its own funds and that the calculation is being made for the period of one academic year, involving 100 first-year students and 10 instructors.
- A laptop computer costs US$ 1,000. Thus the costs for extra hardware are US$ 110,000.
- The institution will not have to replace their 40 old desktop computers (at US$500 per computer): a benefit of US$ 20,000.
- Benefits for instructors (who do not have to buy a new desktop computer) equal US$ 5,000.
- Benefits for students equal US$ 50,000.
- In the new situation the completion rate will raise and at the same time the dropout rate will go down. As a consequence 10% more students are predicted to enter their second year than before.
- The institution is paid by the university according to the numbers of students in each year. Further assume that on the average 60 out of 100 first students graduate to the second year, which now will increase with 6 students. When the university pays the institution US$2,000 per student, the new situation creates a benefit of US$ 12,000.

9.4.2 Comments

Although the arguments in this paper focus on the institutional actor, data for other actors (instructor and student) are included in Table 1 as well. This makes the table more interesting as it shows that a negative ROI for one actor can be complimented, as is shown in this example, by a positive ROI for other actors. This can be useful information for the decision-making process. It is clear that identifying the major differences causing costs and benefits but also allocating them among the three actors are the major challenge in the simplified ROI calculation. In that perspective the simplified ROI calculation can be interpreted as a decision-support tool for the management.

Table 2. Economic argument, simplified ROI (intangible costs and benefits items)

Actors:	**Institution**		**Instructor**		**Student**	
Items:	Costs	Benefits	Costs	Benefits	Costs	Benefits
Potential growth in enrolment	-	+2	+1	-	-	-
Marketing value	-	+3	-	+1	-	+1
Extra time needed because of malfunc-tioning of systems	-	-	+2	-	+1	-
Total	-	+5	+3	+1	+1	+1
ROI (benefits–costs)	+5		-2		0	

9.4.3 Assumptions

- Values in table 2 are chosen on the basis of an estimate of a positive (benefit) or negative (cost) impression or expectation, based upon a scale from +5 to –5.
- Giving for free a portable computer to students will attract more students and raise the enrolment. The incentive therefore is positive and the (subjective) evaluation on the scale for the institution is +2. However a larger enrolment will result in a larger effort and larger classes by the instructors. For them this item will result in a negative incentive, further estimated with a cost of +1.
- The 'free' portable computer will certainly positively contribute to the general image of the institution and is therefore an important marketing instrument. The incentive is estimated positively (as a benefit) at +2. In the long term working at a highly appreciated institute will contribute to the 'personal value' of the instructors as

well as to the 'value' of the diploma of the students. Both are values as positive (benefit) with a scale value of +1.

- The new hardware and systems will certainly create extra malfunctions, leading to frustration and investment of extra time by instructors and students. Both are evaluated as negative (costs) with a scale value of +2 respectively +1.

9.4.4 Comments

Of course each of the scale values are subjective and therefore open to debate. This debate can be a benefit in an institution. Also, by quantifying the costs and the benefits of the items mentioned, it becomes necessary to form an opinion about these issues. Furthermore and because of the splitting of the different actors, it becomes visible who is getting a positive ROI and vice versa. So in Table 2 it is clear that the institute gets a very positive ROI out of what is been proposed while the instructors seem to pay the bill. This is certainly an interesting issue in discussions about the proposed policy change, but also an interesting issue to compare with the results in Table 1.

Comparable tables can be set up for dealing with items related to the quality and efficiency issues. In those cases and given the difficulty (even impossibility) to convert results of those issues into monetary values, the use of a scale as in Table 2 is an appropriate approach. A crucial issue when trying to combine values within a table, but certainly across tables, is the implicit assumption that all of the items have an equal weight in the decision-making. Of course this is not the case. The simple solution then is to give a weight to each of the items involved.

In practice, the tables mentioned above can be set up using a spreadsheet program. Items in the different tables could be listed in pull-down menus to be chosen by the executor of the simplified ROI approach. And databases with known practical results can be made available to help the user to make a justifiable guess about the scale values he wants to use. All of this can be combined into a software program. Such a program will be developed in the near future at the University of Twente.

10. CONCLUSIONS

Colleges, universities, regions, governmental agencies and private foundations are making large investments in instructional technologies on the assumption that technology will somehow lead to improvements in educational quality and an eventual reduction in costs through greater efficiency. Although there are no concrete data available (yet) to prove this assumption, the likelihood of this claim is certainly realistic. However, efforts should be made in order to move from the potential to the reality, for instance by calculating the return-on-investment (ROI).

Calculating ROI, however, is a complex matter leading to major objections for its use in practice. A potential solution is to reduce the complexity by using a kind of simplified ROI whereby the focus is on those items that differ significantly in a new situation, using ICT, versus the traditional situation. In a simplified ROI, an intuitive and predictive approach is used, supported by a software tool to suggest options. Major benefits of the simplified ROI approach will be the discussion and debate it triggers and the awareness it stimulates among those involved in policy making for an educational institution.

REFERENCES

Bacsich, P., Ash, N., Boniwell, C. and Kaplan, A. (1999) *The costs of networked learning*, Internal report. Sheffield, UK: Sheffield Hallam University.

Bates, A. (2000) *Managing technological change*, San Francisco: Jossey Bass.

Brynjolfsson, E., and Yang, S. (1996) *Information technology and productivity: A review of the literature*, Advances in computers, 43, p. 179-214. Also [http://ccs.mit.edu/erik/itp/index.html]

Business, 2.0 (2000, March) *The 10 driving principles of the new economy*, Special section of the magazine Business 2.0, p. 193-284.

Collis, B, and Moonen, J. (2000) *Report of the study trip (September-December 1999)*. Internal document. Enschede: University of Twente, Faculty of Educational Science and Technology [http://users.edte.utwente.nl/collis/StudyTrip/home.htm]

Edith Cowan University. (1998) *The Edith Cowan University Strategic Plan 1998-2002*, Perth, Australia: Edith Cowan University

Fisser, P. (1999) *Theoretical framework*, Internal document. Enschede: University of Twente, Faculty of Educational Science and Technology.

Gustafson, K. and Watkins, K. (Eds.) (1998) *Return on investment (ROI): An idea whose time has come again?* Educational Technology, 38(4), p. 5-6.

Jewett, F., and Young, F. (1998) *Evaluating the benefits and costs of mediated instruction and distributed learning*, [http://www.calstate.edu/special projects/mediated instr/]

Jongbloed, B., Maassen, P., and Neave, G. (Eds.) (1999) *From the eye of the storm. Higher education's changing institution*, Amsterdam: Kluwer Academic Publishers

Moonen, J. (1994) *How to do more with less*, in S. Wills and C. McNaught (Eds.), Interactive multimedia in university education: Designing for change in teaching & learning. Amsterdam: Elsevier

Moonen, J. (1997) *The efficiency of telelearning*, Journal of Asynchronous Learning, [http://www.aln.org/alnweb/journal/issue2/moonen.htm]

Moonen, J. (1998) *Potential of MESH technology for high-quality and flexible tele-collaboration*, MESH project. Enschede: University of Twente, Faculty of Educational Science and Technology.

Moonen, J. (1999) *Cost, efficiency and effectiveness of ICT in higher education,* in Collis, B.A. and M.C. van der Wende (eds.). The use of information and communication technologies in higher education: An international orientation on trends and issues. Enschede, The Netherlands: University of Twente, CHEPS. Also [http//education2.edte.utwente.nl/ictho.nsf/framesform]

Moonen, J. (2000a) *A three-space design strategy for digital learning material,* Educational Technology, 40(2), 26-32.

Moonen, J. (2000b, 28 January) *Is there a new economy in education?* Presentation at the Idylle conference, University of Twente. [http://www.oc.utwente.nl/oc/i3conference]

NCHEMS (2000). *Technology Costing Methodology,* [http://www.wiche.edu/telecom/projects/icm/index.htm]

Reid, J. (1999) *The shape of the future. A structure for UWS in the 21st century,* Internal document. University of Western Sydney. [http://www.uws.edu.au/html/future.html]

Rower, J. (1999, 22 November) *The numbers game,* Fortune, p. 263-266.

Rumble, G. (1998) *The costs and economics of open and distance learning,* London: Kogan Page.

Russells, T. (1999) *The no significant difference phenomenon,* North Carolina State University.

Shepherd, C. (1999) *Three roads to cost-effectiveness or ... how to have your cake and eat it,* [http:/www.fastrak-consulting.co.uk/tactix/features/roads/roads.html]

Southern Cross University. (1999) *Online Learning Strategic Plan,* Internal document. Lismore: Southern Cross University, p.17.

Taylor, T. and White, V. (1991) *The evaluation of the cost effectiveness of multi-media mixed-mode teaching and learning,* Australian Government Publishing Service, GPO Box 84, Canberra ACT 2601, p.36.

Vries, P. (Ed.) (1999) *Telelearn. Costing issues in flexible and distance learning,* Hertogenbosch, The Netherlands: CINOP. [http://www.ellinet.org/telelearn/default.html]

BIOGRAPHY

Jef Moonen is a pioneer in the design and development of educational computing resources. He is frequently called upon to advise decision makers in strategic choices relating to technology use in educational institutions. Cost-benefit assessment is one of his major areas of expertise. He is Professor of Educational Instrumentation in the Faculty of Educational Science and Technology, University of Twente in The Netherlands. Previously he was Director of the National Centre for Educational Computing in the same country [http://users.edte.utwente.nl/moonen/]

Exquisite complexity

Rethinking the learning process and the learning environment in the Information Age

Gail Marshall

Gail Marshall & Associates, 2393 Broadmont Ct., Chesterfield, MO 63017 USA.
74055.652@Compuserve.com

Abstract: Schools are based on organisational patterns and on beliefs about how learning occurs. Both are grounded in a community's social, economic, political and cultural values. As the School of the Future is planned attention must be paid to the powerful influences exerted by those values. Sharing plans, examining practices, and discussing policies within and across communities will be important as School of the Future advocates begin their reform efforts.

Key words: Curriculum development, politics, economics, culture

"Oh what a tangled web we weave." Wm. Shakespeare

1. INTRODUCTION

Schools are defined by organisational patterns and by beliefs about how learning occurs. Those patterns and beliefs are rooted in social, economic, political and cultural values, a mix that provides 'exquisite complexity' when it comes to designing, implementing and institutionalising the School of the Future. Different values, held at different times by different countries, have resulted in different models of schooling. Some types, the academy and the trade school/vocational school for example, have persisted because they continue to serve felt needs, while other models have left few traces, in part because their values and practices were not continually viewed as consonant with social, political, economic, or cultural values. So the School of the

Future must confront those complex social, economic, political and cultural forces.

This paper is based on the following points of view:

1. We can only go forward by looking backward, by reviewing different organisational patterns and different theories of how learning occurs, and by examining the social, economic, political and cultural factors operating to support or oppose patterns and theories;

2. We should think about Schools of the Future and not The School of the Future given the differences in social, political, economic and cultural patterns in different countries. Schools of the Future will probably be based on several different models, each created in the crucible of a country's conflicting and competing goals, existing resources and general climate for acceptance of change.

3. Conditions in some countries may perpetuate existing models, while in other countries existing patterns may be broken by internal or external forces. The specifics in this paper are American. While many other countries have different histories for their educational system and so will have different issues to deal with in envisioning schooling, the ubiquity of the "factory" model in many countries and the perceived need to be competitive economically will yield conflicts and challenges similar to those experienced by American educators.

Technology has often been treated as an innovation and so sociological approaches, looking at how and why technology has not been adopted, have been at the forefront of many discussions. While this approach may elucidate some problems it is also important to view technology within the framework of a learning community and focus on the organisation and conceptualisation of learning, so beliefs about how learning occurs and is assessed, and how learning is organised within schools should be addressed when we discuss Schools of the Future.

2. ORGANISATIONAL PATTERNS OF SCHOOLING

Discussions of Schools of the Future must be based on ways of delivering content and process to large numbers of children and adults if the challenges of the future are to be met in each country. But since the Industrial Revolution school has been viewed as an instrument of social control where students are taught prescribed social mores.

> Mass schooling was in the first place set up and paid for by societies to see that cultural imperatives, and especially knowledge, skills and forms of behavior demanded by the Industrial Revolution, were transmitted and that certain characteristics such as social strata, were constantly reproduced and renewed (Owen, 1985).

Prior to the Industrial Revolution many schools in America were not compulsory, locally based and grounded in religious values. They emphasised the canon of western thought. Students were judged by the quality of their thinking and reasoning; other schools aimed to produce workers skilled in crafts or specialised skills and, again, the emphasis was on the quality of students' work.

But the Industrial Revolution, with its need to organise and control workers, led to significant social, economic, political and cultural changes, not only in the way work was produced but also in the way other social agencies were organised. The factory system, suiting the needs of employers, was designed for the production of materials quickly and cheaply, and was adopted in classrooms as well as in factories because, according to Ure (1835), the benefits of the Industrial Revolution are derived less from mechanisation and more from the social control of those who stood at the machines. Ure and other social commentators saw that such a system of control and standardisation must occur across society and not just on the factory floor. Frederick Taylor's strategies for improving efficiency — centralised control of manufacture, breaking down the process into discrete steps, separating concepts (the role of management) from execution (the role of the worker), and standardising the process — began to serve as a model for delivering learning.

Callahan (1962) points out that Taylor's efficiency movement was adopted by American schools in the early 1900's as waves of immigrants arrived and threatened to flood the marketplace with cheap labour. Since the early 1900's the factory model has become a "template" for Americans of how schools should be organised and how learning should be delivered, both for "academic" studies and for "vocational" studies.

As a result what is to be learned was broken down into short segments, teacher directed learning was emphasised over the imperative for students to read and synthesise on their own and assessment by means of short answer quizzes instead of essays became the norm in American schools, educational procedures fostered by the growth of behaviourist psychology. The model has since been adopted in other countries and, with the growth of the World Wide Web (WWW) and the globalisation of educational publishing promises to become an Internet norm.

In contrast to the factory model John Dewey and others proposed a "community" model, which emphasised personal and social development within school and viewed the work place as offering more than factory based jobs. The model, rooted in a psychology of learning and thinking that is fundamentally opposed to behaviourism, has been tried in different ways over the last century but has never replaced the factory model.

In the late 1950's a new method of organisation, the school as "shopping mall" (Powell, Farrar & Cohen, 1985), and a new approach to learning, enquiry across a wide range of topics, gained currency because of social, economic and political factors operating at that time. School was viewed as a place to keep students from flooding the workforce and, since students rebelled against traditional schooling and many subjects were viewed as irrelevant, courses outside traditional curricula were offered. Students were encouraged to set their own goals for what they learned and how they learned. Teaching and learning theory was basically instrumentalist, whatever was thought to work was tried even though many approaches seemed to have no theoretical basis.

But, over time, the majority of the models of schooling emphasise "tightly bound" course content, i.e., traditional curricular subject matter presented via textbooks. Content is taught with teachers lecturing and students listening during 45 - 60 minute time blocks.

Now, in the late 1990's, "wired" versions of schooling are being devised. Online courses, offered primarily but not exclusively to fulfil work preparation goals, are becoming more frequent. Some are based on the factory model of moving students quickly through courseware; others are a form of web-based school as shopping mall, where students construct their own course schedule. Table 1 shows several different types of schools and their essential features.

Some "wired" school models attempt to replicate the community model by explicitly building in assignments that call for student-to-student collaboration. Other 'wired' school models are based on the factory system, delivering discrete bits of material and testing via short answer quizzes while ensuring the isolation of each student from the others who are working on the same materials.

When economic conditions call for rapid training of large numbers of students, it is difficult to resist adopting the behaviourist/factory model but if economic forces pull away from the model of tightly bound schools in order to emphasise collaboration and divergent thinking, it may be difficult for the public at large to accept loosely bound schooling.

When computers were first introduced into schools, some educators believed that the very nature of computing would change schools, i.e., providing for individualised work, automating routine tasks, enabling teachers to introduce new topics or teach old topics in new ways. Instead, Becker (1983; 1986) and others have found that schools, especially secondary schools, have shaped computer use to fit existing organisational patterns and prevailing belief systems about learning. Most American high schools continue to work with tightly bound courses based on textbook topics, teacher dominated instruction and short quizzes.

Table 1. Types of school organisation

Type of school	Organisational/learning features
Academy/dame school	Individual or small group settings; mix of age and ability groups; curriculum emphasises religious values and/or mastery of the "canon"; reading, recitation and repetition; written and oral presentations for qualitative and quantitative grading;some collaborative work arrangements but most situations are 'tracked' and competitive.
Factory type schools	Large groupings; grouping by age; tracking by ability level; curriculum emphasises reading, writing and arithmetic, with "lower ability" students often tracked into low skill vocationally oriented courses; competitive; reading, repetition, some recitation; worksheets and standardised exams emphasis on quantitative grading.
Vocational school	De-emphasises "academic" subjects and either presents a range of skills needed for entry into the labour force or teaches sets of highly specialised skills in an apprentice-type program; manual dexterity emphasised over mastery of traditional subjects such as reading and writing; assessment tends to be performance based; group instruction with some time for individual work/ consultation; competitive.
Community school	Mix of ages and ability groups; curriculum emphasises personal and social development; collaboration emphasised over competition; project method often used in teaching/learning situations and as a basis for qualitative assessment of students.
Wired school	A wide range of options currently available—factory model, community model, vocational model and shopping mall model; each model may replicate itself completely on the WWW; organisation into discrete classes or options for widely distributed sources of information, collaboration and dissemination; quantitative and qualitative assessment.

The economics of information delivery over distances may lead to many different types of course offerings but the politics of centralisation and standardisation may mitigate against more complex types of courses being supported by government. At the same time, some social forces may call for conformity in curriculum while other social forces, like those of the 1960's, may demand a diverse set of options, which may be opposed by segments of the community on cultural or religious grounds.

Similarly, the economics of delivery and certification mean that some courses will be designed so that students acquire specific information delivered in a step by step fashion and the economics of grading will call for short answers to multiple choice or fill in the blanks type questions as a means of certification; on the other hand, the almost inexhaustible resources of the World Wide Web offer many course developers the opportunity to pose novel and challenging problems, the answers to which require significant time to assess and the implications of which diminish rather than support social conformity. What this bodes as the global village shrinks, competition for resources rises and demands for a highly skilled work force increase is interesting to contemplate. Surely many countries will adopt wired school procedures consistent with their own successful past practices in non technology settings without examining the implications of such decisions.

Question #1. How does each of the organisational models provide a framework which best achieves a country's goals for technology?

Question #2. Which model most accurately reflects one or another country's prevailing social, economic, cultural, political and religious forces currently prevailing?

Question #3. How does a country alter its prevailing models of schooling to accommodate to technology's contributions?

Question #4. How do the belief systems about learning in each country — especially with regard to discrete vs. systems approaches — affect goals for learning about technology and learning with technology?

Question #5. Which set of beliefs is consonant with each country's goals and objectives for schools or initiatives for technology and implications for change efforts?

3. SCHOOLS' ATTEMPTS TO MOVE TOWARD THE FUTURE

Over the last twenty-five years many large and medium scale initiatives for using technology to change what is taught and how it is taught have been implemented. Some of those efforts were evaluated, some were not but we can glean some ideas about the problems the initiators faced through both print and anecdotal records.

The IBM Model Schools Project, 1983 - 1984, was based in the 24 largest school districts (mostly urban districts) of America. The project was designed to encourage the use of tool software across a wide range of school subjects. At least one high school per district participated.

Within and across districts several interesting and exciting applications were developed by teachers. For example, one secondary school science teacher created a database of the periodic table for his students to analyse, add to and study from. The database stimulated interest in the topic and seemed to aid students' learning since the use of the database was viewed by students as an aid to study and as an organisational principle for information acquisition and retrieval. In another school the entire staffing of English classes was changed to allow one teacher, skilled in 'process' writing, to model teaching strategies in tandem with other English teachers. As a result, the entire secondary school began to emphasise writing in all subject areas. Neither application/innovation was adopted by other secondary schools in the district, and few of the individual and interesting applications of technology developed by other teachers survive, in part because many of the districts at the same time adopted Instructional Management System software programs that were viewed as the districts' preferred technology solution. Hadley and Sheingold, who interacted with Model Schools Project members during meetings at Bank Street College, make interesting observations on some of the teachers in the project that they followed over time (Hadley & Sheingold, 1993) but the evidence shows that the project did little to shift American teachers away from drill and toward the use of more open ended educational activities.

The Apple Classroom of Tomorrow (ACOT) project (Dwyer, Ringstaff & Sandholz, 1991) was another attempt to create a nation-wide laboratory for developing and implementing technology based learning experiences. While the evidence shows that some participating teachers did make changes in what they taught and how they taught, the larger school in which each ACOT classroom was located seldom adopted the changes, and the project's effects, both in terms of teacher behaviour and student learning, have not spread very far beyond the confines of the immediate ACOT classrooms because of the deeply held beliefs about classroom management and learning theory.

The JASON Project (OTA, 1989) was designed to explore the ocean floor and promote data analysis and evaluation activities between members of the science community and the school community. The wealth of data is stimulating some contacts but analysis and evaluation is limited to a small group of students and calls for collaboration that current organisational patterns and belief systems about what is to be learned and how it is to be learned cannot support.

A major state-wide project, Nebraska's plan to connect schools to the Internet (Topp & Grandgenett, 1996), is an important component of the state's Systemic Initiative in Mathematics and Science. While viewed positively by participants, the project did not generate the widespread use of the Internet envisioned by developers. In part this was due to the hardware and software problems that compromised so many other change initiatives but also because principals did not believe in Internet use by students, another example of the mismatch in learning goals and methods of achieving those goals. Such results have been found in other states in spite of government and industry's attempts to increase schools' Internet access.

In each of the cases cited above the tradition of schooling in the participating schools was modelled on the factory — where subject matter is tightly bound, where education is directed from the teacher to the student, where short blocks of time are available, where social conformity is valued, and economies of measurement are the norm — exerted powerful influences to contain the movement toward change and retain policies and practices that are consonant with the "template" of schools as factories.

4. FACTORS EXTERNAL TO SCHOOLS AFFECTING POLICIES

Given the within school and within community expectations of what schooling is and should be, the problem of forecasting what Schools of the Future will look like is complex. Governments are increasing centralisation of education. So curriculum development, professional development, assessment, planning and procurement are being centralised in state operated schools while cultural and religious groups are opting out in greater numbers than before to establish small schools that resemble the home or village schools of a previous century.

On the social side, the competitive, one size fits all isolation of students from one another in the classroom model based on the factory, has been shown to be less effective in promoting learning than collaborative work. Business and industry are abandoning the traditional model of factories in favour of team-based operations, flexible organisation and flat not hierarchical structure. But here a dilemma exists. One goal of schooling is the creation of socially conforming individual. That goal is assumed to be achieved in the factory mode of the school. Collaboration can produce workers skilled in creating and producing in teams, the latest corporate mantra, but collaboration may also lead to a rejection of social conformity, a major goal of schooling for many community groups. So the public at large is equivocal when it comes to calling for changes in school patterns.

The advent of the World Wide Web may not change the situation. The availability of small or large communities on the Web creates a powerful pull away from topics/issues associated with "school" and towards the interests/goals of adolescents disenchanted with traditional schooling. But fundamentalist groups and many community leaders are opposed to organisational patterns and curricula that promote social and personal development. Instead, they opt for "mastery of the canon" models that emphasise social or intellectual conformity, although there is little agreement about who should conform to what. Each day there is a call for librarians and school personnel to "block" WWW sites to students. Blocking is not merely based on fears of access to pornography but also access to issues deemed unsuitable for students. Witness the latest set of school board decisions abandoning the teaching of evolution in several states!

Such has been the situation in America. Other countries, with more stable histories may not experience the same pressures, although it is interesting to note that England has moved away from "Open Classrooms" and investigative learning situations to a more structured and hierarchical plan; some countries, with less stable histories then America's may have experienced either wider swings or the perpetuation of one and only one model, regardless of its utility.

As the World Wide Web and the networking of the world becomes a reality one might expect greater destabilisation with the concomitant possibility of government imposing increased standardisation as members of the public seek one, two, three, four or more options depending on the social, religious and cultural entities represented.

Changing schools is not an endeavour to be undertaken without forethought about the multiplicity of factors involved. It may be necessary to consider the literature of school change for guidance in solving within school system problems that will be encountered but that will not be sufficient to ensure productive change. External to school factors may loom as large, if not larger, than within school factors. For example, in commenting on "The

Great School Wars" that roiled New York City during attempts to change school governance during the 1960's Diane Ravitch captured the situation.

> The public school operates on behalf of the community, but how 'community' is defined is the source of political and ideological controversy. A child lives simultaneously in many communities: his (sic) neighbourhood, city, state, and nation; his ethnic group, race and/or religion; his parents' occupation and interests may place his family in other communities as well. ... Respecting common values and common humanity need not imply the pursuit of homogeneity; no one wants to be a faceless figure in a mass society (Ravitch 1974, p. 402).

As mobility increases and even the most homogeneous societies become increasingly diverse the strains of accommodating to different social and cultural mores will pose a major challenge for educators as they decide what is to be taught and how it is to be taught.

Designers of Schools of the Future must grapple with the exquisite complexity of balancing the schools' goals for students with, on the one hand, the ever expanding possibilities offered by telecommunications and, on the other hand, the competing social, economic, political, and cultural forces in mass societies. Overarching all of these issues is the fact that in the past the move toward change has often neglected the question of what is to be taught and how is it taught, becoming bogged down instead by the issue of who or what should be in control. The centrality of the schools' mission — to teach meaningful material in ways that increases students' knowledge and understanding and makes them thoughtful, productive, responsible members of society — must not be lost in the move toward creating Schools of the Future.

Question #6. Given a country's history of curriculum development, which current economic, social, political, and cultural values will serve to promote which kinds of technological integration/infusion in schools? And which values will work to constrain which types of technology use?

Question #7. How will each country work with the prevailing social, economic, political and cultural values to move toward Schools of the Future?

Question #8. What is central, in terms of what is to be learned and how it is to be learned, for each country's Schools of the Future?

5. RECOMMENDATIONS

Given the discouraging results of curriculum building and reform based on IT use in American high schools, making recommendations about curriculum and change for the 21st century is risky business. But a few ideas can be gleaned from past successes and failures.

Examples of successful uses of technology in other countries' schools should be made available to all participants in the educational decision making process — government, business, school administrators, teachers, students and parents.

The implications of successful uses of technology must be discussed within and across countries as widely as possible, with both the positive and negative aspects as they apply to social, economic, political and cultural issues studied carefully.

The means by which successful uses of technology were planned, implemented and institutionalised must be specified, carefully studied and discussed across communities.

Discussions of "technology" in the abstract must be replaced by carefully considered models and methods of technology where the match between organisational patterns of schooling and belief systems underlying the use of technology on the one hand and the outcomes of technology use on the other hand is addressed.

The implications of current models of schools and current ideas about how learning occurs must become part of a national discussion. British newspapers, for example, are presenting "snapshots" of the ways different schools are using technology with brief but interesting discussions of rationales and outcomes.

Learning goals and outcomes must become a central focus of technology based planning and delivery. It cannot be assumed that technology use will automatically ensure achievement of a country's or a community's goals. Instead, the steps needed to ensure the best use of technology for each student must be analysed and implemented.

Planning for Schools of the Future must anticipate social, economic, political and cultural shifts that will impact how technology is used and what impacts, realistic or not, are expected as a result of technology use.

REFERENCES

Becker, H. (1983, 1986) *School uses of microcomputers. Reports from a national survey.* Baltimore, MD: Center for the Social Organization of Schools. The Johns Hopkins University.

Callahan, R. (1962) *Education and the cult of efficiency*. University of Chicago Press, Chicago.

Dwyer, D., Ringstaff, C. and Sandholz, J. (1991) Changes in teachers' beliefs and practices in technology rich classrooms. *Educational Leadership,* 48, 45-52.

Hadley, M. and Sheingold, K. (1993) Commonalities and distinctive patterns in teachers' integration of computers. *American Journal of Education*, 101, 281-315.

Owen, J. (1985) Belgian education. In *Issues in Comparative Education*. (eds. K. Watson and R. Watson). Croom Helm, London.

Powell. A., Farrar, E., and Cohen, D. (1985) *The shopping mall high school: The second report from A study of high schools*. Houghton Mifflin, Boston.

Ravitch, D. (1974) *The Great School Wars: New York City, 1805--1973*. Basic Books, New York.

Topp, N. and Grandgenett, N. (1996) Year 1 evaluation of Nebraska's statewide plan: Connecting schools to the Internet. *Computers in the Schools,* 12(2), 115-129.

Ure, A. (1835) *The philosophy of manufactures: An exposition of the scientific, moral and commercial economy of the factory system of Great Britain*. Charles Knight, London.

US Congress, Office of Technology Assessment (1989) *Linking for learning: A new course for education*. OTA-SET-430. US Government Printing Office, Washington, D. C.

BIOGRAPHY

Gail Marshall has taught Latin and World History in secondary schools in New York City, New York. A graduate of Marymount Manhattan College and Washington University in St. Louis, Missouri, she obtained a Ph.D. in Child Development and Psychometrics, and has worked for the St. Louis Public Schools both as a member of their Division of Research and Evaluation, where she evaluated Career Education programs, and as the director of the IBM Models Schools Project. She also worked at a federally funded educational laboratory (CEMREL) as an evaluator of the Comprehensive School Mathematics Program, the Midwest Regional Exchange and similar reform efforts. Currently she is consulting with the Evergreen Project on distance learning courses.

Networked technologies and other stories: New paradigms for learning

Alnaaz Kassam
8 Burnt Bark Dr., Scarborough Canada.

Abstract: This paper examines the role of networked technologies in transforming education from a teacher-centred, text-book driven and mono-cultural world view within one classroom to learning across national borders, where students become investigators, thinkers and knowledge creators reflecting upon the problems of the world. This papers reports on a research project which linked Canadian students with experts to study diverse cultures of the world. Through the research study, it was discovered that achieving a reflective approach to studying "others" is not merely a matter of breaking classroom walls and making contact, but rather includes changing attitudes and acquiring an ability to approach knowledge in a more constructivist manner.

Keywords: Internet, inter-cultural understanding, constructivist learning

1. BACKGROUND

A few years ago, an IBM ad on TV showed a group of nuns discussing the latest program from IBM. "I just read about it in Wired," explains one nun. "You get true multitasking and easy access to the Internet" to which the Mother Superior replies: "I'm dying to surf the Net" The picture fades as the pager tucked under her habit starts to beep.

Another ad for the IBM Aptiva portrayed Africa - the computer stood in the middle of a lush field. A choir practised a song and was unable to find the right musical note on which to begin singing. A child playing some music software on the nearby computer, gives them the right note. The choir breaks into happy smiles, singing again.

What is the symbolism here? We see Africa as it is always portrayed - happy, smiling people, its countryside, no sight of the complex, cosmopolitan cities, Africans singing. We see also that it takes a child on a foreign computer to find the solution to a simple problem - a problem that surely any African is infinitely more capable of solving than a computer. These ads formed part of a series that was running on TV - ads that presented people from varied cultures, varied occupations and distant countries - all relying on the technology and the support that IBM provides.

What did these advertisements portray? From the point of IBM they portrayed access. They portrayed technology that is accessible both geographically but also across cultural, social, ethnic, national and even religious boundaries. And it is a theme that is echoed throughout the literature on the Internet - whether in the arts, business or education. The underlying message around all the promotion attempts is: the Internet will provide access to information, to communication and to dissemination. Without it, you will be left behind. You will not be able to participate. At the same time, the ads seem to proudly proclaim that all people - regardless of national, cultural, racial or even physical ability can participate in, benefit and access the new technology. But is the phenomenon we just described access? Is it access when those being portrayed do not own, produce nor direct their own portrayal?

Porter (1994) would argue that the medium of television and its ads belonged to the older broadcast model of media where a small number of producers sent information to a large number of consumers. However with the new computer networks, this is changing In fact, with the information highway and the integration of satellite technology with television, computers and the telephone, the broadcast model will change to a system with multiple producers, distributors and consumers.

In the new media age that Porter describes, Africans could participate in conveying their own views of themselves - but if Africans can, so can all the cultures of the world. However, what is even more frightening in its power, is the potential for everyone - including our students to join in the fray. When this technology moves into the traditional teacher-centred, text-book driven classroom, knowledge dissemination has to change too. Eurich-Fulcer and Schofield (1995) explain that WAN technologies challenge the transmission mode of knowledge as facts to one where knowledge is based on individuals' perspectives and opinions. According to them, students will have to evaluate information, rather than simply absorb facts.

For Cummins and Sayers (1995), the root of the problem is the mismatch between industrial and post-industrial organisation of society, wherein students need to be perceived as autonomous beings who will use technology in a process of critical collaborative inquiry.

Similarly, Keating (1995) explains, we are in the midst of a technological change that will demand a transformation in societal functioning. This transformation is arising from already existing information technology that includes instantaneous global communication, unlimited knowledge storage and retrieval, sophisticated data analysis and simulation along with artificial intelligence that includes robotic manufacture.

Keating (1995) in this context, describes the transformation of society in the information age (as opposed to the industrial age) as being one where:

- pedagogy moves from knowledge transmission to knowledge building;
- the prime mode of learning being individual to one where it becomes more collaborative;
- where educational goals geared toward conceptual grasp for the few and basic skills and algorithms for the many, move to conceptual grasp and intentional knowledge building for all;
- there is a developmental model of life-long learning for everyone not just for an elite;
- vertical bureaucracies are replaced by collaborative learning organisations.

And in the kind of Internet projects described by Riel (1996), we can see that new learning provides for forms of integration very different from reading a text, watching a video or listening to a teacher speak. Students can interact with exhibits in a museum, take a walk through the White House, aim a telescope out into space, dissect a frog, take a stroll through a zoo and visit cities around the world. For Riel these connections are possible when we accept the Internet not as a physical context but an evolving social construction - when one accepts that it is not technology but people that form communities. Similarly, in the building of Internet networks, it is not the technology that will build relations but rather the social connections and constructions that will form the communities.

But it is not merely through social contact and the building of communities that one acquires true inter-cultural understanding. This is achieved through a change in attitudes and engendering in students an ability to carry out critical inquiry and the collaborative *creation* of knowledge through dialogue in their classrooms and with classrooms across the globe. This is not achieved through a passive acquisition of facts or even complex literary styles or historical analysis in the cultural literacy of socially powerful groups. (Cummins & Sayers, , 1995, p. 13). For Cummins and Sayers (1995, p. 170), it is a pedagogy of collaborative critical inquiry which will make schooling relevant to marginalised populations of students and engage them in academic effort. This pedagogy is achieved through fostering students' ability to think critically about complex social issues and take collective action to shape their societies (Cummins & Sayers, 1995, p. 170).

In fact, as this paper will demonstrate, one can break down classroom walls, one can change knowledge from a top-down to a collaborative model, one can bring in the perspectives of less dominant peoples into the classroom but none of these will affect attitudes and ways of critically approaching issues. These aspects of human development go beyond technology.

2. THE NEED FOR INTER-CULTURAL UNDERSTANDING IN THE GLOBAL CONTEXT

It is clear that as we enter the new millennium, global relations between peoples of the developing and developed world will become more and more frequent. In this context, inter-cultural understanding between peoples of the world becomes critical. As Cummins and Sayers (1995, p. 10) explain, Marshall McLuhan's "global village" is upon us. There is unprecedented inter-cultural contact globally resulting from a variety of factors: economic and political migration, technological advances in transportation and telecommunication, economic and political interdependence between countries of the world etc. This increasing inter-cultural contact both within and without national borders cries out for more two-way communication between cultures and an understanding of divergent cultural perspectives.

3. INTER-CULTURAL UNDERSTANDING AND THE OTHER STORY PROJECT

The paper reports the results of a research project entitled: *The Other Story: Research in the Development of Telecommunications Materials to Promote Inter-cultural Understanding.* The Ontario Ministry of Education and Training funded the project for two years. The Principal Investigator of the project was the author of this paper. Co-Investigators Dr. Rina Cohen and Dr. Brian Durell participated in the project. There were 3 on line conferences during this time, two explored issues of the impact of the TV on the Caribbean region and one looked at Canadian history from both a First Nations perspective and the traditional text book version.

The main objective of the Other Story project was to bring the "Other" into the classroom through the Internet. The first episode of the project (on which this paper reports) involved linking students in the Caribbean and in Canada through an online virtual conference. The conference participants also included a teacher and Canadian students of Caribbean origin, as well as experts in various aspects of Caribbean culture. All online data was captured and analysed. Most classrooms were also observed by trained researchers. The project was further enhanced by in-depth teacher interviews.

The project brought issues of social justice, cultural survival and the fair portrayal of all cultural, social and national groups into the classroom. The project's first premise was that the people whom we studied would create the materials that were developed and distributed in schools.

The project was carried out in the form of a simulation with each classroom posing as the government of a fictitious Caribbean island. Each government was posed with the task of debating whether they wanted to regulate TV on their island or not. Each classroom was divided into 4 groups representing the Ministries of Culture, Tourism, Finance and Information. Each Minister received a portfolio of materials relating to the Ministry.

The Other Story was a program that introduced students to the rest of the world from an "issue-centred" perspective. When students debated the issue of the impact of global TV on the Caribbean, the Ministers of Tourism read amongst other things, the work of Jamaica Kincaid, who describes one aspect of tourism in her home of Antigua in the following way:

> "The word 'emancipation' is used so frequently, it is as if it, emancipation, were a contemporary occurrence, something everyone is familiar with. And perhaps there is something in that, for an institution that is often celebrated in Antigua is the Hotel Training School, a school that teaches Antiguans how to be good servants, how to be a good nobody, which is what a good servant is. In Antigua, people cannot see a relationship between their obsession with slavery and emancipation and their celebration of the Hotel Training School (graduation ceremonies are broadcast on radio and television)."

Students also read an article on tourism which gave figures of how much of the tourist dollar is already spent in the tourist's home country towards the airline ticket. Often the hotel where the tourist stays, is owned by the airline and the food consumed by the tourist during his visit is bought overseas, before the tourist even gets to the Caribbean.

The students correspondingly watched a film called *The Dish Ran Away with the Spoon.* The is part of a series on issues of development put out by the BBC. It explores the issue of cultural domination and TV through the perspective of the people affected: artists, writers, teachers, religious leaders, politicians, school children and other ordinary people.

In this film, the director visits Cuba and laments its poverty but then feels that at least the Cubans have been able to keep their culture, whereas, he on his own island is bombarded with images of snowy weather forecasts on CNN and episodes of an afternoon soap opera. The film also interviews a priest who is trying to ensure that the cultural heritage of his people is preserved through music, dance and drama.

Students also read stories, poems, commentary and newspaper articles on the Caribbean region. Students as part of the conference that was held on a listserv on *Schoolnet,* a Canadian educational online network, also had the opportunity to pose questions to members of the Caribbean culture who were available online and who offered comments to students. A classroom in Barbados was also linked to the project.

All Canadian schools in the project were inner-city schools with students from working class neighbourhoods. Students, in classroom observations, carried out before the project commenced, tended to be apathetic, uninterested in school and classroom discussions. An interview with one classroom teacher, Keith, revealed that he was depressed by the apathy and disinterest of his students. He had tried everything, including having students watch films on social and economic inequities, classroom discussions on everyday life, even career discussions. Students were in their last year in school, ready to join the workforce as soon as the semester was over and school was largely irrelevant to them.

4. INTER-CULTURAL UNDERSTANDING

The materials provided the students with online conference experience and the online presence of the Caribbean experts were carefully selected for authenticity, wisdom and a true reflection of the culture. The researchers were not prepared for the extreme racism and narrow-minded views of the students who formed part of the conference.

4.1 Incident 1: the Caribbean as a resort

Amongst the first comments to emerge online were students' pre-conference impressions of the Caribbean.

> "The Caribbean gives me a lot of different impressions. For example, Jamaica. When I think of Jamaica I think of holidays, honeymoons, sun, fun and sand. Also I think that the people would be very happy (high), because marijuana is legalised."

In one class, the teacher lists comments from students on the board:

> "Goats and pigs running around, surfing, people living in grass huts on beaches, street markets, low paying jobs, no electricity, nude beaches, cruise ships, dreadlocks (hair style), alcohol, tropical storms, tropical

fruit, say 'Hey man' (like we say 'eh'), black, bare footed people, dress in grass skirts, colourful clothes, hot/nice weather, seafood, parties, sun tanning, drug problems, reggae, lots of tourism, sandals."

In this example, we see illustration of the typical stereotypical views of the Caribbean, which are by no means isolated.

Why would Canadian students have these images of the Caribbean? A research report, which analysed the portrayal of minorities in Canada, showed that in general they are under-represented among the newsmakers, experts and citizens presented by the news media. Where attention is received in the media, minorities are portrayed as villains and victims than as newsmakers, experts reacting to contemporary events (Ungerleider, 1991).

Television ads, especially during the harsh winter months, show swimsuit clad white couples frolicking on beaches that have deep blue water and pure white sand. Black waiters in impeccable white suits carry trays of delectable fruit drinks to white women lounging on deck chairs by the swimming pool. The ads are invariably accompanied by loud music from the Caribbean.

And as we observed above, this portrayal of the Caribbean is not so very different from the portrayal of Africa, a model of media dissemination that is reminiscent of the older broadcast model of TV. It does not encourage questioning, nor a discussion of issues.

4.2 Incident 2: The Caribbean as a third world country

Later in the same day, the researcher in Keith's classroom observes the following conversation:

Student 1: "Let us discuss the other responses from the other classes to see what is realistic and logical."
Student 2: "Did you watch the American music awards the other night, it was neat."
Student 3: "The video we watched on the Caribbean was propaganda: they only focused on the problems of a little TV."
Student 2: "I think they are lucky to have TV: some people cannot even afford to eat."
Student 3: "I have been there, they live in shacks and don't have TV."
Student 2 says: "What do we write, we just need one response." and writes: "I think they are lucky to have TV. Some people cannot even afford to eat."
Student 2: "We have finished."

An online quotation from another school reflects similar patronising attitudes and disdain for the Caribbean. When asked if watching the video has changed his mind about the Caribbean, the student replies:

> "My impression of the Caribbean has not changed because I found the video to be somewhat unrealistic. I have been to the Dominican Republic and saw what it was really like, I mean I actually went out of the American resort that I was staying at and looked around. I visited the market and the beach and the mountains. The video portrayed the Caribbean as this great place where everyone is happy and only worried about what the children watch on TV when they are lucky to even have a TV."

Here once again we see the deep ignorance of the response, the idea that the Caribbean people are so poor that they have no right to complain about TV and its domination of their culture. They should be happy that they have a roof over their heads. It is an attitude that is both arrogant and simplistic.

4.3 Incident 3: The Caribbean as poor

Our final excerpt from the Other Story research project is the following comment placed on the listserv right at the beginning of the conference by a young female student who has been to the Caribbean:

> "The images that come to my mind when I think of Caribbean culture is hot weather and a third world place. I think of people living in plastic tents on the beach, eating the hard fruits that fall from the trees. During the day they spend all their time making little boxes and braiding the tourists' hair. The tourists barter with them and cheat them of their profit. The people of the Caribbean know this so they raise the price sometimes by a couple hundred pesos. A golden coloured pendant is almost never real gold. The people are so desperate to sell that they carve 14k into the bottom and fool all the tourists. The children are made to work from whenever they can walk and talk until they can no longer work, their children will now take care of them. The schools are very expensive so no one goes. All the money that the tourists spend at the resort goes to the United States. None of the tourism money goes to the people. Not many of the people have real paying jobs and those few who get picked to work in a rum factory earn less than 20.00 American dollars a month. Most of them even have a big family to support."

From this excerpt can be observed the stereotypes of the developing world. People living in plastic tents on the beach, poverty, people cheating on tourists, too many children and child labour.

We also see that a certain view of the Caribbean is emerging, a view that reflects the environment of the North American attitude of superiority, of ignorance of the rest of the world. At the same time, there is a flaunting of that ignorance. This is the perspective that will be observed in almost mirror-like reflection in the popular films that will be discussed below.

In the next section these three incidents will be analysed to demonstrate how the virtual networking aspect of the simulation permitted the exposure of different views, more complex analysis and most importantly, the perspective of the members of the culture which was being studied.

5. THE INTERNET'S ADVANTAGE FOR INTER-CULTURAL UNDERSTANDING

The above section demonstrated quite adequately that students in the classes were quite ignorant of the Caribbean, had succumbed to stereotypical views and were totally influenced by the tourist image of the Caribbean as a beautiful but primitive place to visit.

In this section the interactivity of the listserv will be displayed. This was a conference that insisted on the presence of members of the Caribbean community, both as students and as "experts". This resulted in other images of the Caribbean emerging. This perspective would have proved impossible, had students only had access to textual or video material, especially if these materials did not reflect the cultures that they proposed to study, which is what occurs in most cases. However, as seen in the above incidents, while the technology brought in different perspectives and allowed an issue-oriented perspective, students were for the most part passive, interested only in the most superficial of discussions.

ICT cannot change approach to learning, only schools or teachers can contribute toward this process. ICT can certainly facilitate that process by providing resources in the form of text and visual resources, linkages between peoples of different cultures, but as Riel pointed out earlier, the building of social relationships, the building of human communities is the work of human beings. And as Cummins and Sayers (1995) also concluded, inter-cultural understanding must be based on critical collaborative inquiry. We shall discuss the power of ICT within this context.

5.1 Analysis of Incident 1

The following is the response of the students from a school in Barbados, who are reacting to the comments from students about their pre-conference perceptions of the Caribbean as a primitive but "paradise-like" place to visit.

> "One of the misconceptions about the Caribbean is that the people live in grass huts on beaches and that there are goats and pigs running wild. This is in no way accurate. Caribbean people live in regular wood or brick houses just like everyone else and like most people we build pens and sties for our goats and pigs, if we have any. Considering that we live in regular houses, it is safe to assume that we have electricity and running water.
>
> "Freedom is very important to Caribbean people. We are not thrown into prison for giving our opinions on political matters, neither is the press under the control and direction of the government. Barbados is very politically stable. Our parliament has been in existence for over 350 years. We experience much less crime and drug use than urban societies in Canada and the U.S.A.
>
> "Tourism is also important to the Caribbean but the images which people are given about the Caribbean create their own misconceptions. The tourists are led to believe that tropical life is one long party but the truth is that it is not. There is more to these islands than tourism. We are real people with real problems."

Here we see that the Internet provides, over the quick images of TV and of the stories created in movies, *voice*. The interactivity of the listserv brought the views of people (students just like the ones in Canada) actually living in the Caribbean to challenge the stereotypical views that were thrown at them. Thus the first advantage of the Internet for education in inter-cultural understanding is that it provides *interactivity*.

Secondly, because the interactivity is available to everyone who is a node on a network, it is a level playing field and so Internet provides *equality* between participants. It is important to note that the school in Barbados is a high-cost school which promotes high academic skills and university entrance. It is not a school which has technology, but it is not the technology which promotes higher thinking skills and critical collaborative inquiry but rather the approach to constructivist learning, where students become researchers and independent thinkers. It will also be noted below that Caribbean students in Canada admonish their Canadian counterparts for making blanket observations without really having conducted any independent research.

5.2 Analysis of incident 2

In the second incident students are dismissing the fears of the Caribbean people in losing their culture through TV. Their comments are essentially that because these people are so poor, they should count themselves lucky that they even have TV. This incident illustrates the usefulness of the online discussion. The project only has access to this conversation between students because there was a trained researcher available to listen to these comments, but this is only rarely the case in classrooms. In fact, for the most part, the teacher may also be in another part of the room, when students come up with these racist and patronising comments. However, the second comment in the same incident was online and so captured, transparent and available for response, available for comment from other students, from experts of the culture and from students in Barbados too.

Thus we see that the third advantage of the Internet is that it provides *transparency* to people's comments. However, it also provides audience for more racist comments as discussed in the next section.

5.3 Analysis of incident 3

In this incident, a young student used the forum of the listserv to voice her impressions of her visit to the Caribbean. This student with her comments on the poverty, lack of education and dishonesty of the Caribbean peoples aroused a storm of protest from students outside her classroom.

The first response is from Keith's class, which has no students of Caribbean background, which is in fact only a few blocks away is:

> "As far as I'm concerned, the comment from Island A is a disgrace. Your views on Caribbean culture are a disgrace and borderline racist. You are portraying the people of the Caribbean as lazy and having nothing better to do than 'rip-off' tourists."

Keith is pleasantly surprised; he has been working for months on getting his students to be less biased and here he sees them reacting to another student. This means that the Internet provides a forum for students to debate and discuss issues. Here we see an example of critical collaborative inquiry.

The second response is from two students who have just arrived from the Caribbean. They are new students in a class participating in the project.

> "I found these comments very biased and untrue. I have lived in the Caribbean and have never seen plastic tents on the beaches except for cub scout excursions. Education in most islands is free and many have high literacy rates and some higher than Canada. I want to know what island you visited because in all of the islands I have visited, I have not seen these conditions. Where are you learning all of this?
>
> "Not since the Arawaks and Caribs (about the 15th century), have our people lived in huts and we only see them as a form of diversion for the tourists. Students should research the region before stating these false stereotypes that could influence people's decisions on visiting the islands."

The final response is from one of the Caribbean "experts", a professor from a nearby university who has volunteered to participate in this project, offering comments to students' online discussion.

> "Some of you have raised the issue about 'ripping-off' tourists. Do some people in the Caribbean 'rip-off' tourists. Of course this happens! But it happens everywhere else in the world as well. Does this happen more in the Caribbean than in other parts of the world? No one really knows, but probably not. Quite often, however, the Caribbean is advertised to tourists in a very unrealistic way (is it paradise?) and this creates a problem for tourists when something 'wrong' happens. Does it rain in paradise? Maybe not. But it sure does in Jamaica."

This excerpt slowly but surely breaks down the stereotypes that the students have come up with, discussion must be based on issues and cannot be a simple listing of prejudice. Thus one student, through the power of a listserv receives three different types of responses. The first is from students who are of the same socio-economic background (and in fact from a school a few blocks away) as she is. The second is from students who come from the country of which she has such a low image. Finally, the third is from a reasoned and well-informed "expert" who is from the region she is speaking of. While it is difficult to gauge the long-term effect of this type of input to individual students, it is important to realise that this type of interaction was impossible until the technology broke down the traditional walls that existed between the classroom and the outside world.

ICT also allowed the creation of an online inter-cultural communication, where each was provided equal access in the forum. This was a situation that was never available before; traditionally students relied on information from teachers and textbooks, sometimes from the library. Here they now had contact with the cultures they were studying.

But it must be made clear that it was not the technology, rather it was the careful setting up of the experience. Students were exposed to the highest quality materials, which were based upon research on issues, research on historical and present day political background. Students could not succeed unless they read the background literature. But if the outside world provided insights to students to cultures to which they did not have access before, the racism of the students *within* the classroom also reached the outside world.

It is interesting, however, that Janet, a teacher of Caribbean background who formed part of the simulation, posited that these views were very much part of the majority culture and that it was better that they were aired and dealt with in the safety of the classroom than if they were simply ignored and swept under the rug.

6. FURTHER ANALYSIS

In the Other Story project, researchers set up a learning network which promoted an opening up of communication between students of various cultures. While the technology provided an open and level playing field, each user being an equal node in a vast network, it was the narrow minded views and knowledge which portrayed the developing world in disparaging ways, which dominated the discourse.

At the beginning of this paper, two commercials were presented which portrayed the use of technology as neutral and in fact indispensable to global and universal happiness. In the course of the description of the simulation, it has been discovered that technology does not hide prejudice, it sometimes highlights it and renders it more transparent. ICT however also provides a way of opening up new avenues of communication.

It was demonstrated that there exists a deep psychological feeling of superiority over the developing world. In the next pages, an analysis of the larger context of the media that dominate the Western world is undertaken.

6.1 THE CONTEXT OF INTER-CULTURAL UNDERSTANDING

Mukherjee and Achebe have pointed out that while non-European cultures are regarded as “other”, they are also often used as a backdrop to the playing out of the lives of the story's main characters, who are invariably white and of the dominant cultures. Thus we have Conrad's *Heart of*

Darkness, where Africa serves as the primitive background of the struggle between civilisation and the jungle in the meaning making of the main character. This use of others, their land, their culture and their lives as just the backdrop to the sometimes meaningless romps of Hollywood actors and actresses is a tradition that continues today. It is portrayed in films like *Out of Africa* where the hauntingly beautiful African countryside becomes a romantic scene for the mating of two colonisers. The display of proud Africans who are masters of their own country and their own destiny as mere servants who cry and grovel in front of their white masters is ignored and arouses no comment. And as shown, it is precisely this unquestioning but demeaning and degenerating portrayal of the Other that comes through in classroom observations of students participating in the Other Story project.

While one may lament the level of awareness and lack of sophistication around issues of cultural imperialism and developing countries on the part of Canadian students, it does not seem surprising when one considers the diet of literature, films and TV programs that our culture feeds them continuously from birth. The Other Story project, however, provided Canadian students with an opportunity to see another perspective, that of the "other" whom they had considered voiceless until now.

While the Internet poses new opportunities for minorities to express themselves and to have a voice in the classroom, it is an achievement that can be marred because our students are not ready for this experience. The Other Story was saved from being a purely racist expression of student views because of the way it was constructed. Students were provided with high quality background materials, articles, films and stories written by the Caribbean people, and they had the presence of Caribbean students and "experts" available online to steer them away from problems.

Thus the Internet for inter-cultural understanding provides interactivity, transparency and equality, each of which can be abused unless we provide an experience that is carefully constructed, that reflects the views of the people we study. How then can we use the Internet in ways that will promote respect and communication between peoples of the world, a prerequisite for the future prosperity both economic and political of the globe?

7. RECOMMENDATIONS

As discussed above, it was the interactivity, transparency and equality provided by the technology which provided deeper and more intricate webs of meaning to inter-cultural understanding in the classroom. As such the following recommendations relate to each of these phenomena:

Interactivity: Internet projects of the future which claim to promote intercultural understanding should ensure that there is interactivity between students of different backgrounds such that not only is each an equal node on the computer, but also that the learning experience which they undergo is not trivial or unexamined.

Transparency: Because ICT renders all communication transparent, it is vital that the teachers and organisers of the virtual conferences or any other form of communication between classrooms, ensure that an atmosphere of mutual respect and politeness pervade the discussions. On line privileges should be removed for all those who abuse this rule.

Equality: Because the Internet provides each with a node on the computer, it should not be assumed that classrooms across the globe have the same access, freedom of expression and even the bandwidth that Canadian students might enjoy. Internet projects should emphasise issues, discussions, even text based activities which then call upon other resources in the classroom environment rather than depending upon huge memory reserves with WWW-technologies. The emphasis should be on the egalitarian exchange of views, such that students may learn from and about each other.

Finally it is recommended that in opening up the classroom walls across geographical and national boundaries such that countries and cultures come together as equals, the following guidelines should be kept in mind:

a) Respect for all people of the world should be the basic premise and ground rule of all online discussions.

b) This respect can be engendered through a revision of all curricula, from textbooks, literature, documentaries and posters used in schools.

c) Ensure that traditional media which do not reflect this respect will be used to train students in developing critical analysis and humanistic views.

Students need to learn from a constructivist viewpoint. Classrooms are places where students might explore, analyse, question and challenge teachers on questions of cultural imperialism around the world. In classes where students are passive, awaiting the passing out of knowledge, untouched by discussion and questioning, the potential of the Net to teach others to understand people from their own perspectives becomes difficult.

While this simulation took place in the Canadian context, its recommendations are applicable to students in Westernised countries. It is important that students everywhere be exposed to a sympathetic but complex view of the developing world and this can best be achieved through direct contact possible through ICT technologies.

ICT offers a promise of allowing the "other" into the classroom as an equal. However the educational system has not done an adequate job of preparing students to be critical collaborative learners, thinking, questioning and learning. ICT can provide the circumstances which allow human beings to grow socially, ethically and intellectually but it is the teachers who need to bring the excitement and involvement back into the world of learning. Without having students as ethical, active, involved and intellectually challenged knowledge creators, there is no future for networked technologies except as vehicles of commerce or exotic travel.

REFERENCES

Cummins, J., and Sayers, D. (1995) Brave New Schools: Challenging Cultural Illiteracy through global learning networks, New York: St. Martin's Press.

Eurich-Fulcer, R. and Schofield, J. (1995) Wide-Area Networking in K-12 Education: Issues Shaping Implementation and Use, Computers Educ. 24 (3), 211-220.

Keating, D. (1995) The Transformation of schooling: Dealing with developmental diversity, Lupart, J., McKeough and Yewchuck, C. (Eds.), Schools in Transition: Rethinking Regular and Special Education, Toronto: Nelson, 119-139.

Mukherjee, A. (1988) Toward an Aesthetic of Opposition, Essays on Literature Criticism & Cultural Imperialism. Toronto: Williams-Wallace Publishers.

Porter, M. (1994) A Second Media Age, ARENA Journal, no. 3, 49-91.

Riel, M. (1996) The Internet: A Land to Settle Rather Than an Ocean to Surf and a New "Place" for School Reform through Community Development, ISTE SIG/Tel Technology in Education Newsletter, Winter 1996 [http://www.gsn.org/teach/articles/netasplace.html].

Said, E. (1979) Orientalism, Vantage Books, New York: 1978.

Ungerleider, C. (1991) Media, Minorities and Misconceptions: The Portrayal by and Representation of Minorities in Canadian News Media, Canadian Ethnic Studies, XXIII (3), 158-163.

Warschauer, M. (2000) Technology and School Reform: A View from Both Sides of the Tracks" in Education Policy Analysis Archives, 8 (3), January 7, 2000, [http://epaa.asu.edu/epaa/v8n4.html].

Wells, G. (in press) Dialogue about Knowledge Building, Smith, B. (Ed.) Liberal Education in a Knowledge Society. La Salle: Open Court, [http://www.oise.on.ca/~gwells/OpenCourt.html].

BIOGRAPHY

Alnaaz Kassam is a high school English teacher in Toronto, Canada. Her professional experience includes being a Senior Research Officer at the Ontario Institute for Studies in Education of the University of Toronto. She has worked with computers since 1983 in various capacities: training teachers in computer literacy, researching the first impact of computer technology in Ontario classrooms and using the Internet to link classrooms to promote inter-cultural understanding. She has been an English and computer literacy teacher for the past two years and has taught in the private and public school systems and at the elementary, secondary and adult levels.

Values and competencies in the school of the future

Humberto Maturana and Eduardo Cabezon
Facultad de Ciencias, Universidad de Chile, Santiago, Chile.
Universidad Metropolitana de Ciencias de la Educacion (UMCE),
Av. Jose Pedro Alessandri 774, Ñuñoa, Santiago, Chile.
ecabezon@umce.cl

Abstract: The purpose of this paper is to present a concept of education that stems from the theory of cognition of one of the authors. From this concept the values and competencies (abilities and skills) are proposed that the School of the Future ought to develop as a new learning environment. The following basic statement is discussed: "Education is a process by means of which adequate relational behaviors (i.e. cognitive, affective and psychomotor behaviors) are triggered through which another (or oneself) arises as a legitimate other in coexistence with oneself." If this emotion is conserved as the fundamental culture that we live together, it is more likely to observe an educational environment in which human beings (adults and children) can live together in autonomy, responsibility and respect for themselves, for others, and for their ecological environment. If these conditions are fulfilled, human actions will be developed with trust and mutual acceptance. We can expect that within this educational and learning environment, persons will interact with enthusiasm in their daily life, they will show creativity when proposing new ideas, ability to assess themselves with equity and to conserve their adequate social behaviors with responsibility and self-respect.

Keywords: Culture, languages, learning environment

1. INTRODUCTION

Different cultures vary according to different configurations of emotions that characterize them as different closed networks of conversations. What characterizes the different behaviors as different kinds of actions, are the different emotions under which they arise or are received.

We claim that living under the emotion of love, i.e. under those relational behaviors through which another (or oneself) arises as a legitimate other in coexistence with oneself, we can expect intelligent behaviors. That, which we call intelligence in daily life in our culture, is an expression of an assessment of the capacity to participate in a new or an old consensual domain that a person, or in general any living being, may exhibit in the course of its interactions. In all cases of intelligent behaviors, the biological condition that makes those different intelligent behaviors is the same: structural plasticity as the fundament for a changing adequate behavior in a changing medium.

In order to understand more deeply the fundamental notions of this paper, we firstly present some of the ideas that have been developed by one of the authors, Humberto Maturana, who has rooted his research from biological and systemic thinking and experiments.

2. THE LIVING SYSTEMS

In 1970 the word "autopoiesis" was introduced (Maturana and Varela, 1972) in order to connote the organization of living systems as closed networks of molecular production. The fundamental thing that happens in the constitution of a living system as a molecular autopoietic system is its constitution as an autonomous entity that has a singular existence as such in the continuous flow of molecules through it. Biological phenomena occur in the actual realization of living systems as singular unites, not in the particular nature of any of the molecular processes that realize them. "Autopoiesis" is not something that can be called a property of living systems. Rather it is their actual manner of being as the organization that constitutes them as singular entities in the molecular space.

The claim that living systems exist as singular autonomous molecular autopoietic unites through interactions in a medium with which they are in a continuous molecular interchange, is a claim about how they exist in their internal composition as well as about how they exist as totalities. Systems as composite entities have a dual existence, namely, they exist as singularities that operate as simple unites in the domain in which they arise as totalities, and at the same time they exist as composite entities in the domain of the operation of their components. The relation between these two domains is not causal. They do not intersect, nor do the phenomena, which pertain to one, occur in the other. The generative relation between the two as seen by an observer is a historical relation. The totality arises together with the relational domain in which they exist as such. More details about these statements can be found in Maturana (1980, 1988 and 1990).

2.1 Language and languaging

That which we connote as we speak of language is usually seen in terms of what we do while "languaging" (using language), and therefore, we usually speak of language as if it is an instrument we use to communicate. Thus, it seems acceptable to say that language is a symbolic system of communication. But language cannot be explained in terms of notions such as communication or symbolization, because these notions refer to operations that entail language. Communication is a commentary about the flow of the interactions between systems. Also symbolization is secondary to language, because it takes place in the explicit distinction that one particular operation will participate in the flow of the co-ordinations of behaviors for some other operation in such a flow. Languaging occurs in the flow of recursive co-ordinations of doings, not in any isolated coordination of doings in particular. Language arises as a manner of living together in a new operational domain that did not exist before.

Human beings exist in language. That means that they are the kind of beings that operate in a manner contingent to the course of our languaging in the flow of our recursive "consensual co-ordinations of consensual co-ordinations of behaviors". In other words, human beings exist in closed dynamics of languaging, and everything that they do as humans takes place in our languaging as a flow of consensual co-ordinations of consensual co-ordinations of behaviors. For example, a minimal operation in languaging in which we may understand what this means, takes place when one attempts to take a taxi through gestures. If one meets the gaze of a taxi driver on the other side of the street and makes a gesture to stop him, and then one makes another gesture indicating to him to do a U-turn around, what one does is coordinating the first consensual coordination. Actually, what has happened is an operation of coordination of coordination of behaviors in which the taxi as a carrying operation had arisen. The meeting of the gazes by the first gesture constituted an interaction in which the client and the taxi driver entered in an initial coordination of behavior. While the gesture of the client as seen by the taxi driver, coordinated such initial coordination in a sequence that an observer would call an act of hiring the taxi, so the next gesture for turning around was the coordination over the first coordination of behavior.

As languaging beings, living immersed in languaging, we do not easily see that in this episode two things have happened. One is the flow in co-ordinations of co-ordinations of behavior that are not innate, but are consensual (that is, learned). The second thing is that the taxi as a carrying device arises in the coordination of coordination of behavior, and is not an independent entity by itself. So, all that we say or may say, all that we may distinguish as we do what we do as observers (as human languaging beings), takes place as an operation in consensual co-ordinations of behaviors, without making any reference to anything outside our languaging.

2.2 Emotions

What we distinguish in daily life as emotions are all kinds of relational behaviors, not particular doings. And what we connote biologically as we speak of emotions referring to ourselves or to other animals, are body dynamic dispositions (involving the nervous system and the whole body). They determine what we can do or not do, in what relations we can enter or not enter, at any moment. As a result, different emotions can be fully characterized as different domains of relational behaviors or as dynamic body dispositions for relational behaviors. For example, love is the domain of those behaviors or dynamic body dispositions through which another arises as a legitimate other in coexistence with oneself. Aggression is the domain of those behaviors or dynamic body dispositions through which another is denied as a legitimate other in coexistence with oneself. And fear is the domain of those behaviors or dynamic body dispositions through which one moves away from the circumstances in which one finds oneself. In these circumstances, love is not a virtue or something special. It simply is a biological phenomenon as the domain of those behaviors through which social life arises and is conserved. Love is the biological dynamic system that constitutes trust and mutual acceptance in body and spiritual relations of nearness and intimacy.

3. HUMANS AS LANGUAGING AND LOVING ANIMALS

Humans are languaging animals. That means that they live in language as a manner of flowing in coexistence in consensual co-ordinations of consensual co-ordinations of behaviors. This manner of living must have arisen in the history that gave origin to humans some three million years ago. At the same time humans are loving animals. That is apparent in daily life in that they fall ill, at any age, when they are deprived of love because of demands, pressures or any relational behavior that denies them. Gerda Verden-Zöller (1993) has shown in her studies of the early childhood, that it is fundamental for a child to grow in a relation of total trust and body acceptance in free play. At first in the relation with the mother (female or male, since mother is a relation of care), and then as the child grows in relation to other persons with which he or she lives (in nursery, kindergarten and school), to become a self-respecting and socially integrated adult.

The evolutionary history of human lineage is a history of social life centered on consensuality and cooperation, not on competition or aggressive strife. As such human evolutionary history is a history of expansion of the capacities for consensuality, and hence, of expansion of intelligence. Intelligence is not primarily the capacity to solve problems, but it is the capacity to participate in the generation, expansion and operation in consensual domains as domains of co-ordinations of behaviors through living together. Languaging, indeed, living in conversations as humans do, requires such an enormous capacity for consensuality, that humans are all essentially equally intelligent. The differences in intelligence that seem to exist between humans are not due to differences in their capacity for consensuality, but in their "emotioning" (having emotions). In fact, due to the nature of intelligence as a relational biological phenomenon, different emotions affect it differently. Thus, ambition, competitiveness, anger, envy, aggression and fear reduce intelligence because they restrict the domain of openness for consensuality. Only love expands intelligence, because love as the domain of those behaviors through which the other arises as a legitimate other in coexistence with oneself, opens a human being to see and to enter in collaboration.

3.1 Culture

When we speak of culture or cultural affairs in daily life, we mean a closed network of conversations. That network constitutes and defines a manner of human living as a network of co-ordinations of emotions and actions that is realized as a particular configuration of interlacing of doings and emotions of the people that live that culture. As such, a culture is constitutively a closed conservative system that generates its members as they realize it through their participation in the conversations that constitute and define that culture. To pertain or belong to one culture is an operational condition, not an intrinsic quality or a constitutive condition of the human beings that realize that culture. Any human being can belong to different cultures in any different circumstances of his or her living, according to the conversations in which he or she participates in those different moments.

3.2 Values

"Values are distinctions of relational configurations in the living together, which obtain their legitimacy from love" (Maturana, 1990). Values can also be understood as linguistic commentaries that missed the particular aspects of living together under the inspiration of love. All the values referred to in the literature are founded in love, such as honesty, cooperation, respect, loyalty, generosity, responsibility, justice. Why does in our cultural environment the necessity arises to identify and establish explicitly the values that we would like to live? One explanation from our perspective is that this is due to the fact that we belong to a particular culture (patriarchal culture) which has a fundamental contradiction, which in great proportion is the source of the suffering in which we live now. In other words, our present culture is the encounter of two cultures based on emotions which contradict to each other. One is the ancestral "matristic" (not "matriarchal") culture founded in the emotion of love. The other is the patriarchal culture, which was initiated with shepherdess some ten thousand years ago, founded in the negation of the other, that emphasized relationships of appropriation, competitiveness, struggle, success and control, in contrast to the values lived in the relation of child and mother. This negation of what was learned in infancy that arises in adulthood, gives origin to suffering. Thus the question about values arises from living within this contradiction, as a reflection to recover the matristic life of the infancy for the life of adulthood.

4. EDUCATION FOR THE FUTURE

First of all, we have to state that from this biological point of view, to learn is to live together. That means that the learning happens in any way the transformation that takes place in the living together. Human beings, for their condition of living in language, are open to learn anything. However, not every learning can be considered as educative. The term "education" is derived from the action that takes an implicit ethical sense. The ethical preoccupations are related to living in a free and non-contradictory environment, under the mutual acceptance and respect. Meanwhile, the moral preoccupations have to do with social norms, which have been established as legitimate by an authority. The norms of actions are not necessarily accepted with enjoyment. It is more likely that what is realized from the inspiration of love and reflection, can permit us to act with freedom, and then develops as a responsible act from our understanding.

4.1 Values, competencies in a new learning environment

We think that probably now our basic statement about education could be understood in the following terms: "Education is a process by means of which adequate relational behaviors (i.e. cognitive, affective and psychomotor behaviors) are triggered. Through that another (or oneself) arises as a legitimate other in coexistence with oneself." This means under the emotions of love. Maybe this simple statement might also be considered simplistic. But our experience with different kinds of students and with teachers is that they have understood that their most important task is to live together with others in the acceptance of themselves as legitimate others. Finally, if the emotion of living in love is conserved as the fundamental culture, it is more likely to observe an educational environment in which human beings (adults and children) can live together in autonomy, responsibility and respect for themselves, for others and for their ecological environment. If these conditions are fulfilled, human actions will be developed with trust and mutual acceptance. We can expect that within this learning environment, persons will interact with enthusiasm, they will show creativity when proposing new ideas, ability to assess themselves with equity and to conserve their social behaviors with responsibility and self-respect.

4.2 The role of ICT in future education and schools

Under these conditions ICT will not be a problem for education. On the contrary, we could use ICT as an expansion of our body in terms of mutual trust and acceptance. We claim that from our experiences for the last 8 years, working with teachers and students. Our actual work has been done mainly with teachers in the Master Program of Education at the "Universidad Metropolitana de Ciencias de la Educacion" (UMCE) in Santiago, since 1992. Every year we have had some 30 teachers as graduate students in each semester in our course named "Biology of Knowing and Biology of Love".

This course, with a duration of 18 weeks, consists of lectures and workshops, which permit the students to understand and reflect about the ideas expressed in this paper. In the beginning we usually hear from the students that these ideas cannot be applied to education. Around the middle of the course, we observe that many teachers can apply in some creative and personal way the discussed strategies. For example, we see the application of one of the main notions of the biology of cognition that "in the experience one cannot distinguish between perception and illusion", and that then that errors or mistakes are not committed "a priori", but afterwards as a commentary of one observer. We think that these ideas can be understood in a way that many of the teachers can really apply procedures of formative evaluation on their students in different. If these relatively simple interactions that before seemed difficult to apply, are easily applied after a few weeks, we think that the emotioning that we can elicit from these students with the understanding of the basics of the theory of cognition, are good signs for teachers to be open to operate with more enthusiasm with ICT devices at their schools, than their colleagues without this experience.

We are beginning to follow up our teachers in their actual environment. Some proportion of them, after their graduation as Master of Education, have been promoted as supervisors giving technical support in their schools. Our hypothesis is that when some theory is provided on reflection and understanding under the emotions of love, it is more likely that the students can operate in daily life and in their professional activities with more freedom in a creative way.

REFERENCES

Maturana, H. and Varela, F. (1972) *De Máquinas y Seres Vivos*, Editorial Universitaria, Santiago, Chile.

Maturana, H. and Varela, F. (1980) *Biology of Cognition, in Autopoiesis and Cognition,* edited by D. Reidel.

Maturana, H. (1988) *Reality: The Search for Objectivity or the Quest for a Compelling Argument.* Irish Journal of Psychology (Issue on Constructivism) 9 (1): 25-82.

Maturana, H. (1990) *Science and Daily Life: The Ontology of Scientific Explanations. In: Self- Organization: Portrait of a Scientific Revolution,* W. Krohn, G. Kuppers (eds.) Kluwer Academic Publishers, Dordrecht, Boston, London.

Verden-Zöller, G. and Maturana, H. (1993) *Amor y Juego: Fundamentos Olvidados de lo Humano,* Instituto de Terapia Cognitiva, Santiago, Chile.

BIOGRAPHIES

Humberto Maturana is professor in biology at the Universidad de Chile as a specialist in perception, neurobiology and cybernetics. He teaches at the Universidad Metropolitana de Ciencias de la Educacion (UMCE) in the graduate program for teachers. He invented the notion of "autopoiesis" applied to the living systems and his theory of cognition has been applied in education since 1989. In 1994 he won the National Prize of Science in Chile.

Eduardo Cabezon is a professor in evaluation and curriculum at the Universidad Metropolitana de Ciencias de la Educacion (UMCE). He has been working with Humberto Maturana since 1990 and is applying the theory of cognition in his undergraduate and graduate teaching and research.

The impact of modelling in informatics education on collaborative learning with school Intranets

Sigrid E. Schubert
Informatics XII – Didactics of Informatics, University of Dortmund,
D-44221 Dortmund, Germany.
schubert@cs.uni.dortmund.edu

Abstract: This paper examines the potential value of modelling in informatics education. Learners understand that they must collide with the principle restrictions when they use these artificially created model worlds which have now become real systems within their environments. Computer supported learning processes often fail because the learners do not understand the informatics models with which they directly or indirectly interact. Chances in German secondary schools made it possible for learners to collaborate in their learning, even when remote from each other in space or time. A research project that started at the University of Dortmund during the academic year 1998-99 investigated the detection of the difficulties of these learners. Useful observations about the experience and the technology used to support groups were made. The study showed that collaborative learning requires modelling skills and competencies of informatics. Therefore examples of typical modelling tasks are presented from the view of the needs of learners.

Keywords: Collaborative learning, Internet, school Intranet, informatics modelling, data security

1. INTRODUCTION

During the past few years, the teaching and learning in schools has changed significantly due to the influences of informatics. It is to be expected that the future development in the direction of pupil orientation and their ability to learn throughout their life is mainly supported by informatics. Experts describe this overall development as the Information Age. There is a contradiction between the requirements placed on pupils to master complex informatics systems and the lack of a standard, obligatory place in the school curriculum, which can be used for learning informatics. Nievergelt analysed this contradiction at Swiss schools and formulated the following observation: "In the age of applications, programming is no longer merely required as a tool but is basic knowledge for the reasonable application of tools produced by the others. A similar statement is just as valid for all forms of general education" (Nievergelt, 1999, p. 368). For this requirement which was disregarded for a very long time, a new type of informatics education must be tested that places the emphasis on the acquiring and construction of informatics models.

Hubwieser and Broy have introduced a special curriculum for this purpose: "The emphasis lies on the representation of information about complex systems, which we call modelling. In our opinion these techniques support the students in nearly all problem solving tasks, within informatics as well as within all other subjects" (Hubwieser & Broy, 1999, p. 166). The term informatics modelling is used in this article in order to avoid confusion with the very narrow view of programming as a tool. Informatics modelling opens up general educational methods of access to the understanding of informatics systems. This article is linked to this knowledge and tries to illustrate how informatics education supports new school developments.

The informatics education working group at the University of Dortmund carried out research into:

- the basic concepts of informatics and their implementation in informatics education (Humbert, 1999),
- tele co-operation as an object and means for informatics education (Schubert, 1998; Schubert,1999), and
- the development of collaborative learning via a school Intranet (Rüdiger, 1999).

The theoretical concepts was empirically examined in discussions with school heads and teachers, performance tests, by interviewing pupils and the video recording of lessons. It has been shown that informatics education has a strong influence on learning. This includes both the contents (Oberschelp, 1998) and the learning methods (Taylor, 1997).

2. MODELLING IN INFORMATICS

2.1 What is special about this way of modelling?

Model formation and system development differ from other sciences enormously. Computer scientists construct descriptions (programs, software), which are designed to differentiate space for action. When required, the description is applied and it controls processes in the real world. These actions should not be left to coincidence but should turn human objectives into actions. This can only succeed if the real world is described in the informatics system as precisely as possible.

This is exactly the problem. In principal, informatics systems are only able to take in a specific part of the world they model. These synthetic sections form the model. It was always the case that the human being had to decide what was of importance for him in the case of a concrete application and what he could dispense with, or believed that he could go without. If the decisions are successful, then the user hardly notices that he is having an effect on real life by use of his model. He is satisfied if he completes his tasks, is able to achieve his objectives.

In the most unfavourable situation, the model proves to be useless. The informatics system cannot be implemented. Obviously, one hopes that such models can be amended and improved so that they can be used. However, there will always be some disagreement about the specific advantages and disadvantages that a model has in principle. The specification for the model is developed and it summarises the desired system characteristics. The correctness of a system is determined by comparing it with the specification.

The connections with the real world cannot be completely included for testing, as they can also not be fully included in the informatics model. Therefore, user demands are only taken into account if they are included in the specification. This influence at the system development stage is made more difficult for a class of tasks that are processed by persons who do not personally participate in the development process. Users are accordingly dissatisfied with solutions that are designed to cover large areas of responsibilities. Beginners find it difficult to understand that they must collide with the principle restrictions when they use these artificially created model worlds that have now become real systems within their environments.

2.2 Informatics models provide general education

Pupils are often not well prepared to take their future personal responsibility as emancipated citizens for the creation of the Information

Age. They should deal with interactive media in a critical manner although they may never have learned how to understand them. If one analyses the mysteries of these systems, we have two basic problems:

1. The pupils do not have an application strategy which releases them from the specialities of the single systems and which, in principle, provides them with access to the solution of a task class which has a similar functionality. For this, a functional system model is required.

2. The expectations that the pupils have deviate from the real system situation so that a cognitive gap prevents the interpretation of the system process. To this end, a situation transition model supports the orientation in complex and non-deterministic process sequences.

The promotion of the basic understanding of informatics systems is one of the most important educational objectives of informatics education. We start with the simplest acquaintance of typical information and process sequence representation structures. The more demanding design function should not be missing. This has to do with an exemplary penetration of the development process. The best way to learn informatics modelling is in a handling-oriented manner. Knowledge of informatics structure concepts (Hubwieser & Broy, 1999) which can be applied and modified is required for the transitions of sections from reality to model.

Computer-supported learning processes often fail because the pupils do not understand the informatics models with which they directly or indirectly interact. One example for the direct confrontation with an informatics model is the regulation of interaction rights. If the pupils understand the principles, methods, and tools, then they can to make and implement decisions independently. As far as selecting the functionality of classes in an object-oriented informatics system is concerned, the pupils only have an indirect access to the application model. The development team made decisions which can no longer be influenced within the learning process and it is possible that they can be restricting or impeding.

3. CHANCES IN GERMAN SECONDARY SCHOOLS

3.1 Schools on the Internet

In Germany, many teachers brought schools online long before media-effective campaigns existed for this purpose. Colleges and universities promoted the development of a school-specific telecommunication structure. Therefore, in the beginning teachers and pupils only had a restricted access to the Internet. The participants produced their electronic documents on the school computer without an active network connection. These documents were collected and stored in the world-wide network at regular intervals.

In the beginning, a small number of teaching projects made use of the new communication possibilities. The foreign language lessons in the subject English profited from the fast overseas e-mail. The collection and evaluation of environmental data required learning that encompassed both states and subjects. The discussion of globally political themes opened the way to intercultural learning.

Telecommunications leads to an opening up of the schools, provides access to new materials and opinions. It can promote the substantial growth of learning groups and the exchange of experiences between teachers. However, these potential advantages do not open up automatically but require new capabilities. The design of electronic documents, the effective search through the information offered world-wide, and the responsible handling of the action radius which is heavily expanded are all a part of this.

From 1996 to 1999 many schools which provided secondary education were connected to the world-wide Internet via a single telephone line and with only one single workstation (one single computer). For the approximately more than 1,000 pupils and more than 100 teachers at such a school it quickly became clear how unsatisfactory this situation was. Many teachers solved the problem by installing a Linux server themselves in order to connect the local school network to the Internet. A considerable number of regional and countrywide training courses about this subject took place as the inhomogeneous school technology made the administration much more difficult. In the meantime, the neglected school network administrators founded a regionally subdivided group in the German Informatics Society (GI) in order to bring about a reasonable level of support for this unpaid service and to promote the exchanging of experiences.

3.2 Development of school Intranets

The term school Intranet encompasses a wide range of performances. It is now the case that a local school laboratory is able to make internal and external use of Internet technology in almost all German secondary schools. Parents and teachers attempt to gain promotional funds for equipping additional rooms. Exemplary solutions exist which provide Intranet access from all classrooms and staff rooms. Learning concepts, which make use of this, are still rare. Good examples are presented via the regional education server and school presentations.

Equipment recommendations were developed by the members of the aforementioned GI-Group. It is often the case that the school administration is overtaxed as far as making future decisions concerning the content and financial aspects. School failures with donated used company computers and discarded administrative computers did not help to save up money. It is amazing that so many teachers attempt to create or expand a school Intranet system in their free time. The support by school heads and colleagues is by no means routine. The replacement of missing concepts by technically enthusiastic teachers and pupils is only possible as a temporary measure.

At the time this article is being written in November 1999, the external access to learning materials on the school Intranet is still an exception for most of the pupils and teachers but the development here is so fast that the author expects that this access will be the normal situation in the near future. The typical situation today is that teachers and learners continue with their work at home, each for themselves. The networking of these homework stations has started. The exchange of experiences between the teachers is enriching. In learning processes, these networks are still playing a background role. The submission and return of homework is no longer carried out within the school. Solutions that can easily be copied must be analysed. Extensive collections of digital materials are being created in the schools. However, they are often very isolated next to the education concepts and hardly influence the overall school programme.

It is especially the case that as a form of preparation for life-long learning process, they enable new thinking and working methods to be created and must be anchored in the school profiles and curricula. Traditional tasks such as examination revision can be very effectively and individually supported. The unclear administrative tasks initially impair the systematic development of the existing school Intranet. There are still closed laboratories. School administration networks are organised and administered across all schools.

3.3 Computer supported collaborative learning - CSCL

The BSCW system (GMD, 1995-99) is a software system for CSCL in schools which is very comfortable to use and free of charge. It has been criticised by teachers for not being easy enough to use. CSCL is a sensitive process that requires complex models in order to provide support via divided systems which are independent of time and location. This gain in handling quality has its price. One is not concerned with highly complex informatics systems, but with the daily life at a secondary school. The spiral curricula which has made a name for itself over generations because it ranged from the simple to the complicated is confronted by the challenge of opening up the access of to these complexities which cannot be reduced by any means.

The Dortmund didactics group researched CSCL in two initial stages. In the first case, CSCL was introduced to the informatics education as a tutorial package together with BSCW systems (Humbert, 1999). The motivation resulted from the founding of the concept and implementation of technically elaborate processes on the basis of general education. As far as this is concerned, ambitious informative educational content can be included in a handling-oriented manner, for example:

- the design of an order structure for the organisation of the information,
- the activation of system signals for group co-operation,
- the linking of internal and external information structures,
- the version check for information administration,
- the access rights for security demands typical for the group, and
- the working techniques for information transfer.

The pupils successfully learn how to use a model-based access.

In the second case, research was carried out into the transition from the traditional group work to CSCL with teaching material both in informatics lessons and in subject-specific projects. This research project was carried out within the scope of the pilot project to introduce the field of information and communication technology at a special kind of grammar schools in Saxony (1998-2002). In this project, a school form are being developed in Germany in which the "teaching of principles of informatics" was emphasised in the teaching-learning process in order to examine the influence of informatics-related thinking and working methods through all subjects.

The results of the CSCL in project training with Web-based systems showed an unusually high level of pupil motivation and independence (Rüdiger, 1999). The comparison with other developments showed that this positive experience is not dependent on a specific CSCL system (Leinonen et al, 1999) and that the limited view of the place of informatics systems in the school in the category of media formation is incorrect.

4. SKILLS AND COMPETENCIES

4.1 Learning scenario

CSCL promotes project work with the following phases: 1) motivation, 2) objective orientation, 3) planning and recording of the activities, 4) allocation of roles, 5) information acquisition, 6) selection of tools, 7) setting up of solution hypotheses, 8) recommendation of working strategies, 9) documenting the agreements, 10) designing the solution, 11) securing, presentation and evaluation of the results, and 12) reflection on the learning process.

Simpler exercises for accessing information, structuring information, and tending to information security details which enable a transfer from the computer supported group work are necessary prior to this complex learning scenario.

4.2 Access to information

The pupils analyse group learning processes so that they are able to implement elementary CSCL tasks such as reading, conveying, writing and complex actions such as the searching and administration of documents with a process-oriented model (e. g. action diagrams). The differentiation according to roles (e.g. owner of a document) within the group by access rights is presented. This includes changing the groups and roles.

Searching must be based on strategies and tools. The catalogues with numerous hierarchical levels are based on expertise, the search machines on staying power. Both of these are search systems which include rules for dealing with meta-information (e.g. search paths). In order to understand the directories, one must have an insight into their logical structure. Search machines form extremely large databases without being able to evaluate the usefulness of this flood of information to the user. Carefully considered criteria must be developed that can be used to restrict the range of the search and to control the automatic, blind search which the Web-crawling robots carried out. The information evaluation is researched on the basis of the possibility of checking information sources.

An allocation of meta-information to the documents thus displaying the processing of information in the group is concealed behind the administration. At all times, who or what has changed and when it was changed must be recognisable at all times. The version control achieves this in many systems but does not secure the legal and ethical protection. For this reason, the group's public area must be separated from the personal area which each pupil has. The pupils should be able to administer the access to their documents themselves so that they develop the responsibility for the authorship and sense of legality.

4.3 Structuring of information

The pupils learn how to construct complex structures from elementary information and how to apply them to networks, for example:

- trees for the directory structure in order to organise the files,
- graphs for planning multimedia documents, and

- semantic networks for illustrating the workflow.

A basic understanding of the installation and functional method of distributed systems is preparation for the design of distributed documents as a linking of local documents on the school server with global modules on the Internet. The fault vulnerability of absolute information addresses is recognised and relative links are reduced via a calculation algorithm. The pupils collaboratively construct the knowledge which is new for them in the form of documents and software. The linking of learning to modelling and knowledge construction can be used in all subjects but the informatics education as a prerequisite for this requires a fixed place in the curriculum.

In informatics, CSCL is used in the project work in order to develop a complex piece of software within the workgroups. The members of the group initially develop their thoughts and suggestions for solutions within their personal network learning area. The group reaches agreement as to when the intermediate results (analysis, specification, draft, program module) are to be placed for discussion in the mutual area. After an evaluation has been successfully completed, the modules are connected to form the complete system and group documentation. Thus, the division of labour is much more successful by the production of documentation than in traditional group lessons, this being due to the fact that all members really are active (Schubert, 1998). The normally unattractive recording of the interface and design decisions reached becomes a necessary component of group communication due to the CSCL system and is now immediately available in the digitised form which is required at a later date. It simplifies the evaluation of the learning outcomes.

Group communications is a field of experience which the pupils have and which they can model themselves with informatics methods. Taking awareness as an example, they understand how the traditional possibilities of directing attention to alterations in the learning process can be implemented in CSCL by means of an informatics system. This commences with the addition of meta-information (e.g. notes as learning instructions, icons with a signal effect) to the documents. Pointer structures combine the workflow document with the learning results. Progress and omissions within the learning process become transparent for the complete group. By changing the roles between leading the discussion and participating in the discussion the pupils make use of various CSCL functions in order to argue, evaluate, and motivate. With this they learn to understand the various CSCL layers.

4.4 Information security

Requirements which are easy to understand but which are difficult to realise exist in the group communications:

- It should not be possible to falsify the message.
- It should not be possible for confidential information to reach unauthorised persons.
- It should be possible to prove who a message comes from.

The pupils recognise the limits of information security and the risks for the group resulting from carelessness (e.g., passing the password on to others). They learn how to differentiate between securing against accidental events and against intentional attacks with the following basic threats:

- Loss of confidentiality leads to an unauthorised gaining of information.
- Loss of integrity means a falsification of information.
- Loss of availability makes itself known in the form of an impairment of informatics systems functionality (e.g., by viruses).

By protecting against access or encrypting information it is possible to ensure that only the group of persons who are intended to read the information are able to do so and that the information is unable to reach the destination in an altered form without this being noticed. Protection against access should completely, permanently and correctly guarantee access rights in accordance with security requirements which typical for the group. In a security strategy, the pupils determine which persons are permitted to carry out certain operations with certain objects. These rights and prohibitions must be controlled by the system on the basis of a database, in which the access rights are store. Therefore, mechanisms are required for the authentication (identification and verification) of group members on the basis of ownership, knowledge or biometric characteristics.

The pupils use the digital signature and acquaint themselves with the basic principle. Only the owner of a secret cipher key is able to create a signature. Every other person can use the public cipher key in order to determine whether the signature is genuine. Mathematical functions exist which are easy to compute with polynomial complexity, the reversal of which being practically impossible without additional information (called trap-door) being made available. One-way functions such as the factorising method and the discrete logarithm method can be used in a signature algorithm. After the document has been electronically prepared, the digital signature can be calculated and included. After the receipt of a signed document, the identity of the sender must be checked. One advantage is that the electronic signature is disconnected from each bit of the message, which is to be signed. For longer messages it makes sense not to sign the message itself, but a functional value of a certain length which can be allocated to it. This compression regulation is referred to as cryptographic hash function.

5. IMPLICATIONS FOR THE FUTURE

CSCL provides the pupils with many ideas which must often be dealt with. It is often the case that the teacher has almost no time for the moderation of new group communications. A new learning culture looms. It requires adequate prevailing situations that are currently missing. It is typically the case that pupils and teachers separately continue with their work at home after mutual lessons have taken place. Work has commenced on the networking of these home workstations but in Germany, these are not yet connected with the school Intranet.

Collaborative learning requires transparent and understandable teaching-learning actions. Pupils are subjected to higher demands to the effect that they describe their actions and document their activities, them therefore being hardly able to withdraw in the group. Teachers must release themselves from routine methods, learn how to master new informatics systems and therefore notice that they have much more work dictated the preparation and evaluation of group learning.

Informatics modelling is experiencing a Renaissance and is becoming a prerequisite for successful projects, even outside informatics. However, this implies that the pupils who do not have suitable access to informatics education of this kind might have a negative attitude to learning. These application situations are not suitable for the trial-and-error method. The Department on Informatics Education of the German Informatics Society recommends a systematic introduction to the informatics modelling for all pupils from 10 years of age.

CSCL is an application process in which the pupils especially understand and actively co-design demanding informatics concepts. They are provided with a problem and handling-oriented system including abstract structures and complicated mechanisms for rights administration, awareness, workflow management, and data protection.

> The capability of structuring information space in a network with informatics methods and navigating such structures in order to determine a required information with an acceptable level of effort is a part of the general education of all students in the Information Age. Pupils use informatics modelling in CSCL in order to structure their learning activities in an increasingly independent manner, to plan their learning process within their own responsibility, and to understand the curricula coherence better. It is exactly these capabilities which characterise life long learning.

REFERENCES

GMD (1995-99) Basic Support for Cooperative Work (BSCW), http://bscs.gmd.de

Hubwieser, P., and Broy, M. (1999) Educating surfers or craftsmen: Introducing an ICT curriculum for the 21st Century, in [ComNEd] Communication and Networking in Education in a Networked Society. Proceedings of the IFIP Open Conference, Aulanko, June 13-18, 115-121.

Humbert, L. (1999) Grundkonzepte der Informatik und ihre Umsetzung im Informatikunterricht. Informatica Didactica,[http://www.didaktik.cs.uni-potsdam.de/InformaticaDidactica].

Leinonen T., Raami, A., Mielonen, S., Hakkarainen, K., and Muukkonen, H. (1999) FLE - Tools Prototype: A WWW-based Learning Environment for Collaborative Knowledge Building, in [ComNEd] Communication and Networking in Education in a Networked Society. Proceedings of the IFIP Open Conference, Aulanko, June 13-18, 376-377 [http://mlab.uiah.fi/fle].

Nievergelt, J. (1999) Roboter programmieren – ein kinderspiel. Informatik-Spektrum, 22(5), 364-375.

Oberschelp, W. (1998) How informatics and discrete thinking return to school. in Information and Communications Technologies in School Mathematics (eds. D. Tinsley and D. Johnson), Chapman & Hall, London.

Rüdiger, B. (1999) Von der traditionellen zur computerunterstützten Gruppenarbeit. LOGIN, 19(3/4), 36-41, [http://ls12-www.cs.unidortmund.de/ddi/forschung/ruediger].

Schubert, S. (1999) Informatische bildung und telekooperation. LOGIN, 19(3/4), 30-35.

Schubert, S. (1998) Internet-studies communication and information technology (CIT).

in Informatics in Higher Education (eds. F. Mulder and T. van Weert), Chapman & Hall, London.

Taylor, H. (1997) Developing an active learning infrastructure with community involvement, telecommunications, and technology. it+ti, Informationstechnik und Technische Informatik, 39(6), 27-32.

BIOGRAPHY

Sigrid Schubert received her diploma in physics from the University of Dresden (Germany) in 1972 and her doctoral degree in didactics of informatics from the University of Chemnitz in 1988. Since 1972 she has taught informatics in secondary and vocational education. In 1998 she became professor in didactics of informatics at the University of Dortmund. Her research interests are: informatics at secondary schools, collaborative learning, multimedia evaluation in teacher education. She is chairman of the Department on Informatics Education of the German Informatics Society (GI) and member in IFIP Working Group 3.1 on secondary education.

Designing digital learning environments

Paul A. Jansen, Petra Fisser, and Cees Terlouw
SLO, The Netherlands.
P.Jansen@slo.nl
University of Twente, P.O. Box 217, 7500 AE Enschede, The Netherlands.
p.h.g.fisser@edte.utwente.nl, c.terlouw@oc.utwente.nl

Abstract: In this paper an overview is given of current developments in the Netherlands. The second part starts with some educational fundaments for Digital Learning Environments (DLE's). The elements of DLE's are described by the different interactions and communications between the student and participants and materials in learning environments. The paper finishes with some concrete examples and some considerations about choices to make for schools.

Keywords: Learning environments, flexible learning, innovation, policy

1. INTRODUCTION

Starting in 1998 there will be substantial investment in the use of ICT in Dutch schools. One of the major programs from the Dutch government "Investeren in Voorsprong" ("Investing in Progress") was launched in 1997. This program was a strongly governmental steered implementation plan, which aimed at the integration of ICT in education in such a way that it contributes to the actuality, quality, effectiveness and attractiveness of education (Ministry of Education, Culture and Science, 1997). The plan was would eventually result in a ratio of one computer for every ten children.

In April 1999 the new Minister of Education presented the continuation of "Investing in Progress" in the program "Onderwijs online, verbindingen naar de toekomst" ("Education online, connections to the future"). In that plan the responsibility for the implementation of ICT in education is put in the hands of the schools themselves. Schools receive a fixed sum per pupil from the Ministry which is intended to incorporate new media into their curricula. They can decide for themselves how they will make use of this budget for hardware, software and training, while the government only determines the overall policy, promotes relevant training for teachers and encourages the development of methodology and software. One part of the national programs is to encourage all primary and secondary teachers to get their 'Digital Driving License for Education', in order to obtain skills and knowledge in several ICT applications.

Another part of these governmental plans is to provide all ca. 10.000 Dutch schools (vocational tertiary, secondary and primary) with a special extranet, called "kennisnet" ("knowledge-net"). The goal of this project is to connect groups (students, teachers, parents, schools, organisations and other interested parties) with each other, with educational suppliers and with Internet. This plan has to be carried out before the end of 2001.

Giving schools money and a connection to the Internet will not provide a good learning environment for a student. Embedding ICT in education requires more than that, including a didactical way of integrating ICT in education in such a way that ICT supports the learning environment of the student. The questions we want to answer in this paper are twofold:

1. Which is the framework in which a powerful didactical concept is combined with an ICT-approach?
2. Which real existing Digital Learning Environments (DLE) are present in Dutch primary and secondary education which illustrate and elaborate the framework?

We will illustrate our approach with examples of DLE's for Dutch primary and secondary schools. Finally, we will conclude with some points of discussion.

2. THE OVERALL DIDACTICAL FRAMEWORK

Nowadays the continuum teacher-centred <-> student-centred[3] education is an important perspective to consider. The teacher-centred end of the continuum concerns the activities of the teacher in order to stimulate learning of students. The other end of the continuum concerns the own, self-directed activities of students in order to learn.

In general the trend is to move from a more teacher-centred approach to a more student-centred approach in the target situation. Therefore, two types of didactical approaches are distinguished, both examples of metacognitive

[3] The term "students" includes pupils in primary and secondary education.

skills that are needed in order to find the relevant information: (a) self-directed learning in which students create their own learning process, and (b) scaffolding, in which students realise their learning process with decreasing help of teachers. This distinction is also relevant in education in which ICT is involved.

Scaffolding is, as said, a didactical approach in which the metacognitive skills can be learned. Scaffolding can be described as a communication process in which support, given by the teacher, gradually decreases. It is a process of gradual reduction of support until the scaffolding is no longer needed. (Jonassen, 1996; King, Staffieri, & Adelgais, 1998; Winnips, 1998). The instructor monitors student learning in a careful and individualised way and withdraws support when the student can work on his or her own (Collis, Winnips & Moonen, 1999). In figure 1 the process of scaffolding is represented.

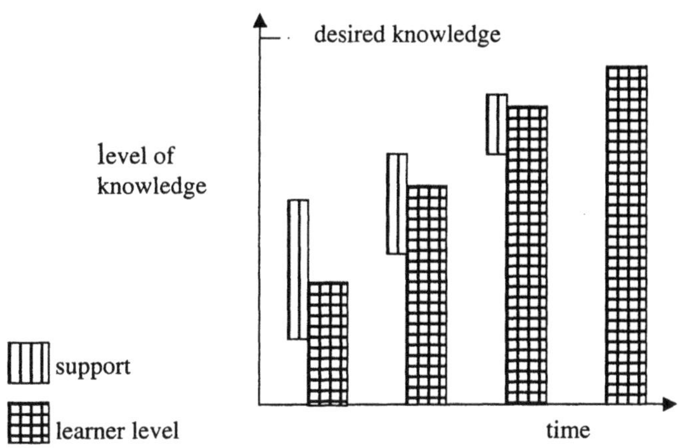

Figure 1. The process of scaffolding (adapted from Winnips, 1998)

The ideas described above follow the constructivist learning approach. The constructivist approach has been described by many authors. We would like to follow Tabbert's description that learning is a process of knowledge construction, learning occurs by interpreting information, people use current knowledge to construct new knowledge and learning is highly adjusted to the situation in which it takes place (Tabbert, 1993). In other words, in this approach knowledge is believed to be actively constructed, tightly connected to the individual's cognitive repertoire and to the context within this activity takes place.

According to Salomon (1998) ICT offers the opportunity of actively constructing knowledge in particular symbolic forms (word, graph, pictures) and structured in particular organisational ways (databases, hypermedia) available for exploration and manipulation. Salomon further claims that not just being exposed to these symbol systems of technology and media, but being actively involved in construction, either individually or collaboratively, makes this possibility a powerful one. Salomon's ideas offer a first handgrip in answering the question of how to combine ICT and a good didactical concept to result in an effective DLE. In the following sections of this paper we will elaborate on this.

3. A FRAMEWORK FOR ICT AND INTERACTION

We will start by giving a frame of reference with regard to ICT in education, focussing on the interactions that are needed in education and can be made possible by using ICT.

3.1 A model for interaction

Communication can be seen as a certain amount of interactions that a student can have with its environment. Sysling and Van Veen (1997) have outlined a model in which the student, according to the latest principles of the before mentioned learning theories of constructivism, is the central person in a learning process. The student has different kind of interactions with his environment. This is shown in Figure 2.

In this model the student is the most important person in a learning process. According to Sysling and Van Veen the student has several possibilities to start an interaction with his environment: he can study learning materials, receive assignments from the teacher, look for information in a library, discuss the material with fellow students, etc. In return, the environment can have interactions with the student: the teacher gives instructions and feedback, students work together on an assignment, the organisation keeps track of study progress, etc. All these interactions can be categorised with the before mentioned distinctive didactical approaches: self-directed learning and scaffolding.

Sysling and Van Veen claim that for each interaction ICT can be used. They also claim that this kind of education, in which the student is the central focus point and in which ICT is integrated in education, leads to DLE's, with sufficient possibilities for interaction and for real learning.

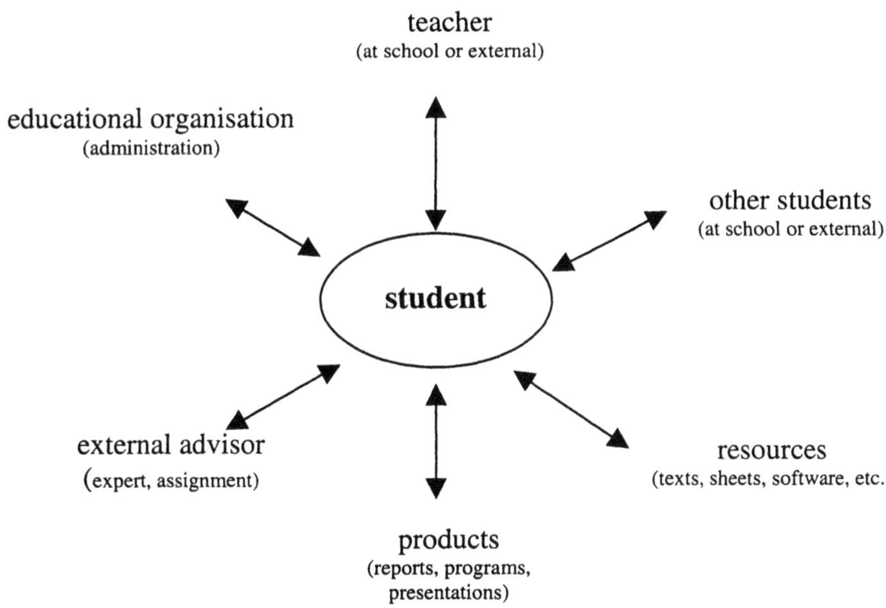

Figure 2. Interactions between student and learning environment (adapted from Sysling and van Veen (1997)

3.2 A digital learning environment

Against this background, we argue that by combining the communication possibilities of ICT and a constructivist didactical framework with effective interactions a Digital Learning Environment (DLE) can be created. A traditional learning environment of a student consists of a combination of means, strategies, persons and facilities to place a student in a position in which he or she can learn. A DLE supports and enriches the traditional environment by functionally using ICT.

Mirande, Riemersma and Veen (1997) give a broad definition of a DLE: each learning environment that uses technology. In the context of DLE's Collis (1996) speaks about telelearning and defines telelearning as "making connections among persons and resources through communication technologies for learning-related purposes". This means that the learner is engaged in learning, but not on his own. The learner makes connections with others (teacher, other students, etc.) or with specific resources (text, video, etc.). According to Collis the persons and resources involved in telelearning may be beyond what the learner could have access to in his ordinary learning context, but they may be also the same persons and resources, made accessible in different ways and at different times than before.

4. METHOD

In order to answer the second research question about real existing DLE's which are present in Dutch primary and secondary education, literature and WWW research has been conducted. Looking at the given framework and the description of DLE's the first step is to describe existing examples of ICT in education and the interactions as mentioned in the model in Figure 2.

We will follow the argumentation of Sysling and Van Veen in relation to interactions and the description of Collis of Telelearning or DLE's and describe each category of interaction with examples from teaching practice.

5. RESULTS

Before we discuss each interaction we will answer the question if interaction via ICT can be used for pupils from primary and secondary schools. We will give a short view on the situation in these schools.

5.1 Current situation

Each year the Research Centre of the University of Twente produces an ICT-monitor. The ICT-monitor reports on the current state-of-affairs of ICT in Dutch education. The latest ICT-monitor (Brummelhuis, 1998) shows that the attitude in primary education towards the educational use of ICT has changed positively over the years. Many teachers are convinced that ICT is useful for education. A third of the teachers find themselves insufficiently informed about the possibilities. Since one cannot implement ICT-practices that one doesn't know, it is expected that the implementation will stagnate in an increasing number of schools. The ICT-monitor for secondary education shows that teachers think they will no longer be the most important source of information. Computers are seen as an important tool for the organisation of the education. Students use computers independently working on assignments or searching for information. Computers will be available to them, just as any other learning material. Although the willingness to change is large and the use of ICT is seen as valuable and relevant, most teachers think they lack relevant information and haven't got enough materials.

By this we see that ICT is a hot topic at both the primary and secondary schools. Although several problems have been observed (especially related to teacher training) there are many possibilities for ICT at these schools. We will describe some possibilities in the next paragraphs, relating to the interactions of a student as described in the theoretical framework.

5.2 Student-teacher interaction

Giving assignments, discussions between teachers and students and giving feedback on assignments are examples of student-teacher interaction, where scaffolding is crucial. One of the most common ways to use ICT for this kind of interaction is e-mail. Students can ask questions about the learning material, teachers can supply information about the course and give feedback, etc. This kind of interaction can also be supported by using the Internet. Usually this is done by providing general course information, such as information about the goals, the schedule of lectures and information about teachers and students.

Examples of the use of e-mail at primary and secondary schools can be found, but it usually concerns communication between students. Examples of e-mail communication between teachers and students are barely found. One example is the project 'Kid E-mail' where students and teachers used e-mail in an organised way to exchange ideas about flying constructions.

A more technological enhanced tool for student-teacher interaction is video- or audio conferencing. With the help of these technologies a teacher can reach a student at a remote site. This is often used if a student cannot come to class easily. These technologies will be used more often, when the infrastructure will be available at the schools.

5.3 Student-student interaction

An example of student to student interaction in a learning process is communication during an assignment. Tasks have to be divided and a product has to be made. Using e-mail and a website as described above for interaction between teacher and student can be used in the same way for interaction between students. Communication with other students in another country is one of the possibilities.

An example of this type is the project " Stuyvesant and Dutch Colonies in the U.S." in which a Dutch primary school and an American Middle School study together (see www.gco.nl/tyr/menue.htm). The project has started by making acquaintance by mail. The educational department in the municipality of the Dutch school provides a lot of information about the period in which Stuyvesant lived. The students from the Netherlands and the USA were matching their results which are published at the website.

Another way for student to student interaction is to put their assignment or product on the web. This can be a simple webpage with information or a more sophisticated digital portfolio. Examples of this on the Internet are drawings of children that are scanned and put on a webpage or a digital school newspaper with short stories or children's songs.

There are more advanced tools for collaboration, such as discussion lists on the Internet or GroupWare. The amount of examples to be found of this kind of collaboration at primary and secondary schools is rising. This is inherent to the way primary and secondary education is organised and to the level of ICT skills of the students. Next to this we believe that the growing use of tools as GroupWare is one of the results of teacher training.

5.4 Student-resources interaction

One of the major advantages of the Internet is the huge amount of information that can be found. There is information about an enormous diversity of subjects. Not all information is well structured or easy to find. This means that students have to learn new skills in retrieving and managing the information. These skills are included in the Dutch curricula.

It is not possible to give an extensive and comprehensive list of all kinds of examples of student-resources interactions. It is sufficient to say that there are many possibilities (searching on the WWW for a specific subject, etc.). The pitfall is the overload of information and the necessary skills to discriminate between useful and second-rate information.

5.5 Student-product interaction

Student-product interaction differs from student-resources interaction. In the latter the retrieval of information is the key issue. In student-product interaction the issue is to use the found information and make an own product. This can be done individually or with fellow students. Again, e-mail, a website and GroupWare can be used to facilitate this process. Working together on a document, developing a homepage or making a presentation or portfolio are all examples of student-product interaction.

5.6 Student-external advisor interaction

One of the possibilities of ICT is to bring an external expert in the classroom. This can be a veterinarian telling something about horses by videoconferencing, asking questions by e-mail to a historian about the Middle Ages, or an artist showing his latest paintings on his homepage. The expert delivers the content and the students can listen and ask questions. An example of this can be found at a website made for primary schools (www.iselinge.nl/Scholenplein/euro/index.htm). One of the course ideas on this site is offering students the possibility to ask questions to people who know a lot about the Euro, for instance banks, Ministries of Finance, etc.

5.7 Student-organisation interaction

It is important for a school to keep track of the learning results of the students. There are several ways of doing this. Common tools are word processors and spreadsheets to save the data. There are more sophisticated tools to keep track of the learning results. One of them is a new developed tool called SPRS, a Study Planning and Registration System which offers a digital platform for contents, planning, assessment and registration.

6. INTEGRATING INTERACTIONS INTO A DLE

As we have seen, there are many possibilities for using ICT for interactions in education. But it is also clear that the interactions as described above are all a specific part of the learning process. Integrating all kind of interactions with particular ICT tools and applications into one environment which is accessible for students and teachers is what every school should aim for if it wants to use ICT effectively.

At this moment there are some examples present in the Netherlands of primary and secondary schools that use such an environment. Discussions are going on about the installation of such platforms in a region, using for example the infrastructure of the university in this region. Therefore it is interesting to look at some examples from Higher Education, because it looks to be a real future for primary and secondary education.

6.1 Existing DLE-platforms

There are several commercial products that can be used to offer a DLE. Recently a research is carried out in the Netherlands in which several commercial products are compared for use in Higher Education (Droste, 1999). As a conclusion, Droste argues that strategic attention has to be paid to the situation in which a platform is used, to the support of specific functionalities in the platform, to the support from the organisation for purchase such a platform, to technical and maintenance issues and last but not least to the costs of such a platform (Droste, pp. 39). We think that this conclusion is also true when choosing a platform for primary and secondary education. Next to this we argue that also the training of teachers is included when different platforms are considered.

Although there are platforms for DLE's available as shown above, there are several institutions that have developed their own platform or DLE. One could say that they are re-inventing the wheel, but some of these projects have good reasons for developing an own product. As an example we give a short overview of the DLE that is developed at the University of Twente, C@mpus+, a Learning Environment that will be used at secondary schools too in the future.

C@mpus+ started as a project of the Faculty of Educational Science and Technology as the TeLeTOP (Telelearning at TO) Project. TeLeTOP is focused on extending the Faculty's innovative technological profile through integrating telematics applications in our own courses for more-flexible learning. TeLeTOP is the implementation project that supports the Faculty's philosophy: Extending the benefits of good teaching and a good campus-based experience to all students: full-time students and part-time students who are not always at the campus. The part-time students can follow the courses at their home or workplace, but have to come to the university once every two weeks to follow lectures, in accordance with the Faculty's philosophy (for more information about the TeLeTOP project see the TeLeTOP homepage http://teletop.edte.utwente.nl/).

The Faculty of Educational Science and Technology choose to develop its own system, after evaluating other existing systems. All existing products had good aspects, but none of them supported the Faculty's philosophy to the extend that was wanted. The TeLeTOP project was carefully evaluated and based on the results of this evaluation the university decided that this system should be used throughout all Faculties of the university. In 2000 several Faculties will start to use the TeLeTOP system, now called C@mpus+, probably including a group of secondary schools in the region.

6.2 Considerations for DLE's at schools

The constructivist approach offers many starting points for a good didactical foundation for making useful usage of ICT in education. With ICT the learner can construct his or her own knowledge in co-operation contexts. As we have seen in the description of the interactions that a student can have with the environment, with ICT knowledge can be constructed through communication with teachers and fellow students. The teacher is still needed in this process, especially at the beginning of the learning process. A student has to learn how to construct his own knowledge. He has to learn how to retrieve the right information and he has to learn how to interpret and deal with the found information. But gradually the teacher's role will change from telling the student what he should do to supporting (coaching) the student in his learning process.

A good DLE provides possibilities for all interactions described by Sysling and Van Veen (1997). These interactions model the learning environment that is needed for a student to gain the necessary knowledge, skills and attitudes. The level of use of ICT for these interactions will depend on both the teacher and the student. The student should have the possibility to use ICT when useful. The necessary skills to use ICT should be acquired in order to use ICT as effectively as possible and face-to-face communication remains important. Both students and teachers have to obtain the necessary skills to use ICT in education. Teachers indicate that they need more knowledge and training in the pedagogical, didactical en organisational aspects of computer use in education (Brummelhuis, 1998).

The support of the government is important. Overall policy should be developed with attention for didactical methodology. Training for teachers should be available to all schools. Next to this the support of the management and the teachers of the schools is important. From the Dutch ICT-monitor it seems that the overall opinion is positive. This is important for the success of the implementation of ICT at schools.

In conclusion, a DLE should correspond with the views of the school towards education and the place ICT will take within it. A school should use ICT not only to the norms of society, but also to educational norms and values. Enough attention should be paid to the appropriateness of using ICT. Some situations are more appropriate then others. All kind of interactions should be imaginable, where possible supported by ICT. When used well, ICT can help a student to become a self-directing, flexible, communicative member of society.

REFERENCES

Brummelhuis A. (1998a) *ICT-monitor 1997/1998, Basisonderwijs en Voortgezet Onderwijs [primary and secondary education],* Enschede, Universiteit Twente, Onderzoek Centrum Toegepaste Onderwijskunde (OCTO).

Collis, B. (1996) *Tele-learning in a digital world. The future of distance learning,* International Thomson Computer Press, London.

Collis, B., Winnips, J., and Moonen, J. (1999) *Scaffolding and the use of the WWW: Does it pay off?,* Manuscript submitted for publication to the Journal of Interactive Learning Research).

Droste, J. (1999) *Advies keuze teleleerplatform,* Stichting SURF, Utrecht.

Jonassen, D. (1996) *Scaffolding diagnostic reasoning in case-based-learning environments,* Journal of Computing in Higher Education, 8(1), 48-68.

King, A., Staffieri, A., and Adelgais, A. (1998) *Mutual peer tutoring: Effects of structuring tutorial interaction to scaffold peer learning,* Journal of Educational Psychology, 90(1).

Ministry of Education, Culture and Science. (1997) *Actieplan and Implementatieplan voor Informatie- en CommunicatieTechnologie in het onderwijs [Action plan and Implementation plan for Information and Communication Technology in education],* OCenW, Zoetermeer

Mirande, M., Riemersma, J., and Veen, W. (1997) *De digitale leeromgeving [The digital learning environment],* Wolters Noordhoff, Groningen.

Salomon, G. (1998) *Novel constructivist learning environments and novel technologies: Some issues to be concerned with,* Research Dialogue in Learning and Instruction, 1(1).

Sysling, M., and Van Veen, B. (1997) *Inventarisatie Teleleren CT&M [Inventory Telelearning Civil Engineering and Management, DOC 98-04],* Educational Centre, University of Twente, Enschede.

Tabbert, B. (1993) Allan Collins, *From inquiry teaching to cognitive apprenticeship,* In Instructietheorie (eds. S. Dijkstra, T. Dillingh, and B. Tabbert), 2, p. 97-147.

Winnips, J. (1998) *Scaffolding van ontwerpvaardigheden voor het ontwerproces van onderwijskundige media door middel van gehyperlinkte ULMs [Scaffolding the development of skills in the design process for educational media through hyperlinked units of learning material (ULMs)],* Internal report, Faculteit der Toegepaste Onderwijskunde, Universiteit Twente.

Winnips, J., and Collis, B. (1999) *Examples of scaffolding in the practice of tele-learning environments,* Presentation and panel session at EDMEDIA '99, Seattle.

BIOGRAPHIES

Paul Jansen graduated in 1973 in mathematics. He became and had several functions in school management. In 1989 he joined the SLO, the Dutch National Institute for Curriculum Development. He has been project leader and co-ordinator for many projects involving ICT as a subject and integrated in other subjects. Since 1999 he is director of 'the School of the Future', an institute specialised in renewing education and business by ICT.

Petra Fisser is a scientific staff member at the University of Twente, Faculty of Educational Science and Technology, department of Educational Instrumentation. Her research focuses on the factors that stimulate using ICT in education and especially for the university.

Cees Terlouw graduated in 1976 in Educational Sciences at the Dutch University of Groningen, and received his Ph.D in 1987 at the University of Twente on an empirical study on instructional design for problem solving in social sciences. He works at the University of Twente, from 1987 at the Educational Center on topics such as problem solving, course development, teacher training and use of ICT in secondary and higher education. Since 1999 the Educational Center is a part of the Dinkel-institute, where he is a member of the management.

Assisting or creating the future?

Léa da Cruz Fagundes
Laboratório de Estudos Cognitivos (LEC), Instituto de Psicologia, Universidade Federal do Rio Grande do Sul, Porto Alegre, Brazil.
leafagun@vortex.ufrgs.br

Abstract: The goals, methodology and results of the EducaDi Project (Distance Learning in Mathematics and Science) are discussed. This project was supported by the CNPq, the Research National Council in Brazil. The purpose of this project was to develop new models for the educational virtual networks. The project assumed that the introduction and use of digital technologies must be supported by structural, operational and cultural changes in the schools. It required understanding the learning process and the cognitive, moral and social development of the learners. New roles and practices were designed to change communications and interactions among teachers, students and knowledge. The methodology used was a new interdisciplinary approach to learning projects. Key success factors were the ability to cooperate in groups and to create new forms of information search and data organization as well as the flexibility to acquire the skills required for new jobs, including research skills needed for the production process.

Keywords: Virtual networks, school culture, teacher interactions

1. INTRODUCTION

We are, no doubt, living a process of fast transformations in the form of living with great advancements in the area of communication and information processing. It has become almost impossible to plan in advance, to define what has to be learned, and which skills are necessary, in order to inhabit this "new world." When we speak of education, though, we can be sure of some needs:

- To update sources of information and to develop new talents/skills, in all areas.
- To develop attitudes and values for the autonomous and co-operative conviviality.
- To develop new skills for the same profession, whose activities vary, and are easily transformed.
- To develop skills which permit changes from one profession to an emergent one during lifetime.

The great majority of the educational methodologies, and of technologies presently taught in the courses of teacher preparation, has proved inefficient to help the student to learn and to develop new talents.How can we offer opportunities to the new generations to develop their talents in science and beauty, in solidarity and harmony? How can we help them to know, to construct new worlds of distributive exchanges, of positive administration of the conflicts and of the adventures? Such questions disturb and challenge us to search new answers. What should we do?

The necessary shift has occurred from an empiricist practical view, control and manipulation of the changes in the learner's behavior, that has oriented the pedagogical practice, to a problem-solving constructivist view, favouring the interactivity, the autonomy in formulating questions, the search of innovative resources. Some feel that the arrival of the computer technology at schools will not simply introduce the external social changes. Is it possible that this arrival will offer new possibilities for us to search for contextualised information, the experimental confirmation of the critical analysis?

It is called a shift because school systems are organised for a general and standard model of functioning. So, to change from an empiricist view to a constructivist view requires that practising educators put everything we have been trying and dreaming into practice.

In Brazil, only a few teachers working with small groups of students have been able to experiment with innovative practices. These practices have not been disseminated and have not become generalized. May help ICT to enrich the learning environments, to expand the classroom spaces, overcome time barriers, to serve as cognitive "prosthesis"? ICT may help to expand the social-affective processes and the awareness to assist the learners as true agents of their own learning. ICT may guarantee the collective inter-communication, and help to create learning and development communities. How and why can this happen?

Up to now, in the Northern Hemisphere, the evaluations have indicated the denial of these possibilities. Only very recently the need of the change from the empiricist model to the constructivist one started to be discussed.

This is reason we have emphasised the need to investigate how to change the paradigm, and how to apply new technologies to our school system.

This paper analyses some common experiences of the EducaDi Project, Distance Learning in Mathematics, Science and Technology. The project was supported by CNPq, the Research National Council of the Ministry of Science and Technology in Brazil. It was developed with four regional centres, in 29 public elementary and secondary schools during 1997 and 1998. The author was the national co-ordinator and co-ordinator of a regional centre. She worked together on the project with the professors Schiel Dietrich, Mauro Pequeno, and Maria da Glória Noronha Serpa, all researchers from public universities in different regions of our Brazil.

2. THE PHYSICAL AND CULTURAL SITUATION OF THE SCHOOLS

Brazil is a South-American country with a large extension of land, formed by 27 federative states where the population (more than one hundred and sixty million people) lives in diverse contexts. A strong national identity is shared by communities with different historical and geographical backgrounds, all speaking the same language, Portuguese. The possible implementations of the educational system must also take into account the extreme social contrasts. The country has one of the highest levels of concentration of income in the world. There is a great diversity of situations in the public state educational systems.

In the last 30 years there have been successive curricular reforms in the Brazilian secondary level education. One of them, in 1971, consisted of the transformation of the existing secondary level schools, that offered three types of training (scientific, classic or technological studies) into a general secondary school offering a low level professional training, named "professionalizater," to be developed in a short time. The curricular propositions aimed to prepare "auxiliary workers" in different professions. However, study time was cut down and the content of each subject was strongly reduced. The schools did not have the concrete conditions to develop the practical activities. This reform failed in both aspects, basic and professional formation.

One new curricular reform was initiated gradually, whenever the cracks in the educational system started to show and when democratic governments returned to govern the nation. At the present, the system is structured with an emphasis on basic studies, represented by the eight years of fundamental education for all. The professional training has then been assigned to specific technological schools. The three years of secondary level are named "medium teaching" that has to complement fundamental studies. Their legal foundations are in LDB law #9394 / 1996. In search of substantial changes to adapt the National System of Education to the new social, economic and cultural changes in the world, and in search of new solutions available to promote human and social development in our Country, the ongoing reform states in "Diretrizes Curriculares para o Ensino Médio" approved en June, 1998. The Guidelines of the LDB Law point to General Directions and not to Specific Points:

Article 21 - The school system is formed by:

I. Basic education that includes Kindergarten (3-6 years old) Fundamental Level (7-14 years old) and Secondary Level (15-18 years old)

II. High Level Education

In this article of the law, the secondary level must then become a progressive expansion of the fundamental level, the universal public and free education as the right of all citizens.

Article 35 - The secondary level is the final phase of Basic Education. It must then provide the basic preparation for work and citizenship obeying principles of identity, sensitivity and equality by:

A. Stimulating creativity, the spirit of invention and curiosity about the unknown;
B. Developing the acceptance and the ability to cope with the unexpected; and
C. Leading to the recognition of and respect for the individual and group differences and values.

The general preparation for work should be basic, that is, for everybody and for all kinds of work, emphasising the ability to go in learning.

At the moment in Brazil, there is no obligatory sequence of content for each of the school years. Each school receives national general guidelines and chooses content according to the contexts of the community. In spite of this, the textbooks widely used throughout the country present a very similar arrangement of content. These arrangements also are very similar to standard lists from the NCTM Web site (www.nctm.org). The insufficient amount of public schools to meet the needs of the population within the age groups of secondary level is still a barrier for the democratic life.

The major problem remains the educational culture, the conceptions of the educators that resist using these new possibilities. In many schools the curriculum has been designed into parallel, segmented courses, overloading the content of each subject, because the time for teaching is scheduled into pre-defined periods. The teachers teach the same content in the same way, in the same amount of time for groups of hundreds of students.

Some progress has been made. During ten years, for instance, in the SPEC Project/CAPES/MEC/1885-1995 (Science Teaching Enhancing Program) produced new instructional materials and teacher training in accordance with the innovative methodologies of teaching. A large number of texts, books, experimental kits, instructional materials were produced by researchers and experts in the technology of science education.. Teachers were trained. Research projects were developed to test and to evaluate their applications. These results were restricted to the inner groups of their authors. The dissemination was localised and restricted.

During the year of 1996 researchers proposed CNPq, a consortium between four centers in the country to develop the EducaDi project, because they wanted develop experiences connecting teachers and students from different situations to form a learning community. There were some similarities between the schools, such as:

A. All the schools were public and situated in marginal urban zones.
B. The students came from low income population and had little access to ICT.
C. The schools were in the Basic System, fundamental and secondary level, that included 7 to 18 years old students.

On the other hand the cultural, historic and geographic conditions of these populations were very different in aspects such as ethnic, tradition, economic resources, economic production, weather, landscape, work, industrialisation, means of transportation, parents instructional level, and artistic expressions. However, two conditions supported these experiments. First, there were well-defined policies in the Brazilian educational system to favour the use of ICT in the public schools. Second, many teachers wanted to use ICT according to the constructivist approach.

3. THE STRUCTURE OF THE CONSTRUCTIVIST LEARNING ENVIRONMENT

The purpose of this project was to develop new models for the educational virtual networks. The project assumed that the introduction and the use of ICT in the school must be supported by structural, operational and cultural changes.

The rationale of this project was designed using a genetic epistemology which enhances a constructivist understanding of learning process as well of the learner's cognitive, moral and social development. However, the project tried to address questions about the fast transition in the shift of paradigm in the interchange between the partners of the team of educators and researchers. The resources in the space of the server were organised to meet both the needs for a pure constructivist approach as well as the needs for a content delivery service. The difference is more or less control of the activities about information search and the decision making by students.

3.1 Implementation of interactivity

The virtual learning environment is online and utilises a Windows platform, because all the schools use PC compatible computers. We developed the resources to assure interaction in two kinds of interactive communication, synchronous and asynchronous.

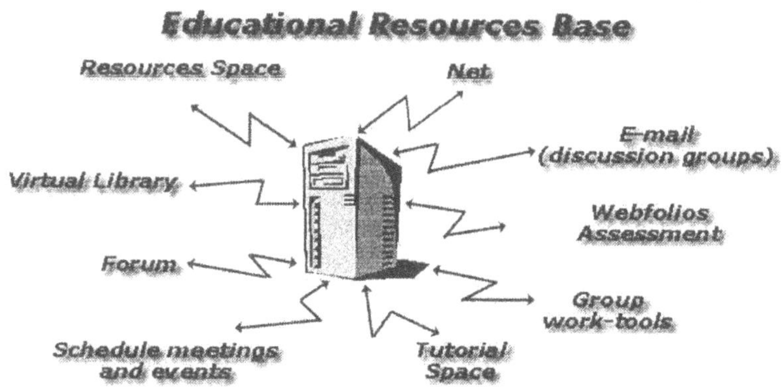

Figure 1. Educational resource base

As shown in Figure 1, free resources were available on the main server in LEC/UFRGS, to enhance interactive communication. Others resources like e-mail, lists, forums, storyboard, forms, CGI scripts were provided to support the collaborative work and to decentralise the decision making. There were also free spaces such called "cafes" for all teachers and students. The project directors used spreadsheets and different databases to made registrations, to schedule activities and programs, and to aid in the management of this learning environment.

The environment included a virtual library with texts, hyper documents and educational materials chosen by educators. It also offered the possibility for each user to edit and to publish their productions as home pages, sites, documents, experimental reports, pictures, photos, music, texts, all sort of compositions, as well as the software that was needed. This included resources for individual use and group portfolio assessment to keep a track of the work of students and teachers. The server also contained the information about the learning environment and the community of users. A special space was reserved for the publication of the Learning Projects.

3.2 Infrastructure and organisational aspects

We have chosen the constructive activity of designing and implementing projects to become a methodology for learning in the EducaDi Project, because the activity of conceiving projects is symbolic, intentional and natural to the human being. Through it, man looks for the solution to problems and initiates a process of knowledge construction, which has generated not only the arts but the social and natural sciences as well.

The word "project" is quite recent in our culture. The word describes both the intellectual effort to devise the project and the multiple activities involved in carrying it out. The devising of a project constitutes the first step in every research, which will then be carried out based on a set of questions, either about itself or about the world. As a student (Mir, 15 years) says: "To me a project is like an architectural project, the guy draws a plan to guess how things are going to turn out in the end, but the difference is that we can keep changing it."

3.2.1 The learning project

When using the expression teaching through projects in school, one might be referring to the school's plan, to the school's project, to the teachers' projects. In this kind of teaching, which criteria would the teacher use in order to select the themes or questions that will define the project? What advantage does the selection of these questions present? Why are they necessary? In which contexts? Which indicators do we have to measure their levels of need? Whom would they satisfy? The curricula? The objectives of the school plan? A training tradition?

In fact, in the field of teaching, every action comes from the teacher's decisions and should return to his control. It is as if the teacher was the sole owner of knowledge to be passed on to the student and, furthermore, as if the decision of what, how and to which extent this knowledge should be acquired by the student was also his unshared responsibility. The student is not given the opportunity of making any choices or decisions. He is supposed to be completely submitted to the rules imposed by the educational establishment.

However, we soon became aware of our mistakes. Research in the area of genetic psychology, mainly on the development of intelligence and on the learning process, have shown the possibility of there existing teaching without learning; that learning can be taken as development; and development results in the subject's operational actions, who constructs knowledge when interacting with his environment, with other individuals and with objects of knowledge which he wishes to appropriate.

When dealing with "learning through projects" we necessarily refer to the formulation of questions by the project's author, that is, by the individual who will construct knowledge himself. For us the student is never a blank page, that is, he was used to thinking before the project began. And it is from this previous knowledge that the learner will set off to interact with the unknown, to appropriate specific knowledge, be it either in the sciences, in the arts, in the traditional culture or in the present changing culture.

A Project to Learn will be generated by the conflicts, by the disturbing interference in these signification systems, which constitute the learner's individual knowledge. How can we access these systems? The student himself is not aware of them! That is the reason why the choice of variables to be tested in this problem solving attempt has to be supported by a survey of questions made by the student himself.

In a Learning Project, who manifests doubts that will generate the project? Who wants to search for answers? The student himself, while acting in a certain context, in his life environment or in a challenging situation, faces such challenges. But can the school allow the student to choose the theme, the question, which will generate the development of a project? It is essential that the students' curiosity, doubt, questionings generate the subject to be researched, and this is not be imposed by the teacher, as motivation is intrinsic to the individual.

The inversion of these roles is extremely significant. When the learner is challenged to question, when he is uneasy and needs to think in order to express his doubts, when he is allowed to ask questions he considers meaningful, and which emerge from his life history, from his own interests, he begins to develop the competence to formulate and solve problems. One, who is able to pose a problem clearly, and sort it out, is learning to define the aims of his activity.

The key statement about the new types of learning in our model of learning environments using ICT is "learning through projects" is quite different from "teaching through projects"? Table 1 illustrates this.

Our strategy is to conduct a preliminary survey on the students' provisory certainties and temporary doubts. And why temporary? When researching, questioning, and investigating take place, many doubts are transformed into certainties and certainties become doubts; or, still, they generate other doubts and certainties which, in turn, will be also temporary, provisory. Teachers and students engage then in negotiations, in a permanent interchange process, for, with each new idea, with each discovery, new paths are open to be investigated and the actions are reorganised.

Table 1. New types of learning

	Teaching through projects	Learning through projects
Authorship Who chooses the theme?	Teachers, pedagogical co-ordination	Students and teachers individually and/or in co-operation
Contexts	Decisions based on external and formal criteria	Student's real life
Whom does it satisfy?	Curricula content sequences	Student's curiosity, desire, will
Decisions	Hierarchical	Heterarchical
Definitions of rules, directions and activities	Imposed by the system, follows determinations; no options	Established by the group; students and teachers reach consensus
Paradigm	Transmission of knowledge	Construction of knowledge
Teacher's role	Agent	Stimulator/adviser
Student's role	Receptive	Agent

There are different paths that lead to the construction of a project, with the students needs as a starting point. It is by inventing and deciding that the students/authors are going to activate and strengthen their motivation. Thus their autonomy must be respected and guidance offered so that the following actions may take place:

- Decide on judgmental criteria about the relevance of a certain context.
- Search/find out/select/collect information
- Define/choose/invent proceedings to test the relevance of the information assembled to the problems and questions formulated.
- Organise the constructed knowledge and make it available.

The introduction of ICT serves to empower the environment and serves also to be useful the Learning Project because we will have not time and space for individual attendance without ICT. We will have not the fundamental aspect of an easier communication and interaction if we will have not ICT in these schools.

3.3 Changes in the curricula

Will the introduction of ICT at school, through the referred methodology, demand changes in the curricula? How have these schools implemented these changes?

In our traditional secondary schools the curricula have been proposed to meet the needs of the greatest number of students. They do not plan for each student but for many groups of students hierarchically organised in levels, according to their ages. This organisation is supposed to reach 40 or 50 students in a class, from whom a uniform response is expected.

In our pilot-experiments with the EducaDi/CNPq Project, with the resources of ICT, we made available some conditions for these schools. Their teachers could choose between "Teaching Projects" and "Learning Projects." The students did not need to study the same content at the same time. The projects could be diversified, but interdisciplinary. There were themes that would run across the totality of the activities. Each student would explore the content in his own time, according to his own pace. His needs could be better cared for, as now they were easily expressed. But, at the same time, he would relate with other students and teachers, with whom he shared interests, in other different spaces and times. These interchanges between partners would allow a permanent activity of construction and "reflexive adaptation."

But how can the teacher manage this "interconnection" between different spaces and times, keeping the identity of the subjects in the collective interaction process, be it an in-class or distance situation? Without technology it is almost impossible. The interactivity afforded by the Web adds a new dimension to the curricula. The student is going to be inserted in the world.

When one intends to bring outside life experiences to the classroom, there are restrictions of time and space, of conceptions and of traditional practices. In the traditional situation, objects of nature and culture are absent from the classroom and the environment is poor with little information and opportunities for exploration and practice. The computer is used to experience virtual environments in simulated situations. When the school itself cannot contain the complexity of all aspects of life, it is then possible to enrich its space with digital objects. With the computer the distant and invisible reality can be accessed and when connection nets are established, new spaces are created.

3.4 Changes in the role of the teacher

Our experience in EducaDi Project shows that the teachers have been surprised with the amount of information the students bring about subjects and technologies not yet discussed at school! Let us see, then, how the students decide for different, original and relevant questions! These questions generate projects with great opportunities for research and experimentation. The search in the Web multiplies chances to get different kinds of information. Differences and contradictions cannot be assimilated without reflective criticism. The students are, then, engaged into discussion and analysis to select the valid information. They may search collaboratively, always present in this virtual net.

Which are the new roles the teacher needs to exert in this new context? In our model new roles and new practices were designed for the teachers, by the teachers themselves in an attempt to change the interaction among teachers, students and knowledge. A teacher may play more than one of these roles (activator, articulator, adviser and specialist) in different moments in our model of learning.

A teacher who never ceases to be a learner, does not do solely cognitively. So, in a constructivist learning environment, some aspects other than the intellect must be activated. The constructivist approach proposes learning of both the physical and the social universe. Activating one's mind and the spiritual conscience in order to learn more about one's interior and subjective world is a fundamental issue under this perspective.

The role of activate the learning process implies the following:

- Work the perception of one's own value by oneself and promote self-esteem and the enjoyment of conviviality and co-operation.
- Develop an environment where respect and self-respect will thrive, which means that the following actions should take place:
  - stimulate free expression about one's special way of perceiving
  - promote the establishment of paradigms concerning interpersonal relationships, and define their rules, taking into consideration the joy of sharing differences;
  - make people aware of the need to evaluate, alone or in groups, their own actions and their consequences;
  - search for transcendental values and consider them as each individual's inherent qualities

The role of articulate real and digital worlds requires good skills for social interplay, besides being flexible with the use of ICT when taking decisions. The articulator will be the fundamental link between the various groups of teachers, students, parents, and could articulate the local interactions and at the same time the interactions in digital word.

To the adviser and to support the Learning Projects development the teachers need to use ICT, but in EducaDi Project they not have need specific training. They have received the assistance of tutors in-service. A constructivist learning environment (software for distance co-operative work) was made available (The TecLec).. The use of the ICT resources as well the Internet server were oriented by tutors, who were high school students or college students, also in distance training at the universities. The production of instructional materials was made by the users aided by the experts of the team researchers on duty in the Web.

3.5 Technological infrastructure of the schools

We show (Figure 2) that the relationship between the number of students and the number of machines and Web connections was insufficient. This was the major challenge for all of us. If we could attain the goals that we have proposed using the minimum of technological resources the model could be replicable in the very restricted conditions.

Local School Technical Infrastructure		RS	SP	DF	CE
Computerised Schools		6	7	7	9
Equipment	Computers for Intranet connection	85	32	46	70
	Computers for Internet connection	50	7	4	19
	Printers	8	5	7	18
	Scanners	1	2	3	6
Attendance	Teachers	85	59	66	139
	Students	2550	1157	1780	4800
Human Resources	Tutors	12	14	6	18
	University experts	28	16	12	30

Figure 2. Relationship between the number of people and resources

4. SHORT TERM RESULTS

Education is a long-term investment. Structural, operational and cultural changes as we assumed in this project proposal occur in a lifelong process for individuals and their communities. Fortunately, the use of ICT gives us new scales in new dimensions of time and space, making possible to accelerate this process. Therefore we could not measure these first results in a credible basis in the period of the last two years.

We have three types of data collected: archives of written interactive communication, hypermedia documents published by users and registrations of processes. The analysis of this data was made during the execution of the activities making possible the feedback. Students made the more formal analysis in different research projects in post-graduate courses.

However the evidence of success of the project can be seen in many ways. First of all, the teachers of different schools in diverse regions of the country used the technology, showing a pedagogical appropriation of ICT. The good results in their published productions spread the wish in the community to experiment with ICT and also decreased the teacher's resistance to change. This wishes spread out appeared in the new PROINFO Project from MEC: during 1998/1999 (http://www.psico.ufrgs.br/mec-nte2 and http://nte.ferj.rct-sc.br) conquered a post graduate degree 1400 public teachers. These specialists are working now in 240 Nucleus of Educational Technology (NTE) that was already created in 27 states to train other public school teachers. The public school demand is growing too fast every day and the EducaDi' schools became a permanent reference for it.

The teachers have free access to all of the production of EducaDi' s server. We used the Learning Environment (software TEC-LEC) and other tools developed by the users and the experts of this EducaDi Project, to train the team teachers (named multipliers) of many NTEs . The University in other virtual course experiences for Distance learning developed in EducaDi is used the resource.The methodology model of the Learning Project (Fagundes, Macada, & Satto, 1999) been adopted gradually by the training staff of many NTEs. The teachers trained also used this model in their classrooms. This work can be seen in the homepages in WEB.

The data collected in a short time (1997/1998) showed two different attitudes by teachers in EducaDi classrooms. Some teachers engaged easily in the Teaching Project model, others engaged directly in the Learning Project model. Many teachers tried to work in Learning Projects but they had great difficulties to understand and to practice all the aspects of the model, working in a transition process. We could search for relations (Figure 3) between the number of students in projects, the number of projects developed, the number of teachers engaged, or not, in projects. The measurement of these relations in a short period of time would not be reliable because this changing process is too dynamic. This scenery changes continually and nowadays the number of homepages that publish Learning Projects hyper-documents is growing. These materials have students' ownership.

Centres	Schools	Students in Projects	Projects	Teachers in training	Teachers in Projects	Computers
RS	06	2550	263	85	80	85
SP	07	1157	45	59	43	32
DF	07	750	19	66	60	46
CE	09	4800	32	571	139	70
Total	29	9257	359	781	322	223

Figure 3. Statistics on participation

We realised that a learning community was established where everyone could became a spontaneous partner when interested in the planning and development of similar projects with the use of ICT. All the partners were autonomous to choose the problems to solve and to search for answers. in collaborative way to learn, to co-operate and to create. This ability consists also in the flexibility to acquire the new skills required for new jobs, including research skills.

5. THE FUTURE

The acquisitions of EducaDi project became support to the development of the new project I VEN (Internet Virtual Educational Networks), for the preparation of 50 schools by Knowledge Enterprise, Inc (BID) for the Brazilian government. IVEN proposes, as our own experiences do, the following characteristics for the programs:

- Hands-on: Students are actually allowed to perform science
- Minds-on: Activities focus on core concepts, allowing students to develop high-order thinking, process and skills
- Reality-on: Students are presented with problems solving activities that incorporate authentic, real-life questions and issues in a format that encourages drawing on multi-disciplinary knowledge, collaborative effort, dialogue with informed expert sources, and generalisations to broader ideas and application.

This new project will be an integral part of continuing the development of schools in the future in Brazil.

REFERENCES

Fagundes, L., Satto, L., and Maçada, D. (1999) Aprendizes do Futuro as Inovações Começaram. SEED/MEC -Brasilia.

Piaget, J. (1977a) L'Equilibration des Structures Cognitives. Presse Universite de France, Paris.

Piaget, J. (1977b) Recherches sur l'Abstraction Réflechissante. Presse Universite de France, Paris.

Piaget, J. (1974a) Reussir et Comprendre. Presse Universite de France, Paris.

Piaget, J. (1974b) La Prise de Conscience. Presse Universite de France, Paris.

BIOGRAPHY

Lea da Cruz Fagundes received her Ph.D. in psychology and masters degree in education. She is full professor at the Psychology Institute of the Federal University of Rio Grande du Sul (UFRGS), Brazil. She is a professor of education and teaches courses in cognitive psychology and computing in education. She is a fellowship researcher of the National Council of Research (CNPq) of the Science and Technology Ministry. She is the founder of the LEC, Cognitive Studies Laboratory, where she has been the scientific director since 1980. She has developed projects about the integration of teaching of mathematics and sciences since 1976. At the same time, she has been conducting research studies in epistemology and genetic psychology. Since 1981 she has been investigating the effects of the interaction of the learner with digital learning environments, having co-ordinated national projects in distance learning and digital networks. She has been a member of the assistant committee on Computing in Education of the Education Ministry since 1984.

Building the evidence base for macro-systemic change

or...creating the bookmark of the future

Jim Ridgway
School of Education, University of Durham, Leazes Road
Durham DH1 1TA, England.
Jim.Ridgway@Durham.ac.uk

Abstract: The theme of Chile 2000 is 'The bookmark of the school of the future'. This paper sets out ways to develop the content of the bookmarked sites. A global trend can be detected towards evidence-based policy and practice. There is a great deal of evidence on exciting ideas concerning the application of ICT in education, but rather little in the way of structured critique of this evidence. ICT faces two major challenges; first, the need to assemble existing evidence in a way that is accessible to users; second, to develop working methods that are appropriate in fields that are not only changing very rapidly, but which are also changing in radical ways. The challenge of creating the contents of the 'bookmark of the school of the future' in the face of macro-systemic change is the focus of this paper.

Keywords: Systems; macro-systemic change; assessment; vision; evidence based policy and practice; the meta-generation.

1. INTRODUCTION

It is notoriously difficult to bring about desirable changes in educational practice, even when the desired changes are to shift the centre of gravity of the bulk of educational practice towards the existing practices of a significant number of excellent teachers. ICT poses problems which are qualitatively more difficult. New educational goals are radically different to old ones, and the base of craft skills on which to build is very modest. The problem is exacerbated because new technologies with exciting educational potentials continue to emerge, and so educational reform must continually address new challenges. These new challenges require a novel approach to the creation and utilisation of knowledge; existing paradigms are not appropriate for a climate of rapid change. The chapter sets out some ideas on appropriate ways to create and use new knowledge under these circumstances of rapid intellectual change. This requires an analysis of current approaches to change, with some critical analysis of the strengths and weaknesses of these approaches, and an account of ways in which an evolving evidence base can be constructed. A goal of the paper is to go well beyond an overview of key concepts and themes on ways to make good uses of emerging technologies. It sets out first to problematise these themes, and then to argue for a different style of knowledge creation and utilisation. The valuable contributions from the IFIP community need to be presented in a variety of ways for a variety of audiences if they are to become useful to a broader educational community. The paper begins with a brief account of global trends which influence education obliquely, then an account of the global trends which influence education directly. The conference theme is 'The bookmark of the school of the future', and so it is important to ask about the content of the URLs that the bookmark points to. As well as considering the contents of the URLs, it is essential to consider the ways that the evidence to be presented in these URLs is created, critiqued, and displayed. The paper concludes with a review of the challenges and opportunities that ICT offers for further research.

2. GLOBAL TRENDS

This section sets out to identify some global trends, in order to contextualise work in education.

Evidence based policy and practice. In fields such as medicine, there has been a dramatic movement away from a dependence on the wisdom and craft skills of local experts towards the use of large scale literature reviews of effective practice, which are then embedded into local practice and national policy. In the political arena, one can identify trends away from politics towards a technology of improved social functioning. Central issues of public concern, such as health, crime, poverty and economic well-being are addressed by looking for methods that are effective, rather than by assuming that the answers to these problems can be deduced from political principles of either the political right ('get the economy in good shape, and everything else follows'), or the political left ('address the problems of social justice, and everything else follows'). A major lesson from these trends is that both politicians and practitioners are likely to demand high quality evidence on which to base their decisions.

Accountability. Accountability is now a major theme in all areas of professional practice (e.g. Moonen, 2000). This theme can be seen in the increased use of statistical data to account for the performance of governments, and government agencies – such as those concerned with health and crime. In education, it is reflected in practices such as the publication of 'league tables' of the performance of schools and school districts. League tables are only possible if one has a single measure of performance. The development of a single measure of complex performance requires value judgements on how qualitatively different aspects of performance (such as cognitive gain, emotional development, social functioning) should be weighted (Rapley and Ridgway, 1998; Moonen, 2000). A major lesson from this trend is that, without considerable work, agents in educational systems are likely to be judged on an increasingly narrow set of performance measures – notably those associated with conventional academic performance. A key activity for the IFIP community must be to design measures of attainment which relate to new educational goals. Without them, new educational ambitions are likely to be ignored.

Shared rhetoric on education. An interesting development world-wide has been the emergence of a shared set of educational goals. These can be observed in the similarities of statements related to National Curricula or their equivalents from different countries, and the statements of educational aims from government ministers around the world. Curriculum ambitions can be summarised (with heroic brevity). There will be an increased emphasis on mathematics and sciences. Within these subjects, there will be an increased emphasis on problem solving, and communication skills, with a focus on solving practical problems. Global political rhetoric can also be summarised (again, heroically). Low-skill, high-wage economies (such as those associated with car production during the 1950s, for example) can no longer be sustained in a global economy where capital (and jobs) is easy to shift from country to country. Economic success will depend on a 'knowledge economy' where high wage economies depend on high skill levels, and on 'adding value'. Education must respond in three distinct ways. First, students must be equipped with high-level intellectual skills, in order to contribute to the new knowledge economy. Second, they must be aware of the complexity of acting and making decisions in a complex and changing world, in order that they cope personally with a fast changing environment, and in order that they are 'informed citizens' functioning in a democratic society. Third, there must be a provision to support life-long learning.

An increased focus on education. Governments are aware increasingly of the importance of education to economic performance. However, the education community should not be complacent about this increasing political focus on education. It is worth remembering the adage 'War is too important to be left to the generals'. By analogy, as politicians attach greater value to education, they are also less likely to allow important decisions on the practice of education to be left in the hands of educators. If the educational community is to retain some autonomy in this critical arena of national policy, there is a need to demonstrate professional expertise. Developing an evidence base for policy and practice is an essential component in demonstrating expertise.

Academic capitalism. There is an emerging body of evidence tracking changes in the ways that knowledge is created and used (e.g. Slaughter and Leslie, 1997). Universities are less dominant in the creation of new knowledge than before; corporations increasingly are devoting considerable resources to basic research as well as to product-oriented research. Industry-academic links are being fostered, as the emergence of on-campus Science Parks testify. Internationally recognised qualifications are being created, such as Microsoft certification of the ability to use different software products. Courses are being franchised internationally, and accredited world-wide. Universities are forming alliances globally to collaborate on teaching, and to recognise courses as being equivalent. Non-traditional providers are entering the educational arena. These trends show that the whole area of education is in flux; old assumptions and values are undergoing revision. Of particular note is the emergence of assessments based on competencies defined by commercial demands, and possible conflicting views of the ownership of knowledge. Traditionally, universities have focussed on the creation and free dissemination of knowledge throughout the academic community. Such approaches are alien to commercial practice, where knowledge is guarded jealously. These trends towards academic capitalism contradict many of the ambitions expressed in this volume, such as the desire for education tailored to local circumstances and needs, and open access to knowledge.

3. THE NEW INTELLECTUAL AGENDA

A number of important themes have been developed throughout this volume. The emergence of a consensus on educational goals from papers written independently around the world is exciting, and evidence that the new vision is clear and appropriate. However, in the implementation of any new vision, one must work out what can go wrong, and plan appropriately. This section sets out to problematise some of the visions presented earlier.

A clear theme in this volume is that students will no longer be the passive recipients of other people's knowledge. The new educational agenda requires students to gather evidence, to evaluate the quality of that evidence, and to interpret it in new ways. This requires considerable intellectual sophistication. In particular, it requires: the development of meta-knowledge, that is to say, knowledge about knowledge creation and use; the acceptance that knowledge exists only in relation to some purpose and not in any absolute sense; and an acceptance of constructivism as a philosophical stance (Azinian (2000); Collis (2000); Downes and Zammit (2000); Fagundes (2000); Isaac (2000); Jansen, Fisser and Terluw (2000); Midoro (2000); Nikolova (2000); Passig (2000); Schubert (2000); and Westbroek (2000)). While these ideas reflect much current thinking in education, they are not shared universally, nor is it clear that they are easily acquired.

From product to process. Educational reforms in mathematics in the USA provide some evidence on the difficulties of shifting the balance of educational activities from an emphasis on technique to a balance of activities where mathematical processes. notably problem solving and communication skills, play an important role. Despite extensive consultation and consensus building on the nature of mathematical reforms across all manner of stakeholder groups, there has been a back-lash from conservative university professors of mathematics, who advocate 'back-to-basics' mathematics. Congressional Hearings are now taking place in the USA to investigate the educational validity of current reformed curricula.

From truth to relativism. Another lesson from reforms in the USA is the emergence of the religious right as a significant reactionary force. Here, the thrust of the resistance is that to teach problem-solving is to corrupt young people. If students are taught to examine evidence critically, to create multiple interpretations and multiple solutions to complex problems, they are likely to generalise this to their religious beliefs. Received wisdom will be challenged, and students might no longer accept scripture as absolute truth.

Even without this radical critique of new educational ambitions, there may be considerable problems in promoting relativism. A study conducted in the 1960s (Perry, 1970) on undergraduates studying humanities at Harvard and Radcliffe College illustrates these challenges. Perry tracked the intellectual development of students via a series of interviews, and identified a number of stages of intellectual development. Many students entered college with a view that knowledge existed in an absolute sense – things are either true, or not true. When this standpoint broke down, it was replaced by a nihilistic (postmodern?) stance, where any theory was viewed as the equivalent of any other theory. At a later stage of development, for some but not all students, a relativist position emerged; rival accounts can be judged against each other in terms of their power to account for the available evidence. Perry's study suggests that current ambitions to develop meta-knowledge in school may be too optimistic. The emergence of a nihilistic phase may pose extreme problems for classroom management. As a counter argument, one might argue that few attempts have been made to develop a relativistic approach. Competent use of the new technologies requires this intellectual development, which may occur seamlessly.

Promoting meta-knowledge. A number of authors emphasise the importance of the development of metacognitive knowledge. These include self-monitoring skills, and self-knowledge. Developing these skills may well be difficult; studies of expert-novice differences (e.g. Schoenfeld, 1985) suggest that the time line for the development of metacognitive knowledge is likely to be decades rather than years. However, this evidence is based on earlier, pre-ICT based learning activities in schools; it may well be the case that metacognitive knowledge can be developed far more quickly, once it is taken seriously as an educational goal (e.g. Adey and Shayer (1994).

Modelling via new representations and symbol systems. A number of contributors argue for the development of the ability to work with new representations and symbol systems. Schubert (2000), for example, argues that modelling will become increasingly important as the use of ICT grows. Existing evidence from international surveys (e.g. TIMSS: http:/www.csteep.bc.edu/timss) shows that students find it very difficult to solve problems which require abstract representations (such as the use of algebra). It is to be hoped that students exposed to ICT-rich curricula will perform better than their predecessors.

Modelling complex processes and problems. This challenge takes students to the forefront of academic work. Almost by definition, developing the skills to model complex processes such as those associated with society and our environment are likely to be difficult.

Learning to know; to do; to live together; to be. Both Cornu and Danon (2000) and Machado (2000) discussed the Report of the International Commission on Education presented in the Delors Report (1996) to UNESCO. These important ideas draw attention to the need for education to go way beyond the development of cognitive skills. Delors, and many contributors to this volume, argue for an educational focus on the development of ethics and morality; a knowledge of self, and the role of the individual in society; and the responsibility that different societies have towards each other. It should be remembered that this vision of the functions of education is not shared, universally. Margaret Thatcher famously once stated that 'there is no such thing as society'. While educators might have no sympathy for such views, they illustrate the need for those concerned with innovation to have a clear view of the wide range of beliefs about the nature and functions of education.

Despite the cautionary tone of this Section, a general conclusion can be drawn that ICT poses a major challenge to current accounts of human development. Learning environments can be created which are qualitatively different from earlier learning environments, and old theories might not be robust in these new settings. There are exciting challenges to revisit major theories of development of knowledge in all of its forms.

4. EVIDENCE AND MODELS

The major focus of this paper is to explore ways in which an evidence base can be developed which will support the introduction of different and more appropriate educational practices. This section explores the nature of evidence, and some styles of modelling.

4.1 Evidence based policy and practice

The conference title is 'The Bookmark of the School of the Future'. This title contains an implicit challenge to the IFIP community to explore ways in which knowledge can be presented in a way that is useful to a variety of users. Examination of the emergence of evidence based practice (EBPP) in other areas – notably medicine – provides a useful starting point.

The Cochrane Collaboration is an international network comprising 15 Centres in 11 countries. Their work is published in the Cochrane Library and several other forms. For example, Bandolier (www.jr2.ox.ac.uk/Bandolier) is updated monthly, and is designed to bring evidence to a wide range of health professionals. The website receives 40,000 hits per week. Issues might relate to the effectiveness of particular drugs, of some surgical procedure, or of a clinical approach such as screening for cancers of different sort. All members of the collaboration aim to discover all the evidence available, and to summarise it (for example by calculating the effect size of a treatment, based on a meta-analysis of every available study). Results are then made public. Tight criteria are set in order to decide which studies can be included in the analyses. In the case of studies on the effectiveness of a particular drug, for example, only controlled randomised trials (CRTs) are considered. Dissemination of results takes place in two distinct ways; first via publication in leading medical journals, and second via the web. Web sites are designed to encourage comment and challenges to the comprehensiveness of the literature surveyed, to the methods used, and to the interpretation of the analyses. A similar approach is needed to support professionals in education. The work of the Cochrane collaboration has been sketched here as an excellent example of an approach to EBPP. However, as a model to support EBPP for the school of the future, it has serious limitations, some of which are set out below.

4.2 Kinds of evidence

Before setting out an agenda for building the evidence base to support new educational ambitions, it will be worthwhile characterising the status of different sorts of evidence. For any topic, evidence can be available in a number of forms, which have different status and power for EBPP. For example, one can consider:

Phenomena. Evidence at the level of phenomenon describes things which happened in particular circumstances, on a particular occasion (which might extend over years). Case studies are examples of such knowledge (see Azinian (2000) and Westbroek (2000) for school development case histories). This sort of evidence can provide insight and can be a rich source of speculation about the generality of the observation to other situations. Alone, descriptions of phenomena are unlikely to provide reliable guides to future practice.

Regularities. Regularities correspond to the idea of 'laws' in physics; they are empirical generalisations which have been observed on a number of occasions, and which suggest some causal links between action and outcome. Regularities can often be expressed in the form: 'when you do <A>, then <B> happens'. Meta-analyses of drug trials provide an example of this sort of evidence.

Models. Models can take a variety of forms, and can include fully-fledged theoretical accounts. In the sense used here, a model is a description of the topic of interest (a particular learner, or a whole school, for example) together with a set of regularities, integrated in such a way as to provide guidance on the most likely effective practice.

Using different kinds of evidence. Phenomena, regularities and models have different status in terms of their usefulness to bookmark users. Phenomena provide a stimulus to thought; the more similar the background circumstances of the example given to those of the bookmark user, then the more likely the description is to be of value in guiding practice. Regularities are likely to be of use when simple decisions are to be made about how to act; models will be essential in planning action is situations where a number of interacting variables are involved.

4.3 Styles of modelling

Modelling is an essential component of every scientific enterprise, and a wide variety of styles of modelling are used in different scientific disciplines. It is appropriate, therefore, to consider different styles of modelling, in order to choose a style that matches the challenges posed by ICT in education.

A model is any kind of representation of a situation. Mathematical models are common. There, some aspect of the world is coded into a mathematical formalism; the formalism is manipulated to draw some conclusions, which are then decoded back from the mathematics into the situation in the real setting which is of interest. It is most important that the model captures the essence of the situation of interest. Consider this mathematics problem: King Henry VIII had 6 wives. How many wives had King Henry IV?

The humour comes from the fact that an inappropriate mathematical model is implicit in the question. The example illustrates a key point in modelling, namely that the formalism must represent the essential elements of the situation being modelled. The sorts of educational reforms associated with ICT have a number of characteristics that make them particularly difficult to model. These challenges are addressed later in the paper. To explore the challenges, it is essential to consider different approaches to modelling. Only a brief description can be given here; a fuller account can be found in Ridgway (1998).

Analytic modelling. Analytic modelling is common in school physics. The approach is to tackle a complex problem by breaking it down into simpler parts, and studying each part in turn. The parts are then reassembled, to create a model of the whole situation. This approach is extremely powerful in situations where variables can be manipulated independently, and where there is little or no feedback between variables.

Systemic modelling. Here, the challenge is to model situations where elements interact. Systemic modelling requires a careful description of all the elements in the system, and a specification of the links between each of the elements. It is a powerful approach for dealing with complex situations where the overall system stays the same, despite dramatic shifts in the values of individual parameters.

Macro-systemic modelling. Some systems change radically over time. Consider the Earth in space. Initially, a cloud of gas cooled to a liquid state, then to a solid state. Water formed on the surface. This created conditions in which life could emerge. One particular life form made use of photosynthesis – whose by-product is oxygen. As a result, the atmosphere of the planet changed to become oxygen rich. This new system made it possible for new life forms to exist, which depend on oxygen for their survival. To describe the history of the world, it is not enough to talk about an evolving system; the world has undergone radical, qualitative changes – the gas cloud, the molten ball, the solid with surface water, the system containing photosynthesising plants, and the current biosphere, are quite unlike each other, in system terms. This shift from system to system is referred to here as macro-systemic change. The characteristics of macro-systemic change are that some changes take place which make other changes possible. In turn, these make yet further changes possible, and the system undergoes change of such a radical nature that it becomes a new system.

Consider an example of macro-systemic change driven by technology. In 1902, there was no powered flight. In 1914, aeroplanes were being used in warfare. In 1945, a single aeroplane was instrumental in ending a world war. In 2000, delegates fly to Chile from all over the world to discuss the impact of technology on education. This example shows that technology has a radical impact on patterns of human activity. A technological change makes certain things possible. Some of these happen, and a new system emerges. The new system makes other things possible, and so on. Current social systems are qualitatively different from those that existed a few decades ago, and many of these differences have been brought about by technological changes. The example also shows that macro-systemic change can occur very rapidly. References to features of macro-systemic change can be found in Machado (2000) and in Saldano and Reyes (2000).

Different modelling styles are not tied to specific disciplines. Most disciplines use most styles of modelling; some examples are shown below.

Table 1: Modelling styles in education and ecology

	Analytic (c.f. school physics)	Systemic (c.f. school biology)	Macro-systemic (c.f. evolution)
Education	Skinnerian conditioning	models of memory	Piagetian and Vygotskian cognitive development
Ecology	field trials	predator-prey relations	ecology changes

Some sorts of macro-systemic change are predictable. The life cycle of the frog or the butterfly provide examples. In some educational settings, the same thing is likely to be true. The development of ICT based education in schools with similar characteristics may well follow a similar course (see Ridgway and Passey, 1995). Other sorts of macro-systemic changes are unpredictable. Neither the emergence of the web nor its social impact was predictable in advance. The example of the social impact of aeroplanes provides a further example. Predictable and unpredictable macro-systemic change pose somewhat different challenges to educational innovation.

5. BUILDING THE EVIDENCE BASE

How might an evidence base be constructed? The core challenge is to design patterns of knowledge creation and knowledge use which are relevant in the context of macro-systemic change. The first subsection considers ways to make effective use of current knowledge; the second section sets out some principles of research applicable to situations characterised by macro-systemic change.

> ICT in education is bringing about macro-systemic change. Collis (2000), for example, describes educational activities that were simply not possible 20 years ago; Passey (2000) describes patterns of home-school working that are impossible without ICT. The IFIP community needs to consider ways in which an evidence base can be built up which will support the educational community. One way to begin is too consider the working methods of other academic communities which engage in macro-systemic change. Ecological restoration will be used as an example.

5.1 Macro-systemic change in relatively stable worlds

One example of ecological restoration is provided by attempts to return land that has been used for agriculture to its pre-agricultural state; as in prairie restoration. The methods used are described in detail elsewhere (Murray, 1993; Ridgway, 1998); the principles, and the lessons for education, are set out here.

Vision. Ecological restoration needs a clear vision of what is to be attained; this has direct analogies with education (see Collis (2000); Hylen (2000); Isaac (2000); Machado (2000); Maturana and Cabezon (2000); Nikolova (2000); Passig (2000); Saldano and Reyes (2000); Schubert (2000); Westbroek (2000)).

Rich and accurate descriptions. Ecologists have a wealth of rich descriptions about individual plants and environments, and about the match between plant and environment. There is also extensive knowledge about entire environments, which include information not just about plants which are found together, but also about pollinating insects, and other features of the ecology. Tools are available for assessing the health of plants, and appropriate ways exist to remedy failure to thrive. There is a good deal of knowledge about the sorts of plants that are easy to grow, the timelines for growth, and the life cycle.

There is an extensive body of knowledge on the possible transitions from one system state to another. For example, to create a spruce wood from two radically different starting points (say, rock and pond) different transitions are required, as follows:

- rock to lichen to meadow to aspens to spruce;
- pond to marsh to meadow to aspens to spruce.

The knowledge base can serve a number of different functions:

- identifying conditions favourable to certain kinds of communities;
- planning desirable changes;
- implementing desirable changes;
- monitoring on-going changes.

Analogies with education demand that we assemble the following information:

- detailed descriptions of different sorts of student attainment
- descriptions of different ICT activities - which should specify what the activities do NOT include – (see Jansen, Fisser and Terlouw, 2000); Kassam, 2000), and which should include a statement of prerequisites (such as teacher and student competencies, and resource needs)
- knowledge of ICT activities that are common (and easy to establish), and which are rare (and perhaps harder to establish)
- knowledge of the relative effects of different ICT activities in terms of their learning outcomes
- ability to recognise inappropriate activities, and to remedy them
- descriptions of different types of community (or systems) – ways in which classrooms, schools, neighbourhoods, school districts and states can be classified in terms of local circumstances, and in terms of ICT use
- knowledge of transition states, e.g. as ICT is introduced into a school.

5.1.1 Understanding systems and system dynamics

A key focus is to understand the dynamics of individual systems. (see Marshall, 2000; Nikolova, 2000; and Westbroek, 2000). In the case of education, there needs to be a clear specification of the elements in a system (political will; curriculum definitions; assessment systems; patterns of professional development; teacher competencies; community conceptions, and the like) and an account of how change can be engineered within such systems. For example, changes in political will are unlikely to have any effect unless teacher skills are developed; curriculum changes are unlikely to occur unless assessment systems are redesigned so as to reward teachers and schools for achieving new educational goals (Ridgway, 1998).

5.1.2 Understanding macro-systemic change in stable settings

Beyond these understandings of system dynamics, there needs to be an account of ways that the transitions between systems can be achieved. In the case of school reform, other schools can provide examples of plausible stages of development and transition states (Ridgway and Passey, 1995). In the case of large scale systems – at school district or state level, for example – studies of analogous systems undergoing change can provide models.

There is an extensive body of knowledge in the ICT community that can be used to begin to build this evidence base. A key to this development is to discover regularities across systems in terms of the key elements, and to look for regularities in terms of the transitions form one system to another.

5.2 Macro-systemic change in unstable worlds

The problems of macro-systemic change in unstable settings need not just better descriptions and mappings, but also some new approaches to research. There is a need to conduct research at the leading edge of change, in order to explore the 'art of the possible'. Such work complements studies on the integration of innovative practices into the main stream of the curriculum. This section suggests appropriate research strategies.

Exploring affordances. The whole purpose of leading edge research is to explore possible educational activities. These cannot be known in advance. Researchers have a responsibility to explore the range of opportunities that new developments allow, and can support. Part of this work must be the gathering of evidence in such a way as to persuade a reasonable sceptic, rather than to inspire acolytes.

Fail forwards. In any innovative arena, it is important to take the steep learning curve seriously. This requires an appropriate mind - set towards failure. Small failures, blind alleys, and wasted effort are an essential component of successful work. Counting on success and punishing failure is in inappropriate strategy. The exploratory style, appropriate to innovate arenas, is summarised in a variety of different mantra, which include 'fail forwards'; 'ready, fire, aim'; and 'fail fast, and fail often'. Fortune and Peters (1995), and Marshall (2000) provide some examples of the lessons that can be learned from failures, and point to the mind-set which chooses to ignore studies of failure.

Cybernetic feedback. I use the term 'cybernetic feedback' to refer to a practice of using feedback to actively steer the course of future work. Conventionally, feedback is used to ensure that work is on target, and as the basis for small changes. Cybernetic feedback is different in the important respect that it is used to set new targets. Once one discovers that certain desirable things are made possible by new developments, they become educational goals.

Fast dissemination. A key element of working with macro-systemic change in unstable areas is the need to need to establish systems for the fast dissemination of results, in a form which is useable by different groups.

6. CENTRES FOR EVIDENCE BASED POLICY AND PRACTICE

Centres are needed which can be visited regularly by users. There are few problems in principle with establishing such sites, given the number of existing sites designed to provide some sort of support for users (for example, Enlaces in Chile; the National Grid for Learning in the UK; the European Schoolnet (EUN) and its partner networks; EducaDi in Brazil; Kenniset in the Netherlands; Interactive Education Strategies for Schools in New Zealand; EuMedia, supporting professional development in Europe), but a great deal of thought needs to be given the nature of information that is provided at these sites, and the ways this information might be made use of. As in the case of EBPP in medicine, the user must be in no doubt about the knowledge claims being made. The sources of evidence, and the routes to access original sources, must be made clear. This section will consider some of the challenges which EBPP faces, and some of the ways that these challenges might be met.

Communicating with users. There are major problems associated with communicating new ideas. All constructivist accounts argue that one sees the world through the lenses of existing knowledge structures. Communication about novel practices, therefore runs real risks that genuine novelty will be 'adapted' (in the Piagetian sense) to existing knowledge structures. Serious attention must be paid to studies of the ways that users interact with information on EBPP (Downes and Zammit, 2000).

Vivid exemplification of processes and goals. A response to this challenge is to ensure that vivid descriptions of phenomena and effects be provided (in the form, for example, of annotated video clips of learning activities, and assessment schemes with annotated student work). Graf and Yokochi (2000) provide an example which goes some way to satisfying this demand.

Quality assurance: countering dilution and corruption. A classic problem with innovation is that initial exemplary practice drifts back to the banal. Users need ways (and encouragement) to check the fidelity of practices at regular intervals. Issues of the quality of learning activities are paramount (e.g. Collis, 2000; Machado, 2000). Useless activities need identification (such as unfocussed browsing; or use of dubious sites (Collis, 2000); inappropriate patterns of communication between students (Graf and Yokichi, 2000).

Distinguishing evidence and theory. Evidence should be kept distinct from theoretical claims (as far as this is possible), to facilitate later reconceptualisations.

Claims on effect size. Effect sizes in education are likely to vary considerably across settings. Even when the overall effect of some treatment is large, there will be schools and classroom that show no gains (e.g. Ridgway, Zawojewski and Hoover (in press)). Politically, at both local and higher levels, this is important; some stakeholders are likely to form a negative view of new practices. It may well be the case that the less sympathetic stakeholders are likely to implement sub-optimal treatments, and suffer weak gains, thus reinforcing their original resistance.

6.1 Conceptualising systems and macro-systems

This is an area where users will need support. Tools for system descriptions are needed, and some are already available . Further, the whole notion of how users set about conceptualising and modelling systems (e.g. Saldano and Reyes, 2000; Azinian, 2000), and conceptualising macro-systemic change (Fagundes, 2000) will need to be explored.

Critiquing plans. There is a need for tools which support users at an early stage of planning. Systems problems should be considered very early on in planning. Some examples are included below; other examples can be found elsewhere (e.g. Checkland, 1981).

Generalisation. Can the practice the user has in mind be generalised beyond the settings in which it has been demonstrated to be effective? A classic failure of planning is to believe that the results from a specially funded project based on highly motivated volunteers with special skills who work far too hard, can be generalised across the education system.

System capacity. Is there capacity within the system to allow a particular sort of practice? For example, it was clear from the outset that LOGO required high levels of teacher preparation, and long periods of time in class with students working in small groups on computers. In most educational settings, these issues of system capacity should rule it out as a sensible educational innovation.

Parameter estimation. It is important to estimate the time lines for change; the effect sizes for different treatments; and costs. These data are available in the ICT community ('it takes about 10 days of professional development to enable teachers to use <x> fluently in class'). These data need to be accessible at the Centre. It is clear that educational benefits are multidimensional, not unidimensional, (Moonen, 2000) and any review of evidence will need to describe attainment along a number of dimensions.

Predicting unexpected outcomes. This apparent paradox can be resolved via both 'what if' analyses, and by fast feedback from early implementation. The likely implications of particular changes can be thought through in advance. Discovering the emerging impacts of new approaches should be a component of the 'fail fast, fail often' research strategy. Examples from the conference include: the accelerated asset stripping of expertise from poor countries by rich countries (Isaac, 2000); support provided for extreme political views (Kassam, 2000; Lai, 2000); dangers that new technologies will lead to increased social exclusion (Fagundes; 2000); and schools getting bigger or smaller (Hylen, 2000).

Challenging the status of 'academic' knowledge. An implication of EBPP is the challenge it poses to conventional notions of knowledge. The craft skills of 'educational engineering' will become far more salient to users than high level theoretical accounts. It is most important that theoreticians stay engaged with these processes of reform; criticism and reflection must be a characteristic of future work. The co-emergence of a strong evidence base linked directly to conceptual analyses, is likely to accelerate progress in both practical and theoretical domains.

7. CONCLUSIONS

The school of the future, as now, will be a complex system located in a local, national and global system. There is a need for a continuous process of addressing systems issues, and issues of macro-systemic change.

Practical Urgencies

- There is a need for visions of possible, desirable futures
- Centres for Evidence Based Practice which explore user uses, and which support all user communities should be created, or built on existing sites
- New educational goals require vivid exemplification, via appropriate assessment tools, descriptions of intellectual processes, and examples of student work
- New educational practices require robust quality assurance systems

Theoretical Urgencies

- Educational engineering is at least as important as theory; its status should be raised
- A new science of change is needed, urgently
- Knowledge creation and implementation need to be better understood

In order to create 'the meta generation', there is a need to review a number of existing areas, in the light of the impact of ICT on learning. These include:

- the development of ideas about knowledge
- cognitive development
- the development of metacognition
- the development of morality and ethical behaviour
- New sorts of mental processes become important as ICT is used. There is a need to explore the development these 'new intelligences'.

REFERENCES

Adey P. and Shayer, M. (1994) Really Raising Standards: cognitive intervention and academic achievement. London:Routledge.

Azinian, H. (2000) Dissemination of ICT and change in school culture. This volume.

Checkland, P. (1981) Systems Thinking, Systems Practice. New York: Wiley.

Collis, B. (2000) The school of the future: The WWW and learning processes/ new learning environments. This volume.

Cornu, B and Danon, C. (2000) Didactics, Information and Communication Technologies, and the Teacher of the Future. This volume.

Delors, J. et al (1996) Education Holds a Treasure. Report of the International Commission on Education for the Twenty-First Century. UNESCO:HMSO/UNESCO Publications.

Downes, T and Zammit, K. (2000) New literacies for connected learning in global classrooms. This volume.

Fagundes, L. (2000) Assisting or creating the future? This volume.

Fortune, J., and Peters, G. (1995) Learning from Failure: the Systems Approach. New York: Wiley.

Graf, K.-D. and Yokochi, K. (2000) Students teach students in telecommunications. This volume.

Isaac, J. (2000) Identifying educational core competencies for the Information Age: Towards conscious transformation from data to knowledge, This volume.

Jansen, P., Fisser, P., and Terlouw, C. (2000) Designing digital learning environments. This volume.

Kassam, A. (2000) Networked technologies and other stories: New paradigms for learning. This volume.

Machado, A. (2000) Current Status and Perspectives for Education in Latin America. This volume.

Marshall, G. (2000) Exquisite complexity: Rethinking the learning process and learning environment in the Information Age. This volume.

Maturana, H. and Cabezon, E. (2000) Values and competencies in the school of the future. This volume.
Midoro, V. (2000) How teachers and teacher training are changing. This volume.
Moonen, J. (2000) Return-on-Investment and On-line Learning. This volume.
Murray, M. (1993) Prairie restoration for Wisconsin schools. University of Wisconsin-Madison Arboretum: Madison.
Nikolova, I. (2000) Teacher development in ICT: Vision and implementation. This volume.
Passig, D. (2000) Taxonomy of IT mediate future thinking skills. This volume
Perry, W. (1970) Intellectual and Ethical Development in the College Years. Holt: New York.
Rapley, M., and Ridgway, J. (1998) "Quality of Life" Talk and the corporatisation of intellectual disability. Disability & Society, 13, 3, 451-471.
Ridgway, J. (1998) From Barrier to Lever: Revising Roles for Assessment in Mathematics Education. National Institute for Science Education Brief. pp. 8.
Ridgway, J. (1998) The Modelling of Systems and Macro-Systemic Change - Lessons for Evaluation from Epidemiology and Ecology. National Institute for Science Education Monograph 8. University of Wisconsin-Madison.
Ridgway, J., and Passey, D. (1995) Integrating IT: How to Use Existing Evidence About Individual Teacher Evolution to Plan Systemic Revolution. In D. Tinsley and D. Watson (eds.). Integrating Information Technology into Education. London: Blackwell. pp 59-72.
Ridgway, J., Zawojewski, J., and Hoover, M. (2000, in press) Problematising Evidence Based Policy and Practice. Evaluation and Research in Education.
Saldano, A. and Reyes, M. (2000) Edunetmatics, education assisted by world telematic net. This volume.
Schoenfeld, A. (1985) Mathematical problem solving. Orlando, FL: Academic Press.
Schubert, S. (2000) The impact of modelling in education of informatics on collaborative learning with school Intranets. This volume.
Slaughter, S. and Leslie, L. (1997) Academic Capitalism: Politics, Policies and the Entrepreneurial University. Baltimore MD: Johns Hopkins University Press.
Westbroek, J. (2000) The Esloo design for digital elementary and secondary education. This volume.

BIOGRAPHY

James Ridgway is professor of education at the University of Durham. He is an applied psychologist whose interests include: educational uses of ICT; assessment; and educational change. When at Lancaster University, he was Director of the Centre for the Study of Advanced Learning Technologies, an inter-departmental research group, and Director of STAC, a project devoted to supporting the use of technology across the school curriculum. Currently, he directs a project developing ICT-based assessment of problem solving for high attaining students, and is a director of the Mathematics Assessment Resource Service (a major project funded by NSF in the USA) which provides practical support to States, Cities and Districts on all aspects of assessment.

Overview of the focus group recommendations

Herminia Azinian and Raymond Morel

At each IFIP Working Group 3.1 working conference, the focus groups constitute a major strand of the program. All participants at these events are actively involved in small group discussions, sharing their points of views and experiences.

At the Chile 2000 meeting, within the scope of "The School of the Future," each focus group produced a position paper in which a forward look was taken at different aspects of the conference themes. They elaborated concrete recommendations integrating participants' individual experiences. The authors of the overview, who served as the co-ordinators of the focus group activities, are convinced that issues identified will be of interest to support decisions for those engaged in all aspects of education in various countries.

The four focus groups kept the domain of this conference, "The School of The Future," as central to their deliberations. Then each group focused on one of the following themes with the starting points listed below:

1. THEME 1: THE LEARNING PROCESS/ NEW LEARNING ENVIRONMENTS

- The context in which learning will take place;
- New understanding of learning;
- ICT as a learning tool;
- Pedagogy and methodology for the learner;
- Etc.

2. THEME 2: THE ROLE OF THE TEACHER

- Teacher education;
- The role of the teacher as related to the learning process;
- Assessments and examinations;
- Pedagogy and methodology for the teacher;
- Etc.

3. THEME 3: SCHOOLING / SCHOOL CULTURE / ORGANISATION OF THE SCHOOL / SCHOOL IN THE INFORMATION RICH SOCIETY

- Resources and resource management;
- New learning environments;
- School structure;
- History / culture - the nature of a school;
- Changes in schooling that may enable ICT developments;
- How ICT may challenge school function;
- What an innovative school looks like;
- Etc.

4. THEME 4: CONNECTIVITY / NETWORKING

- How will networking challenge school function?
- Future skills and required competencies;
- The virtual school;
- The child in the learning society;
- Etc.

This chapter contains the recommendations produced by each of the four focus groups. We wish to thank all the participants and especially the chairpersons and rapporteurs who did very fruitful work in a friendly and challenging environment.

Focus Group 1 - New learning in new contexts

Chair: David Squires (UK)
Rapporteurs: Toni Downes (AUS) and Klaus-D Graf (GER)
Participants: Betty Collis (NL), Paul Jansen (NL), Mike Kendall (UK), Graciela Sosisky (ARG)

Keywords: Change, learning, education, technology, teaching

1. INTRODUCTION

Whenever we talk about 'new' learning the old question arises "Is there really anything new?". The discussants in the focus group agreed that what is new is the rapidly changing context in which today's learners live, work and learn and the social condition that change is now a constant in our lives. These social, economic and technological changes, and the condition of constant change challenge us to re-evaluate, re-engineer and where necessary create new purposes and processes for learning.

The discussants accepted that the purposes of learning we need for an ever changing world are encapsulated in the statement of the International Commission on Education for the Twenty-First Century (UNESCO, 1996). They are: learn to know, learn to do, learn to live together, and learn to be. As a general statement, it is seen to apply across nations, and in different and evolving social, economic and technological contexts.

The processes of learning most associated with 'new learning' seemed to fall into two main categories. Many pick up on processes of yesteryear which lost prominence when learning was institutionalised through the establishment of mass schooling and the paper-based technologies such as text-books shaped the nature of schooling. Such phrases include 'lifelong learning', 'learning through apprenticeships', 'just in time learning'. Others which include 'learning to learn' and 'constructivist learning' and 'scaffolded learning' draw upon new theoretical understandings but are contested in the worlds of government policy and classroom practice. These processes, along with the processes that currently dominate traditional forms of schooling, and which are considered successful by many communities, policy makers and professionals, need to be re-evaluated and re-engineered in terms of how they meet the above defined purposes of education with the changing contexts. The group agreed that the new technologies play a special role in new learning and new contexts because technological change is not only a key factor generating pressure for change, but also a key facilitator through providing new tools to enable such change.

2. THE CHANGING CONTEXTS OF LEARNING

In order to more clearly identify the pressures on 'new learning' we defined some key outcomes of the changing contexts. These are the blurring of traditional boundaries, the redefinition of global and local, the changing role of various social groups and institutions in the enterprise of education, and the trend to client-led from institution-led education.

2.1 The blurring of boundaries

One key aspect of change is the increasing blurring of boundaries between dimensions such as time, space, and informal and formal working learning. Today workers can engage in international transactions from their home offices, children can vicariously experience a volcanic eruption on their television screen while it is actually happening and students in one classroom can co-operatively solve problems with students in classrooms in another city, country or even continent. Similarly boundaries are blurring between informal and formal learning, between levels of formal schooling, further study, work-place learning and life long community-based learning. We observe, older members of the community working within schools to hand on their knowledge and skills and wealth of experiences, younger and older learning and working together in community settings to solve social and environmental problems, and workers undertaking formal study within their workplace.

Another observation relates to the continuing blurring of boundaries between teaching and learning. As well as the recognition of teaching as a reflective practice where teachers increase their own knowledge and understanding from their experiences and their interactions with learners, students are increasingly assuming teaching roles as 'more capable' peers.

2.2 The redefining of global and local

Learners experience school as a place where they access locally known and controlled resources. With the appropriate ICT infrastructure in place, learners are able to access people, content and opportunities for learning on a global basis. The learners' relationship to the local and global contexts is changing to a situation where the distinction is blurred and they are simultaneously in both. It is now common, for students to be working with fellow learners on shared learning objectives, in real time, where they are not readily aware of their co-learner's location. As more people are able to experience both, the learner will need to be able to operate effectively in both, moving effortlessly between the two.

With a redefinition of the local and global, local forms of social community in which people of all ages engage for learning, citizenship and work, will themselves be redefined. The changing forms of social community, with learners' redefining and managing their learning environments, can lead to people forming different local communities that provide shared social values that extend beyond learning. The local forms of social communities can lead to the revitalisation of the village, whereby services that can be accessed from anywhere in the world, such as banking and health care are removed for economic reasons from local communities does not lead to the villages demise, but provides new communities of teleworkers and telelearning. An old African proverb states, "it takes a whole village to educate a child" in the local and global village! The arrival of new technology could make this the slogan of the future.

2.3 The role of other players

So far main players in formal education have been teachers, carrying most of the educational activities, and state or community officials generating policy and distributing resources. Today there is growing influence of other players, such as students, parents interested in the future of their children and other institutions with special interests like churches.

However, business and commerce are rapidly becoming the very influential. They either want to influence education for their own interests (staff training) or want to sell education to make a profit. So education is going to be for sale: public education will compete with private provision. This is changing the range and nature of economic circumstances in schools and the nature of influence on education. We observe increasing numbers of private schools, charter schools run by corporations, industry funded universities, accredited private (for profit) providers of technical and further education. The most recent phenomenon is the trend for Internet service providers to develop educational content, often edutainment, as a marketing tool for their services. Given these scenarios, public schooling will either diminish or change its role and expand.

2.4 A trend to client-led education

There is a discernible move to a client-led focus to the provision of learning opportunities Lifelong learning resonates with the notion that learners will be able to avail themselves of personally relevant learning activities at their convenience. Organisations are increasingly developing bespoke training/learning environments for their members. The implication of this move will be that the balance of control will shift from the provider of learning (the teacher) to the consumer of learning (the learner). Technology-mediated contexts will have a significant role in enabling a client-led focus. The capacity of technology to iron out temporal and spatial boundaries will act as a stimulus in developing an educational market in which clients can purchase educational provision in forms suited to their own needs.

3. RECOMMENDATIONS

The following recommendations follow from the above observations.

- Past paradigms of learning need to be critically appraised in terms of how they facilitate the necessary learning in our changing and increasingly complex world. Teachers must be ready to move from an instructional role to a facilitation role. They need to hold onto what works, while questioning long traditions at the same time.
- New relationships between emerging actors in education need to be explored. Productive partnerships between local governments and industry and between the parents and the teachers will be essential.
- Productive relationships and partnerships need to be brokered. Educators should not wait to react once relationships are imposed.
- Change must be recognised as variable in an increasingly complex and chaotic educational process. The consequence of this is that educators need to be advocates for their own professionalism and for the common good of education for all.

REFERENCES

UNESCO. (1996) *Education Holds a Treasure*. Prepared by Jacques Delors on behalf of the International Commission on Education for the Twenty First Century

Focus Group 2 - Changing roles of the teachers and pupils with ICT

Chair: Bernard Cornu (France)
Rapporteurs: Vittorio Midoro (Italy) and Robert Munro (UK)
Participants: Leonarda Caroca (Chile), Daniel Frias (Chile), Jan Heilmann (Denmark), Alnaaz Kassan (Canada), Iliana Nikolova (Bulgaria), Antonio Saldaño (Chile), Diana Veneros (Chile)

Keywords: Teacher competencies, teacher training, learning, educational innovation

1. INTRODUCTION

Whether the school of the future remains a largely physical entity or becomes a virtual presence in our future society, teachers in such schools will have very different roles from those they have traditionally exercised or play today. Their role will change as well as their relationships with pupils, with other teachers, with teacher educators and the various individuals and groups in society who are stakeholders in the education process.

2. THE CHANGING ROLE OF THE TEACHER

A number of "push" factors are triggering educational change and are helping to shape the way to, and the design of, the school of the future. One incontrovertible result of these synergistic processes is that the school of the future will incorporate a significant ICT component.

In many countries Governments are intent on creating an "Information Society" and are investing heavily to ensure both the technical resource base and the appropriate infrastructure is being put in place to allow complete interconnection of their societies – societies where all their citizens are conversant with, interested in, and able to use ICT in their employment activities and during their leisure time.

Already, many children, right across the globe, have grown up in our increasingly technological age. They have always used computers, electronic games, multimedia resources and the many, different elements of advanced communications technologies. They expect their educational experience to offer them learning environments which are fully supported by ICT. In these environments they can use ICT tools as and when desired – the computer, the Web, the mobile phone, videoconferencing and integrated media production tools.

All teachers adopt a professional approach to education. They are keen to enhance their teaching skills and to improve the learning environments and experiences they create for their learners. Many are convinced of the powerful educational advantages ICT offers and enthusiastically integrate ICT-based activity into a wide range of classroom activities. These teachers have often been a persuasive force in bringing ICT to the attention of their colleagues who, convinced by demonstrations of good practice, are then prepared to adopt ICT in their classroom work.

These pressures to incorporate a growing element of ICT into the teaching and learning process are being exerted at a time when education is experiencing major pressures to change. A number of paradigm shifts including: From a transmissive to a constructivist approach, From teaching based environments to learning based environments, From a hierarchical to a networked structure, New roles and relationships of teachers and teacher trainers, and From control to monitoring are combining to create an educational landscape markedly different from that of a decade ago - a landscape which will inevitably be much altered in the near future.

All of the above multi-sectoral factors will contribute to the shape and structure of the school of the future. They will foster new sets of relationships between learners, between learners and teachers, and between teachers and their teacher educators.

The traditional delivery and establishment of content is becoming less important. Rather it is the acquisition and development of concepts and skills which will characterise the school of the future. This new approach should create flexible, thoughtful and creative learners, skilled in the use of educational resources (particularly ICT tools), as and when desired or required, to access information, mould this information into knowledge and then apply this knowledge to the solution of problems, the assessment and resolution of issues and the appropriate transfer of conclusions to a variety of audiences. In the future learners will be empowered to learn how to learn.

If this learning shift is to be achieved teachers as well as teaching will have to change. The changes to the education system will set new expectations of teachers and modify the portfolio of desirable competencies and skills they will be expected to demonstrate. With an enhanced ICT component figuring prominently in the school of the future teachers will have to be ICT literate – not necessarily technical experts but confident and competent users and deployers of ICT. They will integrate ICT as and when necessary in their curricular activities and should be flexible, thoughtful and creative enough to take on new or emergent applications of ICT, decide how best they can support the learning process, and incorporate them into their teaching and learning environments – in a "just-in-time" way.

Teachers will need to be ever aware of new pedagogical developments and competencies related to improving the learning process. They should be prepared to explore, accept, reject and , where appropriate, integrate these. Like their learners they will need to embrace co-operative and collaborative philosophies and become team players in the education process – able to work across a range of subjects or curricular areas and support an investigative/problem solving constructivist approach to learning. Teachers of the future will have to respond flexibly, thoughtfully and sensitively to the many needs and different learning styles of their learners. They will also need to be able to design and manage new learning environments where the development of concepts and skills can be best promoted.

These new facets of the teacher in the school of the future have important consequences for teacher educators. While many teacher educators have investigated and embraced new educational paradigms and techniques they have often appeared less than enthusiastic in their adoption of ICT. Teacher educators should respond to the challenge of ICT and be leaders in its exploration. They should actively promote ICT as a cross-curricular resource and demonstrate to trainee teachers good practice in the use of ICT. Teacher educators should model best practice and encourage their students to view ICT as a set of powerful tools which assist their personal productivity as well as promoting their professional and pedagogical expertise. Students should leave teacher education institutions aware of new pedagogical approaches, comfortable in the many uses of ICT and prepared to increasingly experiment with its use to support all aspects of learning.

While many powerful push factors bear on education there are other powerful traditional forces in operation which are resistant to "change in the order of things." A new pattern of education is unlikely to appear quickly and the transformation to the school of the future will be slow, unless the energies of these push factors (social, political, economic, environmental, technical and cultural) are focused on breaking the circle of tradition which is prevalent in education.

This circle can be broken in many ways. Any initiative should start from the needs of the teachers and should be designed to build teacher confidence. Initiatives should encourage active participation of parents and social agencies, all of the stakeholders in the educational system and the school of the future. These initiatives are likely to be most effective if they are focused on creating communities at local, regional, national and global levels.

The world is full of such initiatives. Some of the most successful have targeted the connection of schools to allow collaborative and co-operative projects to develop between schools, teachers and pupils (notably the Enlaces project in Chile) or to provide central resource gathering centres (such as the National Grid for Learning in the UK, the European Schoolnet project and a similar initiative in Canada). In Denmark attempts to develop teacher competence in ICT have been based on teacher acquisition of an Educational Drivers Licence – a development which already has included 25% of the teacher work force and has been extremely successful when a whole school approach is used. Co-operative learning initiatives have been established in France and ICT development as a communication tool has been a feature of considerable educational activity in Israel and Iceland.

It would be valuable if these initiatives were brought together and then promoted throughout the educational community. It is also vital that they are implemented with sensitivity for the socio-cultural conditions pertaining in their respective countries.

3. RECOMMENDATIONS

Cognisant of the many interacting factors which influence the development of the school of the future we would make the following recommendations which we consider would assist its creation:

- Define measures to encourage the creation of teacher communities.
- Encourage teacher communities to share ideas, models, methodologies, experiences, and materials.
- Encourage co-operation among the teacher community members.
- Provoke paradigm shifts in Teacher education institutions.
- Disseminate project based teacher training processes based on ICT.
- Develop ICT competencies of teachers in the context of projects in which these skills are required.
- Provide local frameworks in which teachers can find both technical and pedagogical support.

Focus Group 3 - Schooling, school culture, organisation of the school, school in the information-rich society

Chair: Peter Bollerslev (Denmark)
Rapporteurs: Gail Marshall (US) and David Passig (Israel)
Participants: Miguel Aliaga (Chile), Eduardo Cabezon (Chile), Wendy Davies (UK), Jimmy Isaac (India), Jaap Westbroek (Netherlands), Kwok-Wing Lai (New Zealand)

Keywords: Vision, knowledge, wisdom, school

1. INTRODUCTION

The theme of school, the culture of the school, and the organisation of the school in the information rich society energised the Focus Group to consider visions of education that would apply to the many different cultures and many different goals.

2. VISIONS OF THE FUTURE

Moving into the future, the Focus Group agreed, called for a future oriented vision. While this might seem to be self-evident, a discussion of Schools of the Future must, after all, engage in discussions of the future, the Focus Group believed that it was important to begin with what should be and must be in the future instead of an alternative approach which would begin with the present, state the problems and prospects of present practice, and then work toward ameliorative plans and programs that would push toward some eventual goals. Similarly, the Focus Group believed that it was important to establish a vision that had a far reaching time span-ten-twenty, thirty or more years ahead-rather than discussing a future three or four years from now, the standard frame of reference of hardware and software providers. Similarly, the Focus Group agreed that the scope of the schools′ work should be as broadly defined as possible, and goals should be directed toward many different types of school activities, policies and practices while all of those must be global in their focus and impact.

Such a broadly based vision calls for the highest degree of human interaction. So the Focus Group said that in order to achieve its vision the school of the future must strive to achieve co-ordination and connectivity in order to create new knowledge from the old, yielding wisdom, which is acquired through collaboration.

Such a dynamic, comprehensive vision calls for a re-conceptualisation of many different but vital components of schools: their architecture, their timetables, and the types of accountability measures used. Similarly, current ideas about appropriate uses of technology must be broadened and each country′s culture of schooling and of change will need to be re-examined and/or changed. Part of that culture, the role and the dynamics of the "youth culture" in each country, must be analysed with a view toward understanding the ways youth engage themselves in knowing and learning, and the ways that such engagements develop and grow.

It would be utopian to expect that such visions could be achieved without discussion and debate. For example, it is certainly the case that from one country to another and within countries there are dualisms-idealism vs. utilitarianism and the economy as a constraint vs. the economy as a reality. Similarly, looking to the future must address the question of whether a school is a "physical entity" or is an "idea" situated in many different places at many different times. But, while recognising that there would be inevitable debates about key issues, the Focus Group believed that peoples around the world would accept and adopt visions that moved from knowledge acquisition to wisdom attainment. Key factors in knowledge acquistion are students′ interests, skills and roles, teachers′ competencies, beliefs and roles, and the community′s goals, beliefs and resources. Key goals of wisdom attainment are the engagement of students in authentic, important learning, the involvement of teachers with students, the community and each other, and the community′s investments toward change.

Toward those ends, both the acquisition of knowledge and the attainment of wisdom call for models of change, even when those models have been shown to have been unsuccessful because lessons can be learned from both successful and unsuccessful change efforts. Moving towards knowledge and wisdom also calls for strategies for sharing stories of change, and understanding what we are moving from, where we are going and why. Visions for the future also call for identifying the scaffolding needed for change. Similarly, as schools look to the future there must be an understanding of why schools today are designed and organised as they are in order that the implications of past practice may inform future policies.

Since the creation of schools of the future will be more broadly based than today's schools, the Focus Group also agreed that future schools' planning will call for an understanding of the relation between humans but, equally important, will call for an understanding of the relation between humans and nature.

3. METAPHORS FOR THE VISION

It is often difficult to convey a vision in words but metaphors have the power to make comparisons that are visual and/or vital, and so the Focus Group thought of metaphors as a means of conveying the breadth and depth of their vision. Discussions of the ways schools around the world planned for change and the types of schools resulting from the plans led to descriptions of what "school" meant in different cultures. In Sanskrit "school" means "an abode of knowledge"; in Danish "school" has the meaning of "a direction toward a vision" and in China, "a place for acquiring the knowledge of how to behave." Chile envisions school as a community of actors participating in a social enterprise while in Israel the school is " the house of the book"—"beit hasefer." All of the metaphors connoted a process as well as a place where knowledge and wisdom can be attained, and so the Focus Group agreed that such metaphors encapsulated the essence of their vision for the School of the Future—places where students, teachers, and the community would engage in activities directed toward wisdom.

Focus Group 4 - Connectivity and networking

Chair: Ferrán Ruiz Tarragó (Spain)
Rapporteurs: Don Passey (UK) and Sigrid Schubert (Germany)
Participants: Doug Brown (UK), Jan Hylén (Sweden), Jef Moonen (Netherlands), Miguel Reyes (Chile), Jimena Sepúlveda (Chile), Juan Vargas (Chile), Terry White (UK)

Keywords: Networking, challenges, future skills, virtual school, learning school

1. INTRODUCTION

The discussions concerned the concepts of connectivity and networking. The discussions covered factors involved in a range of aspects of developing connectivity and networking in relation to emerging and new educational systems. Four aspects were considered: 1)How will networking challenge school function? 2) Future skills and competencies required. 3)The virtual school. and 4)The child in the learning society.

2. HOW WILL NETWORKING CHALLENGE SCHOOL FUNCTION?

It is clear that the development of connectivity and networking to support traditional and emerging educational systems arises from two fundamental, and different, perspectives: central concerns (such as concepts of how centralist provision might operate); and individual concerns (such as concepts of the benefits and advantages to the individual learner). Currently there are a number of drivers which are likely to challenge current school function. In a number of countries it is recognised that the transition from primary to secondary schools is often associated with a decline in levels of engagement, interest, attendance, positive attitude, and learning attainment of pupils. This decline is associated with shifts towards student dissatisfaction, and towards parental perceptions and expectations of dissatisfaction with current educational provision from schools. Under these circumstances it is clear that both students and parents could opt for what might be considered better alternative systems of education based outside or alongside schools. Changing attitudes towards learning engagement have been recognised when computers have been made accessible in areas on the streets of towns in Brazil, for example. In other countries parents in some areas are already choosing to support their children at home when the time comes for them to revise for.

For schools which have already become involved in shifts towards greater provision via connectivity and networking, it has been found that this has often been associated with circumstances where there have been financial pressures for change. Schools have responded in shifts towards alternative provision when financial resources have become more limited. Even when financial resources are not limited, positive increases in home learning have been found in some countries.

In some countries companies and organisations have already been involved in the production of resources to support school learning at home.Under these circumstances the involvement of stakeholders can shift significantly. The constitution of stakeholder and business involvement will be a need for consideration by schools in the future. Some countries are already considering the potential advantages or needs to shift from a subject-based to a topic-based, or theme-based, curriculum. For a theme-based curriculum, the Internet offers, through resource links to relevant and up-to-date material, ideal opportunities for provision to meet the needs of students who might want to pursue their learning in these ways.

The challenge to school function is based on shifts in power and control. In terms of power, the shift can be from schools towards parents. In terms of control, the shift can be from that held by teachers, towards students.

3. FUTURE SKILLS AND COMPETENCIES

In terms of future skills and competencies required, students will clearly require an understanding of facility of use, in terms of a literacy in handling of information, as well as appropriate skills to use and create networking. Managing continuous change will be a future skill and competency need not only for school managers, and teachers, but also for students themselves.

4. THE VIRTUAL SCHOOL

The development in practice of virtual will require an understanding of both the strengths and weaknesses of virtual schools, if such schools are to retain key strengths as well as to develop other key strategies. An understanding of the costs of setting up virtual schools will also be needed, although costings prepared to date (in Sweden, and in the UK) suggest that costs are comparable to the setting up of traditional schools.

A problem which the setting up of virtual schools may face is that many will need to start from traditional starting points. It seems important that developmental experiments start from different positions: from traditional school, existing virtual school, and 'green field' starting points. Examples already exist of virtual schools in some countries. In other countries, shifts in organisational practices have been identified in traditional schools moving towards more virtual school situations. The production and sale of specialist expertise and resources has also been developed by certain schools at this stage. Revision material, supporting individual endeavour, and offering lesson objectives, linked resources, and schemes of work for courses run in the school, has enabled some students to work on materials outside school and to attain at substantially earlier times than some of their peers. The use of laptops is also enabling some schools to become mobile schools.

A range of factors is affecting, and will affect in the future, the ways in which implementation and practice of virtual schools can develop. There is a clear role of vision, but where schools are subject to successive initiatives that need to be rationalised, this can lead to a response to vision which can lead to a 'crisis vision' rather than an informed vision. Under such circumstances, mechanisms of integration of initiatives become more vitally important. A virtual school development will need to consider the factor of how continuity of training and development will be handled, as developments of this nature will be concerned with continuous change rather than with a period of change moving developments to a new plateau position. Monitoring and review mechanisms, and frequency of review will need to be considered to support appropriate focused continuous change. Hand-over timecan be reconsidered with the advent of virtual (or part-virtual) schools so that the break periods between terms become more fluidic. However, if students do undertake home learning through virtual schools, then who holds the responsibilities for home learning will also need to be addressed. In order to fulfil the needs determined by virtual schools, both the shape of networks and the origin of networks will need to be accommodated. Future natures of physical infrastructures will also need to be included in vision and strategies for the future.

5. THE CHILD IN THE LEARNING SOCIETY

A major issue for learning will be the need to potentially reconceptualise the assessment of outcomes of learning. The origin of control of assessment, and the nature of control of assessment are central to this concern.

6. CONCLUSIONS

A number of key conclusions emerge:

- The potential for alternative systems has to be established.
- A culture will need to be developed which creates both acceptance and use of the new forms of provision.
- Strengths of traditional and virtual schools must be considered.
- Systems thinking needs to be involved, to challenge traditional systems concepts, and to consider integrative potential.
- Possibilities of different forms of virtual schools in different contexts needs to be considered.
- The development of virtual schools raises issues for all those who will be 'touched' (whether they be students, teachers, parents, business providers, project mangers, or education directors).
- Providers of learning environments can be located outside schools, and needs can be sourced by a variety of providers.
- Individual learners can be the central focus for the provision.
- Learner-focused skills will be needed in the areas of using and creating networking, and a literacy of handling information.
- Teacher-focused skills will be needed for maintaining developments of skills over a period of continuous change.
- Physical infrastructure will need to be introduced to match virtual school needs.
- Assessment needs, methods, and mechanisms will all need to be considered in fundamental ways.
- Support of coursework or project work assessment would match the provision offered by virtual schools.

Virtual school developments raise a number of challenges:

- The relationship and linking of the potential actors involved.
- The challenge for leaders and managers to lead transition.
- Ownership of the intellectual property rights (IPR) of resources developed and how the publishing processes are handled.
- Expressing concepts about virtual schools to teacher educators in ways which enable them to become involved actively.
- Appropriate criteria and evaluation of student outcomes.

Index of Contributors

GPSR Compliance
The European Union's (EU) General Product Safety Regulation (GPSR) is a set of rules that requires consumer products to be safe and our obligations to ensure this.

If you have any concerns about our products, you can contact us on

ProductSafety@springernature.com

In case Publisher is established outside the EU, the EU authorized representative is:

Springer Nature Customer Service Center GmbH
Europaplatz 3
69115 Heidelberg, Germany

www.ingramcontent.com/pod-product-compliance
Ingram Content Group UK Ltd.
Pitfield, Milton Keynes, MK11 3LW, UK
UKHW020133290926
15471UKWH00003B/467
9781475754704